Information and Communication
Technologies in the Welfare Services

of related interest

Confidentiality and Mental Health
Edited by Christopher Cordess
ISBN 1 85302 860 6

Innovative Education and Training for Care Professionals
A Providers' Guide
Edited by Rachel Pierce and Jenny Weinstein
ISBN 1 85302 613 1

Boring Records?
Communication, Speech and Writing in Social Work
Katie Prince
ISBN 1 85302 325 6

The Working of Social Work
Edited by Juliet Cheetham and Mansoor A. F. Kazi
ISBN 1 85302 498 8

The Changing Role of Social Care
Edited by Bob Hudson
ISBN 1 85302 752 9

Information and Communication Technologies in the Welfare Services

Edited by Elizabeth Harlow and Stephen A. Webb

Jessica Kingsley Publishers
London and Philadelphia

First published in the United Kingdom in 2003
by Jessica Kingsley Publishers Ltd
116 Pentonville Road
London N1 9JB, England
and
325 Chestnut Street
Philadelphia, PA 19106, USA

www.jkp.com

Copyright © 2003 Jessica Kingsley Publishers

Library of Congress Cataloging in Publication Data
Information and communication technologies in the welfare services/edited by Elizabeth Harlow and Stephen A. Webb.
    p. cm
  Includes bibliographical references.
  ISBN 1-84310-049-5 (alk. paper)
    1. Social service--United States--Technological innovations. 2.Human services--United States--Technological innovations. 3. Information technology--Social aspects. I. Harlow, Elizabeth. II. Webb, Stephen A., 1956-

HV91 .I464 2003
361.2'5--dc21   2002038919

British Library Cataloguing in Publication Data
A CIP catalogue record for this book is available from the British Library

ISBN 1 84310 049 5
Printed and Bound in Great Britain by
Athenaeum Press, Gateshead, Tyne and Wear

Contents

Introduction   Information and Communication Technologies
in the Welfare Services: Wired Wonderland or
Hypertext Hell?   7
Elizabeth Harlow, University of Bradford, UK

Part One: Social Work and Social Care

Chapter 1.   The Caring Professions and Information
Technology: In Search of a Theory   29
Nick Gould, University of Bath, UK

Chapter 2.   Using the Internet for Evidence-based Practice   49
Mark Watson, OLM Systems, UK

Chapter 3.   Real Records, Virtual Clients   67
*Annie Huntington, University of Salford, UK,
and Bob Sapey, Lancaster University, UK*

Chapter 4.   Technology and Systems of Referral Taking
in Social Services: From Narrative to Code   83
Suzanne Regan, St Martin's College, Lancaster, UK

Chapter 5.   Internet Child Abuse   111
*Brian Relph, Luton Borough Council, UK, and
Stephen A. Webb, University of Sussex, UK*

Part Two: Health and Welfare

Chapter 6.   Information Technology and the Organization
of Patient Care   137
*Walter Sermeus, Centre for Health Services and Nursing
Research, the Catholic University of Leuven, Belgium*

Chapter 7.   Health, Collaborative Learning and the Collapse
              of Professionalism? The Information Brothel   157
              Joe Cullen, Tavistock Institute, UK

Chapter 8.   From Self-service Welfare to Virtual Self-help   183
              *Nicholas Pleace, Centre for Housing Policy, University
              of York, UK, Roger Burrows, Centre for Housing Policy,
              University of York, UK, Brian Loader, Community
              Informatics Research and Application Unit, University
              of Teesside, UK, Steven Muncer, University of Durham, UK,
              and Sarah Nettleton, University of York, UK*

Chapter 9.   Consumers, the Internet and the Reconfiguration
              of Expertise   199
              Michael Hardey, University of Southampton, UK

Conclusion   Technologies of Care   223
              Stephen A. Webb, University of Sussex, UK

              THE CONTRIBUTORS   239

              SUBJECT INDEX   243

              AUTHOR INDEX   251

Information and Communication Technologies in the Welfare Services

Wired Wonderland or Hypertext Hell?

Elizabeth Harlow

As information and communication technologies (ICTs) become a part of all areas of life, their impact is of interest to a broad range of academic disciplines, and theorists from a range of different perspectives. Whilst post-Fordists might scrutinize the way in which ICTs contribute to the changing nature of production and consumption (see Amin 1994), cultural theorists, writing from a post-modern perspective, might explore the construction and dissemination of lifelike electronic images and raise questions concerning what constitutes 'the real' (see for example Webb 1998). Social theorists such as Bell (1973), have argued that ICTs have contributed to a social revolution, which means that we have exited the industrial age and entered the information age. Castells (2000) maintains that a new epoch has been entered, but in addition to the importance of information, the electronic network which facilitates its rapid and global dissemination is also of great significance: we have become a network society. Whilst the idea of a new epoch might be contested, social theorists agree that current times are characterized by fragmentation, pluralism and individualism (Kumar 1995) and academics of various perspectives are attempting to understand and articulate the role and significance of ICTs. With its application in social welfare, this book makes a contribution to this developing genre.

The use of computers in the welfare services is not new and literature on the topic was emerging in the 1980s (for example, see Glastonbury 1985).

However, interest in their application, along with ICTs in general, has steadily increased since then (Rafferty 1997). Over the last fifteen years, two international groupings, HUSITA (Human Services Information Technology Applications) and ENITH (European Network for Information Technology in the Human Services), have contributed to the development and understanding of ICTs in the human services by means of conferences and publications (see for example Colombi, Rafferty and Steyaert 1993; Steyaert, Colombi and Rafferty 1996). This interest in and application of ICTs has, however, not been growing evenly. Gould (in this volume) argues that engagement with ICT applications first appeared in health and has only recently been emerging in social care: put another way, health informatics has been breaking ground whilst social informatics is only now mirroring this progress. *Information and Communication Technologies in the Welfare Services* includes chapters on ICTs in the domains of both health and social care. Whilst the book is divided to reflect these two particular domains, there are themes common to both. Main themes which cut across both areas of welfare include: the way in which ICTs are influencing and changing the design of organizations and their management; the contribution of ICTs to the delivery of welfare services; the use and abuse of ICTs in relation to gender and sexuality; and finally, critical reflection on their application. Whilst pursuing each of these themes in turn, this chapter will acknowledge their place within the wider context of the relevant debates and literature.

ICTs, welfare organizations and their management

Reflecting a dominant theme within the literature on ICTs in general, the main theme within the book concerns their role within management and organization. Both the management and organization of welfare services have been of great interest since the consensus over the state as main provider of social services in the UK came into question. Following the oil crisis in the early 1970s, the conclusion of the post-war economic boom and the end of Keynesian economic principles, the foundations upon which the welfare state depended were no longer seen as valid. This coincided with the rise of neo-liberalism, new methods of production, technological initiatives, and the development of global markets (Leonard 1997). Castells highlights the part played by these technological initiatives: 'the availability of new telecommunication networks and information systems prepared the ground for the global integration of financial markets and the segmented articulation of production and trade throughout the world...' (Castells

2000, p.60). Global competition means that financial investment and production shifts to the region of greatest return. Western countries cannot compete with regions of low wages and hope to improve their position by means of advanced production methods, research, information and brand management. A highly skilled and educated workforce is necessary and fiscal revenue is more likely to be invested in policies aimed at achieving this, as opposed to short-term welfare consumption (Hughes 2000). As a consequence, the welfare services that are provided have to be delivered with utmost economy, efficiency and effectiveness, thus leading to organizational restructuring and the introduction of new managerialism (see Clarke and Newman 1997; Cutler and Waine 1994; Kelly 1991; Lawler 2000). Given the rise of neo-liberalism, economy, efficiency and effectiveness are increasingly understood in terms of free markets.

Although the New Labour governments (elected in 1997 and 2001) have, to some extent, modified the free market approach of previous Conservative governments, there is no attempt to return to Beveridge's vision of the welfare state. This is not only because of the economic context indicated above, but also because large impersonal bureaucracies and centralized systems are no longer seen as adequately responsive to the needs of welfare recipients who are increasingly understood as consumers. According to Siddall (2000), who writes particularly about social services, provision in the UK now involves a changed role for central and local government, changed methods of delivery and a changed language:

> Examples of these shifts include change: from assessment of need to consumer demand; from state provision to increasing provision by voluntary and private sectors; from acceptance of existing services to the need to promote quality; and from state direction of welfare to partnerships. The situation now is one where the mixed economy of care is accepted as a legitimate, institutionalised approach to social services provision. (Siddall 2000, p.26)

Although social services departments (SSDs) have never been the sole providers of social care, their role as primary providers is changing as the voluntary and private sectors are expected to play a larger part. Governmental initiatives aimed at improving the welfare of disadvantaged communities have been introduced (for example, Sure Start) and local governments and SSDs are engaged in new partnerships. Partnership is also the key to the developing relationship between the NHS and SSDs. Even within SSDs, the changed principles concerning the provision of care have necessitated re-organization and division into purchaser and provider units. These changes require SSDs to be empowering, participative, decentralized, flexible and networked – all characteristics of the post-bureaucratic organization (Thompson and McHugh 1995). According to some, bureaucracy is giving way to adhocracy (Toffler 1970 cited in Lawton and Rose 1994). Whilst vertical lines of command remain crucial within welfare organizations, attempts to provide services seamlessly mean that horizontal webs of communication become increasingly important. It is easy to see how ICTs might play their part:

> New information technologies allow…for the decentralization of work tasks and for their co-ordination in an interactive network of communication in real time, be it between continents or between floors of the same building. (Castells 2000, p.282)

Electronic communication within and across organizational boundaries gives new meaning to time and space, as both become compressed (Harvey 1989 cited in Frissen 1997). This compression has the potential to facilitate a speedier response to requests for the provision of welfare services or perhaps enable new solutions to problems.

Within this volume, Sermeus, Cullen, Watson and Regan all reflect on the way in which ICTs are being introduced into welfare organizations in an attempt to improve efficiency, economy and effectiveness. Sermeus, applying a systems analysis to the functioning of hospitals in different geographical locations, explores the way in which ICTs might be able to improve multidisciplinary communication and team-working, and thus enhance the delivery of health care. Prior to this, Sermeus sets out the complexity of hospital management, and reveals the problems for which ICT solutions are being sought. This chapter, whilst highlighting difficulties that might be encountered, is optimistic about the application of ICTs. Thus the chapter provides a good illustration of the mainstream health informatics approach. Like Sermeus, Cullen discusses health informatics. He argues that attempts to reduce the cost of medical treatment include: reducing labour costs; shortening hospital stays; and improving primary, community and self-managed care. ICTs have a part in achieving these goals. ICTs can improve efficiency by means of: enhanced research; electronic records; better communication; and 'just-in-time' diagnosis – the latter leading to a shorter waiting time for patients. All of these benefits relate to the principles and practice of knowledge management (see below) and support the argument made by the advocates of this particular approach, that reduced cost does not automatically mean a reduction in the quality of service.

Focusing on SSDs, Regan, as well as Huntington and Sapey, explores the way in which ICTs have been introduced to streamline the tasks of front-line practitioners. For the vast majority of local authorities, generic social services located within the communities they intend to serve belong to the past. Specialized intake teams in central positions are part of the new networked organizational structures. Regan reports on an intake system modelled on call centre principles: that is, the centrally based team rely on telephones, faxes, computers and email as means of receiving referrals from the general public or professionals based in other welfare agencies. Information and referrals are then passed on inter or intra agency.

Emphasis on organizational economy, efficiency and effectiveness has given rise to a series of new approaches to management. Following on from the 'excellence' approach (see Peters and Waterman 1982), total quality management (see Oakland 1989) and the emphasis on group process comes knowledge management (KM) (Abell and Oxbrow 2001). Sometimes described as a philosophy rather than an approach, KM is intricately linked to the principle of the 'learning organization'. Put simply, the learning organization is one that can adapt to meet the challenges of a constantly changing environment. Training courses for the benefit of individuals are no longer adequate. Organizations need to develop a culture and practice where learning, and the sharing of what is learnt, works to maintain the continuous improvement in goods and services. This in turn contributes, for private sector companies, a competitive advantage in the marketplace. Both the learning organization and KM are concerned with the maximization of intellectual capital which, according to Abell and Oxbrow (2001), can be understood as the combination of 'human capital' and 'structural capital'. Human capital is the people, customs, partnerships, expertise and knowledge of an organization. Structural capital, put simply, refers to the infrastructure and processes that support the people. Although difficult to define, KM can be understood in the following way:

> Knowledge Management practice can be broadly defined as 'the acquisition, sharing and use of knowledge with organisations, including learning processes and information systems'. The emerging field of Knowledge Management seems to reflect a constellation of changes –

some profound, some more cosmetic – in the business environment. (BPRC 2000 quoted in Abell and Oxbrow 2001, p.34)

What has been recognized in recent management thinking is the importance of the 'invisible' attributes of the organization: the knowledge, expertise and relationships amongst staff and between staff and customers. Crucial to this thinking, however, is the means by which knowledge is transmitted, and learning and relationships enhanced. ICTs are of central importance to all of this. Although generated elsewhere, these ideas have been taken up by the UK government and are influencing developments within the organization and management of welfare. The Department of Health, for example, has developed systems to support policy making and training on information use, electronic documents and records. In addition, it has encouraged businesses to share information (Abell and Oxbrow 2001). All of which is in keeping with the principles of KM. Within this volume, Gould elaborates on the concepts of the learning organization and KM. He goes on to illustrate their application and the emerging role of ICTs in welfare organizations.

Keeping health care professionals abreast of policy and clinical developments is an important approach to improving the quality of service. With this in mind, the UK government has established the National Electronic Library for Health. This library is an important element in the current policy on evidence-based health care. That is, clinicians can enhance their diagnostic skills and apply the most successful techniques, by means of information and research findings disseminated via the library. The electronic library means that clinicians can access the necessary information from their desk. This networked accessibility, as Sermeus points out, is crucial to this approach to improving the quality of services.

Social workers are also being expected to improve the quality of their practice by means of information and knowledge. Despite sharp criticism (see Webb 2001), the government is encouraging evidence-based practice in this domain also. Watson (in this volume) traces the way in which information for this purpose might be disseminated. With the establishment of the Social Care Institute of Excellence, the enhanced standard of social work practice and the continuance of professional development is encouraged. ICTs have an important part to play as social workers' difficulties in updating their knowledge might be overcome by electronic solutions. As in the case of health, research findings can be circulated by means of electronic journals. In addition, popular journals such as *Community*

Care and *Care and Health* now have websites (see for example www.community-care.co.uk and www.careandhealth.com). Such websites provide information and encourage contributions on topical issues from those in the field of social care. Indeed, Berman (1996) drawing on the work of Goldstein (1992), Carew (1979), Lyotard (1984) and Dyson, Keyworth and Toffler (1994) asks whether specialist internet newsgroups may be the most apposite medium for social workers to share their practice wisdom without the inappropriately 'scientific' constraints of mainstream academic journals. So, by means of ICTs, professionals involved in the provision of social care can, irrespective of geographical distance, communicate about their work and, in so doing, create new virtual communities – or 'cyburgs' as Bainbridge (1995 cited in Giffords 1998) suggests. Put another way, networked society facilitates a new virtual community of practitioners, researchers, policy makers and educators, all concerned with knowledge and the improved provision of health and social care services.

KM and the production and dissemination of services through the electronic circulation of information does not end at the level of professionals and the providers of goods and services: the circulation of information to customers, service users and patients is crucial. In the UK, the government has committed itself to improving the experience of those using the NHS by means of ICTs. By 2004 all patients should have access to an electronic version of their records and by 2005 it should be possible to book appointments electronically. The aim is for patients to have access to their GPs by means of video-link and for all hospital patients to have a telephone and television by their beds (Jellineck, Lambden and Lilley 2000). Currently, some hospitals (or hospital trusts) do have websites but these are usually teaching hospitals where one or two committed individuals take on responsibility for the website's maintenance (Jellineck *et al.* 2000). According to Jellineck *et al.*, good sites contain information on road and transport links, the location of nearby overnight accommodation and the financial performance of the hospital. A significant development, however, has been the NHS internet gateway, NHS Online Direct. This provides the public with information not only about services, but also about health and medical conditions. Cullen (in this volume) articulates developments in telehealth. Within the context of health informatics in general, Cullen explains and illustrates the way in which improving the public's knowledge regarding illness and health care is understood by politicians, policy makers and health care managers as a means of cutting service costs. Instead of needing to seek (expensive) expert advice, the public by means of ICTs can, to some extent at least, engage in the practice of self-care. Hardey also considers the public provision of health information. Pursuing the topic still further, Cullen, by means of empirical evidence, reflects on the way in which lay people and experts can produce knowledge collaboratively. These contributions draw on, and add to, debates concerning expert knowledge and the changing nature of relationships between professionals and the lay public. There will be further discussion of this in the section below where electronic self-care and self-help are given further consideration.

ICTs and the delivery of services

The organizational design, management and delivery of health and welfare services are inter-related parts of a whole. In social service departments, for example, ICTs can be used in the contracting of services from other agencies as well as in budgeting care packages for individual service users (see Catchpole and O'Higgins 1991). Put another way, service delivery can never be isolated from the wider organizational and managerial concerns. At issue here, however, is the use of ICTs at the point of welfare 'consumption'. ICTs in the consumption of welfare is not new. Help, by means of telephone, was first offered to those at risk of committing suicide in 1953 (Wiener 1998 citing Grumet 1979). Computers as a means of communicating with withdrawn teenagers have been advocated (see Hapgood 1988) whilst the use of computer technology and multimedia as a means of offering welfare services is now documented (for example, Freddolino and Han 1999 and Wiener 1998). Such technologies mean that groupwork can be conducted for those unwilling or unable to leave their homes, or those living in geographically isolated locations. The understanding of this latter approach to delivering welfare has become such that a theoretical framework and guidance for good practice is now available (see Schopler, Abell and Galinsky 1998).

The work of Schopler *et al.* is valuable for practitioners planning to set up and facilitate a group where the relationships are conducted by means of an electronic network. However, ICTs have enhanced the ability of those experiencing social or health problems to help themselves, independent of health and social care professionals. Not only do individuals gain information on their situation or condition by means of the Internet, but also by means of this same technology, they might join relevant chat rooms and gain support from people in similar circumstances. In some instances, specialist self-help support sites might be initiated, 'Jooly's Joint' being one example (cited in Jellineck *et al.* 2000). Julie Howell, who suffers from multiple sclerosis, set up this site for the benefit of all those afflicted with this condition. Pleace *et al.* and Hardey (both in this volume) examine this kind of self-help which is also known as computer mediated social support (CMSS). They describe the different methods of giving and receiving support as well as its strengths and limitations. For example, Pleace *et al.* note that in addition to providing information, CMSS has the potential to offer companionship as well as build or maintain self-esteem. What cannot be provided is practical assistance. Nevertheless, CMSS gives individuals the opportunity to provide social care actively themselves, rather than simply receive it.

Neither Pleace *et al.* nor Hardey offer a technologically determinist account of why CMSS has become increasingly popular. Instead, they turn to a model of social change as articulated by Giddens (1991, 1994). According to Giddens, late modern society is characterized by uncertainty and risk. Science and professionals are no longer seen as able to predict or control the social world, therefore the esteem they once enjoyed has diminished. In consequence, citizens become increasingly reflexive and self-reliant, finding their own way to a secure sense of self. Castells (1997), whilst agreeing with some of Gidden's principles, argues that the rise of the network society has fundamentally altered the way in which identity is constructed. For the majority of people, the opportunity for reflexively constructing identity is absent. Instead, argues Castells, there are three types of identity: legitimizing identity; resistance identity; and project identity. Of these, the most significant is resistance identity, which leads to the formation of communities by those experiencing a sense of exclusion. Self-help groups, and the disability movement, are an example of individuals, sharing a particular predicament, coming together to offer each other assistance outside of the frameworks of formal health and care services. They may, in Castells' terms, constitute an example of the excluded excluding the excluders.

Whether Giddens' or Castells' perspective is preferred, one of the current issues for consideration is the nature of the relationship between lay people and professionals. The availability of information on the Internet, plus declining trust and confidence in professionals can lead to tensions. Indeed, Jellineck *et al.* (2000) suggest that the pride of health professionals and their sense of being trusted is under attack. Writing from the perspective of these professionals, Jellineck *et al.* urge patients not to turn up in the surgery bearing armfuls of printouts on their particular condition, and not to test to breaking point their relationship with their GP. From another perspective, it might also be argued that patient access to health information is bringing about a new equality between lay people and professionals. By developing this theme, Hardey explores the nature of 'truth' on the Internet. On the one hand, health and social care professionals are expected to base their practice on the most 'scientific' research findings, whilst on the other hand professional services based on this may be questioned in the light of the personal narratives offered by those in self-help newsgroups.

ICTs, gender and sexuality

Whether paid or unpaid, welfare work is predominantly the domain of women. Within the developed world, however, women are increasingly less available for the unpaid variety as they enter the waged marketplace. During the last quarter of the twentieth century, women's participation in paid work rapidly escalated. This trend can be accounted for by informationalization (the arrival of the information age), networking, and the globalization of the economy, as well as the specific social circumstances of women themselves (Castells 1997). According to Castells, women's relational and managerial skills, which are socially constructed rather than biologically determined, are well suited to the current economic and organizational context. In addition, women command lower wages for the same work as men and, due to their domestic demands, they welcome the flexible working hours that current employment opportunities afford. Within paid work, women are still most likely to be found in the service sector, particularly social and personal services, although increasing numbers of women are being recruited into business services. Given the poor pay, poor promotion prospects and low morale in the social services, alternative employment opportunities in the business sector are likely to be contributing to the recruitment crisis experienced in the social services (see Harlow 2000 and Miller 2002).

Whilst ICTs are impacting upon the changing employment opportunities for women, women do not appear to be attracted to working in the ICT sector itself: 'men outnumber women by over five to one' (Haughton 2002, p.2). This is a problem as, according to Haughton, a million extra ICT professionals will be required over the next five years. Whilst the ICT sector may be working hard to find ways of enticing more women into its ranks, Haughton's concerns raise another question: how are the women employed in the welfare services responding to the increasing application of ICTs? There is a growing body of literature on gender and technology, and feminist theorists such as Wajcman (1994) argue that as a cultural product, technology is not gender neutral: technology is associated with masculinity. Referring to the work of Cockburn (1983) she says:

> Different childhood exposure to technology, the prevalence of different role models, different forms of schooling, and the extreme segregation of the labour market all lead to what Cockburn describes as 'the construction of men as strong, manually able and technologically endowed, and women as physically and technologically incompetent'.
> (Wajcman 1994, p.224)

The implication of this is that women social workers (and welfare workers in general) may feel less comfortable with ICTs or their potential, even when facilities are made available. Wajcman goes on to argue that power relations are implicated as 'technical expertise is a source of men's actual or potential power over women' (p.224). Certainly within the context of social work organizations, the technological experts and senior managers deciding upon ICT applications are most likely to be men, whilst, as noted above, the practitioners are most likely to be women. Whether women are as comfortable as men in their use of ICTs is being empirically explored (see for example Brosnan and Davidson 1996). Despite this, resistance to the introduction of ICTs in the welfare services is not always considered in the light of gendered predisposition or power relations (see for example Riley and Smith 1997; Semke and Nurius 1991). Certainly women today are not computer illiterate, as was being predicted at the end of the 1970s (Tijdens 1999). Middle-class women, in particular, may be developing sophisticated ICT skills and may be the most active users of the health sites of the Internet. The empirical research that does examine gender differences and the use of ICTs at work suggests a complex and nuanced picture (see for example Duncle *et al.* 1994; Parry and Wharton 1994). In addition, the picture continually evolves, as the introduction of new technologies leads to new possibilities in the workplace (Sundin 1998). An example of this appears in this volume when Cullen describes the way in which telemedicine is offering opportunities for nurse practitioners to enhance their expertise and further their careers accordingly. Such developments provide the potential of changing roles within the health services and offering the (predominantly female) nurse practitioners the means of resisting the conventional power relations between themselves and the (predominantly male) consultants.

Debates regarding gender, ICTs and welfare do not only revolve around organizational operations and the segregation of labour, but also around the way in which ICTs facilitate the abuse and exploitation of women. By means of newsgroups men can inform each other of their experiences with prostitutes and recommend where 'value for money' can be found. Adverts for sex tours appear on the Internet. Sex tourism enables men to travel to more 'exotic' places and act in ways that may constitute a risk within the context of their home community (Hughes 1997 cited in Hearn and Parkin 2001). Sex tourism is connected to the trafficking of women, brides and children. For example, women and children from poor countries can be either lured or sold into prostitution, and maintained in brothels accessible to wealthy men from the developed world. Websites on the Internet can be catalogues for the choosing of a bride. Photographs help men to 'pick' their bride with some brides as young as 13 years. Bulletin boards can be used for pornography, including child pornography (Karlen 1996 cited in Hearn and Parkin 2001), with the most violent and sadistic produced by western men in the Third World (Bindel 1996 cited in Hearn and Parkin 2001). The objectification and violation of women and children as described above involves not only sexism, but also racism, colonialism and the exploitation of global economic inequalities. Intricately implicated is the organized crime that Castells (1998) argues has been facilitated by the development of electronic networks.

Organized international exploitation is also highlighted by Relph and Webb (in this volume) in their exposition of global networks and the circulation of child pornography. The fact that the Internet crosses national boundaries means that even when attempts are made to agree principles of censorship or policing, not all countries will comply: for example, Venezuela and Japan have been identified as countries failing to prosecute hosted websites that provide sexually explicit material involving children. Thus, the availability of child pornography via the Internet means that accessing it is easier now than ever before. Whilst doing so might be illegal in the UK, technical innovations can be exploited to avoid or remove evidence that such activity has taken place. Adding complexity to an already difficult area, computer technology allows the generation and circulation of pornographic pictures which have not involved actual children. Civil liberties groups question whether the use of such material should be illegal. However, Relph and Webb are concerned with the way in which all pornographic material, however generated, might contribute towards actual child abuse. They also highlight the way in which chat rooms provide opportunities for potential abusers to meet and groom their victims. Whilst concerns regarding the circulation of child pornography are not new, new ICTs lead to new challenges for agencies charged with the responsibility of protecting the young.

Critical considerations

Much of this chapter, like most of the literature in general, reflects the optimism with which ICTs are usually viewed. They are most often seen as providing solutions to old problems and offering exciting potential. Such enthusiasm can be understood as a consequence of the modernist era in which we live: increased technical rationality is automatically associated with progress (Ravetz 1996). The section above, however, has identified ways in which ICTs might create new difficulties and add to the complexity of problems that are already in existence. This section will highlight still further the critical comment offered by contributors to this volume and elsewhere.

The applications of ICTs are not 'neutral'; they are a reflection of the economic trends, cultural influences and power relations in which they exist. With the rise of 'new managerialism' in the public sector and the challenge to the authority of professionals, it should not be too much of a surprise to learn that ICTs are being used to curtail the autonomy of social workers. ICTs, according to Harris (1998), are being used to assist managers in their control of social workers by constraining the discretion in their work and monitoring their output:

> ...human and information technology surveillance can be combined with workload measurement integrated into the worker's routine on-line recording. The amount of time needed to manage a caseload can then be determined and managerial attention can be given to 'slow workers'. Supervision sessions can concentrate on the worker's 'productivity'. (Harris 1998, p.858)

The introduction of ICTs within the context of a public sector managerialist agenda leads Sapey (1997) to reflect on the implications for social work practice. For example, he suggests that the task of making an assessment has been altered because of the introduction of administrative documents which, once completed, can be analysed by computer. This has led to what is commonly referred to as the 'check list' approach to assessment. Whilst

Sapey locates this development in terms of adult care, a similar change has taken place in children's services. The Looked After Children Assessment and Action Records can also be seen as a research instrument rather than a means of enhancing the sensitivity and reflexivity of social work practice (see Garrett 1999). Therefore, the exchange between social work practitioners and their clients is being shaped by management's desire to generate information that is open to quantitative analysis. Within this volume Huntington and Sapey explain this shift by means of Castells' (1996) thesis concerning the informational age: put simply, within the informational age, the gathering, analysing and distribution of information has become 'part of the new globalized economy'. In consequence, information itself has gained a new meaning and value. As a reflection of this, SSDs devote more attention to gathering information by means of assessment and data analysis than to the delivering of services. Within this exchange, it is the social work agency, rather than the client, that is the recipient.

Like Huntington and Sapey, Regan explores the impact of ICTs on social work practice. Regan, however, is interested in the way in which it is assumed that ICTs will automatically improve economy, efficiency and effectiveness. In keeping with the recent emphasis on e-government and e-business, many local authorities have been re-organizing their referral systems to maximize the use of ICTs. On the basis of empirical research evidence, Regan concludes that whilst there are some benefits, new problems emerge:

> Embedded in the everyday practices of workers routinely using computers to order the referral-taking process were examples of inefficiency, duplication of effort, variability, fragmentation and ultimately new forms of disorder and unreason. (p.106)

Regan explains the unquestioning support for the introduction of ICTs by reference to the work of Baudrillard. For Baudrillard, we are living at a time when the real and the imaginary have become confused. In this 'hyperreality' it is appearance that is valued – in this instance, the appearance of ICTs as efficient. In addition, the use of ICTs in social work can only be justified if complex human situations and involved social work tasks are reconfigured as simple exchanges:

Customer services, 'e-government' business, local e-goverment and system interoperability all rely upon the allegedly transformative capacities of technology to bridge the lacuna between fantasy and the heterogeneity of the lifeworld and public sector organizations. (p.107)

It is also expected that ICTs can improve social work as practitioners update their knowledge by means of on-line journals and the like. However, many social workers do not have access to computers. Even where computers are available, it is often only senior managers who have access to the Internet and email. This situation is not limited to the UK as research conducted in Ohio concludes that welfare workers concerned with direct service provision were significantly less likely to have access to a computer than those in administration (Hughes 1999). Even when all social workers do have this facility, will it be used to update knowledge? As noted above, Berman (1996) raises fundamental questions about social workers' use of literature and research evidence produced from 'scientific' methodologies. On-line journals and databases will not be any more relevant to social workers than their paper equivalent because accessibility is not the key issue. She questions whether internet discussion groups would be a better means of communicating practice wisdom. However, the result of her empirical research suggests that this is not the case. The two social work discussion groups reviewed were dominated by academics whose main concern was with policy rather than practice. Whilst this may change as more social workers have access to computers with telecommunications facilities, they have not been encouraged to engage in theoretical discussion by an education for practice that has become increasingly anti-intellectual (Jones 1996). Although Preston-Shoot (2002) is optimistic about the educational changes that are currently taking place, he also notes the de-professionalization of social work that helps to explain why 'social workers don't read'. Within this context, will the circulation of information by means of ICTs bring about the kind of change that is anticipated?

ICTs may not be able to halt the de-professionalization of social work, indeed they may be implicated in its progress, for example, in terms of encouraging the 'check list' approach to assessment as noted above. Commentators such as Cwikel and Cnaan (1991) have also suggested that the introduction of ICTs may confront social workers with ethical dilemmas, and the question of confidentiality and client information has been raised by Gelman, Pollack and Weiner (1999). Confidentiality is not only an issue for social workers, but for all those concerned with the personal details of individuals. As welfare services become delivered increasingly by multidisciplinary teams, working across organizational boundaries, the electronic dissemination of client data will become commonplace. The principles and practicality of exchanging information and securing its storage on computer will have to be addressed (see Bellamy 1999). Not all commentators are pessimistic, however, and Gould (in this volume) suggests that anxieties over confidentiality might be misplaced.

Whilst the critical reflection thus far has been concerned with the domain of social work, optimism about the beneficial application of ICTs in the sphere of health has also come into question. Cullen considers the emancipatory benefits of ICTs. Information gathered from the Internet might lead to self-care as well as the erosion of hierarchies between lay people and health care professionals. Not only this, ICTs may enable lay people and health care professionals to produce knowledge collaboratively. On the basis of empirical research findings, however, this latter option is resisted: individuals prefer a passive rather than active engagement with the technology. Even gathering health information from the Internet is not as popular as one might assume, with the majority of individuals preferring to go directly to their physician. For Cullen, who draws primarily on a Foucaultian analysis, the social context indicates that ICTs in the health service are more likely to lead to self-regulation rather than self-help. Overall, their application is predominantly reproducing the status quo rather than introducing a new era of empowerment.

Whilst many may prefer a passive relationship with on-line information, there are those who will not enjoy access to it in the first place. As Bellamy says:

> ...in a country where, in several inner-city pockets, the penetration of ordinary telephony remains surprisingly low, we cannot assume that the commercial market will provide universal access to the information superhighway, even in its most basic form. (Bellamy 1999, p.140)

In consequence, concerns have been growing that a bifurcation between the information rich and information poor will arise. However, if services are to be delivered on-line, then the problem is not just to do with the acquisition of information. Although measures funded by urban regeneration grants are attempting to ensure that all communities have access to ICTs (see Carter 1997) the danger exists that social exclusion will be exacerbated.

Conclusion

From the above discussion it is difficult to discern whether ICTs constitute a wonderland of new opportunities or an abyss of electronic oppression: certainly there are both benefits and pitfalls. What is apparent is that ICTs do not exist outside society. Whilst their particular potential makes a distinct contribution, their development and applications are shaped by their cultural context. Therefore, their introduction into the organization, management and practice of health and welfare professionals can be understood in the light of pertinent social and economic theory. With reference to the work of Castells, this chapter has connected ICTs with global economic change and the 'new managerialism' of the public sector. Contributors to this book have also drawn upon the work of Castells, as well as the work of Baudrillard, Giddens and Foucault to explain the emergent issues and trends. The potential implications of ICTs are far reaching and involve the potential transformation of health and welfare services in the UK and elsewhere. How far change will extend remains to be seen.

References

Abell, A. and Oxbrow, N. (2001) *Competing with Knowledge: The Information Professional in the Knowledge Management Age.* London: Library Association Publishing.

Amin, A. (ed) (1994) *Post-Fordism.* Oxford: Blackwell.

Bainbridge, W. S. (1995) 'Sociology on the world wide web.' *Social Science Computer Review 13*, 508–523.

Bell, D. (1973) *The Coming of Post-Industrial Society.* New York: Basic Books.

Bellamy, C. (1999) 'Exploiting information and communication technologies.' In S. Horton and D. Farnham (eds) *Public Management in Britain.* Basingstoke: Macmillan.

Berman, Y. (1996) 'Discussion groups on the Internet as sources of information: the case of social work.' *Aslib Proceedings 48*, 2, 31–36.

Bindel, J. (ed) (1996) *Women Overcoming Violence and Abuse. Research Paper No. 15.* Bradford: Research Unit on Violence, Abuse and Gender Relations, University of Bradford.

BPRC (2000) *Business Process Resource Centre.* http://bprc.warwick.ac.uk/Kmweb.html

Brosnan, M. J. and Davidson, M. J. (1996) 'Psychological gender issues in computing.' *Gender, Work and Organization 3*, 1, 13–25.

Carew, R. (1979) 'The place of knowledge in social work activity.' *The British Journal of Social Work 9*, 349–364.

Carter, D. (1997) '"Digital democracy" or "information aristocracy"? Economic regeneration and the information economy.' In B. Loader (ed) *The Governance of Cyberspace: Politics, Technology and Global Restructuring.* London: Routledge.

Castells, M. (1996) *The Information Age: Economy, Society and Culture. Volume I. The Rise of the Network Society.* Oxford: Blackwell.

Castells, M. (1997) *The Information Age: Economy, Society and Culture. Volume II. The Power of Identity.* Oxford: Blackwell.

Castells, M. (1998) *The Information Age: Economy, Society and Culture. Volume III. End of Millennium.* Oxford: Blackwell (second edition).

Castells, M. (2000) *The Information Age: Economy, Society and Culture. Volume I. The Rise of the Network Society.* Oxford: Blackwell (second edition).

Catchpole, P. and O'Higgins, M. (1991) 'Keying into community care.' *Social Work Today,* 21 March,15–16.

Clarke, J. and Newman, J. (1997) *The Managerial State.* London: Sage.

Cockburn, C. (1983) *Brothers.* London: Pluto Press.

Colombi, D., Rafferty, J. and Steyaert, J. (1993) *Human Services and Information Technology: A European Perspective.* Southampton: University of Southampton and Antwerp, Belgium, UIA-PSW, ENITH.

Cutler, T. and Waine, B. (1994) *Managing the Welfare State.* Oxford: Berg.

Cwikel, J. G. and Cnaan, R. A. (1991) 'Ethical dilemmas in applying second-wave information to social work practice.' *Social Work 36,* 2, 114–120.

Duncle, D. E., King, J. L., Kraemer, K. L. and Danziger, J. N. (1994) 'Women, men and information technology: a gender-based comparison of the impacts of computing experienced by white collar workers.' In V. E. Gattiker (ed) *Women and Technology.* New York: Walter de Gruyter.

Dyson, G. E., Keyworth, G. and Toffler, A. (1994) *Cyberspace and the American Dream: A Magna Carta for the Knowledge Age.* Washington DC: The Progress Freedom Foundation.

Freddolino, P. P. and Han, A. S. (1999) 'Direct service applications of videoconferencing technologies: case examples from Korea and the United States.' In J. A. R. Coe and G. M. Menon (eds) *Computers and Information Technology in Social Work: Education, Training and Practice.* London: The Haworth Press.

Frissen, P. (1997) 'The virtual state: postmodernisation, informatisation and public administration.' In B. Loader (ed) *The Governance of Cyberspace: Politics, Technology and Global Restructuring.* London: Routledge.

Garrett, P. M. (1999) 'Mapping child-care social work in the final years of the twentieth century: a critical response to the "looked after children" system.' *British Journal of Social Work 29,* 27–47.

Gelman, S. R., Pollack, D. and Weiner, A. (1999) 'Confidentiality of social work records in the computer age.' *Social Work 44,* 3, 243–262.

Giddens, A. (1991) *Modernity and Self-identity.* Cambridge: Polity Press.

Giddens, A. (1994) *Beyond Left and Right: The Future of Radical Politics.* Cambridge: Polity Press.

Giffords, E. D. (1998) 'Social work on the internet: an introduction.' *Social Work 43,* 3, 243–251.

Glastonbury, B. (1985) *Computers in Social Work.* Basingstoke: Macmillan/BASW.

Goldstein, H. (1992) 'The knowledge base of social work practice: theory, wisdom, analogue or art?' *Families in Society: The Journal of Contemporary Human Services 71,* 32–43.

Grumet, G. W. (1979) 'Telephone therapy: a review and case report.' *American Journal of Orthopsychiatry 49,* 574–584.

Hapgood, M. (1988) 'Creative direct work with adolescents: the story of Craig Brooks.' In J. Aldgate and J. Simmonds (eds) *Direct Work with Children: A Guide for Social Work Practitioners.* London: Batsford/BAAF.

Harlow, E. (2000) 'New managerialism and social work: changing women's work.' In E. Harlow and J. Lawler (eds) *Management Social Work and Change.* Aldershot: Ashgate.

Harris, J. (1998) 'Scientific management, bureau-professionalism, new managerialism: the labour process of state social work.' *British Journal of Social Work 28,* 839–62.

Harvey, D. (1989) *The Condition of Postmodernity.* Oxford: Blackwell.

Haughton, E. (2002) 'Gender split.' *educ@guardian The Guardian,* 5 March, 2–3.

Hearn, J. and Parkin, W. (2001) *Gender, Sexuality and Violence in Organizations.* London: Sage.

Hughes, D. M. (1997) 'Trafficking and sexual exploitation on the Internet.' *Feminista! The Online Journal of Feminist Construction 1,* 8. Http://www.feminista.com/v1n8hughes. html

Hughes, L. (2000) 'Crossing, building and breaking the boundaries: social work in a global context.' In E. Harlow and J. Lawler (eds) *Management, Social Work and Change.* Aldershot: Ashgate.

Hughes, R. (1999) 'Access and use of information technology by human service providers.' *Journal of Technology in Human Services 16,* 1, 1–16.

Jellineck, D., Lambden, P. and Lilley, R. (2000) *Your Health and the Internet.* Norwich: The Stationery Office.

Jones, C. (1996) 'Anti-intellectualism and the peculiarities of British social work education.' In N. Parton (ed) *Social Theory, Social Change and Social Work.* London: Routledge.

Karlen, H. (1996) 'Child pornography and paedophiles in Sweden.' In M. Jyrkinen (ed) *Changing Faces of Prostitution.* Helsinki: Unioni – The League of Finnish Feminists.

Kelly, A. (1991) 'The "new" managerialism in the social services.' In P. Carter, T. Jeffs and M. K. Smith (eds) *Social Work and Social Welfare Year Book 3.* Buckingham: Open University Press.

Kumar, K. (1995) *From Post-industrial to Post-modern Society: New Theories of the Contemporary World.* Oxford: Blackwell.

Lawler, J. (2000) 'The rise of managerialism in social work.' In E. Harlow and J. Lawler (eds) *Management, Social Work and Change.* Aldershot: Ashgate.

Lawton, A. and Rose, A. (1994) *Organisation and Management in the Public Sector.* London: Pitman Publishing (second edition).

Leonard, P. (1997) *Postmodern Welfare: Reconstructing an Emancipatory Project.* London: Sage.

Lyotard, J. F. (1984) *The Postmodern Condition: A Report on Knowledge.* Manchester: Manchester University Press.

Miller, A. (2002) 'Situations vacant.' *Community Care*, February, II–IV.

Oakland, J. S. (1989) *Total Quality Management.* Oxford: Heinmann.

Parry, L. E. and Wharton, R. R. (1994) 'Networking in the workplace: the role of gender in electronic communications.' In V. E. Gattiker (ed) *Women and Technology.* New York: Walter de Gruyter.

Peters, T. J. and Waterman, R. H. (1982) *In Search of Excellence.* New York: Harper Row.

Preston-Shoot, M. (2002) 'Why social workers don't read.' *CareandHealth Guide 11*, 10–12.

Rafferty, J. (1997) 'Shifting paradigms of information technology in social work education and practice.' *British Journal of Social Work 27*, 959–74.

Ravetz, J. (1996) 'The concept of progress and technological rationality in human services.' In B. Glastonbury (ed) *Dreams and Realities: Information Technology in the Human Services. Papers from the HUSITA 4 Conference held in Finland 1996.* Helsinki: Stakes.

Riley, L. and Smith, G. (1997) 'Developing and implementing IS: a case study analysis in social services.' *Journal of Information Technology 12*, 305–21.

Sapey, B. (1997) 'Social work tomorrow: towards a critical understanding of technology in social work.' *British Journal of Social Work 27*, 803–14.

Schopler, J. H., Abell, M. D. and Galinsky, M. J. (1998) 'Technology-based groups: a review and conceptual framework for practice.' *Social Work 43*, 3, 254–67.

Semke, J. I. and Nurius, P. S. (1991) 'Information structure, information technology, and the human services organizational environment.' *Social Work 36*, 4, 353–58.

Siddall, A. (2000) 'From Beveridge to Best Value: transitions in welfare provision.' In E. Harlow and J. Lawler (eds) *Management, Social Work and Change.* Aldershot: Ashgate.

Steyaert, J., Colombi, D. and Rafferty, J. (eds) (1996) *Human Services and Information Technology: An International Perspective.* Aldershot: Arena.

Sundin, E. (1998) 'Organizational conflict, technology and space: a Swedish case study of the gender system and the economic system in action.' *Gender, Work and Organization 5*, 1, 31–42.

Thompson, P. and McHugh, D. (1995) *Work Organisations: A Critical Introduction.* Basingstoke: Macmillan (second edition).

Tijdens, K. G. (1999) 'Behind the screens: the foreseen and unforeseen impact of computerization on female office workers' jobs.' *Gender, Work and Organization 6*, 1, 47–57.

Toffler, A. (1970) *Future Shock.* London: Bodley Head.

Wajcman, J. (1994) 'Technology as masculine culture.' In *The Polity Reader in Gender Studies.* Cambridge: Polity Press.

Webb, S. A. (1998) 'Visions of excess: cyberspace, digital technologies and new cultural politics.' *Information, Communication and Society 1*, 1, 46–69.

Webb, S. A. (2001) 'Some considerations on the validity of evidence-based practice in social work.' *British Journal of Social Work 31*, 1, 57–80.

Wiener, L. S. (1998) 'Telephone support groups for HIV-positive mothers whose children have died of AIDS.' *Social Work 43*, 3, 279–85.

Part One

Social Work and Social Care

CHAPTER 1

The Caring Professions and Information Technology

In Search of a Theory

Nick Gould

> Information is a fundamental and crucial element in the delivery of quality social care services that meet the needs and expectations of service users. Information drives services and sometimes actually is the service. (Department of Health 2000)

A recent Department of Health consultation document speculated that British personal social services might feel that they are being 'swamped' by an information agenda. This agenda is being driven from several directions. From the centre, or 'top down' there is: an e-government expectation that all transactions should be capable of being carried out electronically by 2005; all records should be held electronically; there must be interoperability (compatibility) of systems, and the service user should experience the delivery of services as seamless; initiatives such as Quality Protects (www.doh.gov.uk/qualityprotects/) and Best Value (www.doh.gov.uk/ssu/gettingbestvalue.htm) support performance assessment and monitoring regimes which have an information component; the emerging health modernization agenda implies the development of information strategies to support national service frameworks; and a range of cross-departmental policy themes, such as social exclusion, economic competitiveness and democratic renewal, all have implications for the social care information agenda. From the local level or 'bottom up', there is a further deluge of information demands: direct payment systems and other developments towards user autonomy; servicing of local partnership arrangements;

co-ordination of the management of care; strategic planning requirements and corporate IT developments, as well as whatever other local political agendas are active. As this author has previously observed, in the space of twenty-five years human service organizations have moved from a position where the introduction of carbon-copied 'ping-pong' memos was seen as a technological solution to the current situation where intranets, laptop computers and mobile phones are becoming standard parts of the practitioner's tool kit (Gould 1996a).

Various phases of technology implementation in the care sector can be identified over this period (Riley and Smith 1997, p.310). First, mainframe-based client index systems began to appear in the 1970s. Then, specialist 'stand alone' databases were developed in the 1980s to meet the needs of specialist services such as child protection or family placements. From the late 1980s more integrated management information systems were introduced, operating over client–server networks, which attempted to capture the decisions, activity and costing implications for the whole organization. Inevitably, this also has not been the 'end of technology'; applications continue to emerge and supersede whatever is the current state of the art, particularly as bandwidth of wide and local area networks increases, and as mobile computing becomes cheaper and more functional.

Whatever the form of the technology, certain imperatives and problems remain in relation to the collection, management and deployment of social care information. Whilst there is a realization that the deployment of information and communication technology is a necessary element in the modernization agenda, a unified and coherent perspective of how this is to be achieved has yet to emerge. Most social services information systems operate over local networks, usually having evolved from in-house developments with very little standardization of data format, other than to service the collection of central government statistics (Glastonbury 2001). Neither is there a national local authority network, such as the equivalent of NHSnet, nor has the social care market been sufficiently lucrative for commercial developers to drive a standardized approach to information management. At a normative level, the intention is that IT should be the servant of improving the quality of care in relation to four objectives (Department of Health 2000):

- Social care should be citizen focused.
- Social care should be accessible.

- Social care should be integrated.

- Social care should be socially inclusive.

However, the road to deploying technology to achieve these objectives is as yet uncharted, even with the publication of the Department of Health's (2000) *Information for Social Care*. Generic reasons why conceptualizing the relationship between technology and service delivery is difficult can be identified at three levels of analysis: individual practitioner, national and global. These will be commented upon in turn:

Practitioner level: social work is an inherently complex and fuzzy activity. The process of social work cannot be modelled algorithmically. Despite the claims of evidence-based practice, the core business of social care cannot be characterized in terms of technical rationality.

National level: the organization of social care has shifted from Fordist to post-Fordist networks. According to this argument the generic social service department operated on the basis of batch processing of service users. Holding a monopolistic position in relation to the delivery and co-ordination of services, departments' information systems had only to be conterminous with the boundaries of the department. The introduction of quasi-market mechanisms, separation of purchasing and provision functions, and particularly the encouragement of independent suppliers of services, has produced a social care environment within which Taylorist or Fordist organization of service production has been replaced by 'network organizations' (Gould 1996b; James 1994). In the UK this was largely driven by the Griffiths report (Griffiths 1988) on community care and the subsequent National Health Service and Community Care Act (1990), but the marketization and reprofessionalization of social care can be identified generally across western welfare states (Steyaert, Colombi and Rafferty 1996; Steyaert and Gould 1999). The organizational segmentation of care places enormous strains upon the capacity of agencies to collect and exchange information across boundaries.

Global level: globalization is producing continuous change in the environment of social care. More technologically deterministic versions of this thesis see the problems as themselves generated by new technology. Contentious though this may be, and arguable though the nature and extent of the interaction between the global macro economy and the local configuration of services may be (Pugh and Gould 2000), it is argued that change has become continuous and less predictable, creating for agencies an ongoing 'catching up' problem between the external environment and the capacity of the organization to manage its informational needs.

Thus, although the technological advancement of computing during the last twenty years has been spectacular, there is substantial empirical evidence that human services organizations are struggling to conceptualize and implement information strategies which serve the needs of service users and professionals in relation to collecting, storing, updating, retrieving, sharing and using information. This chapter attempts to give an overview of three approaches to the attempt to model the place of IT within the organization: social informatics, the learning organization and knowledge management.

The first has been an attempt by (primarily) European academics, consultants and IT workers within human services to build an indigenous model, in particular one that rescues discussions of computing within social care from the cruder forms of technological determinism and preoccupation with technical fixes. By mirroring 'health informatics' it also aspires to make the topic more fashionable and give it the status of a discipline. Theories of the learning organization and knowledge management are drawn primarily from business management but may have applicability for human services, if problems of translation from a commercial context can be overcome. The learning organization is associated with a range of management and organizational change theorists such as Senge (1990), and Argyris and Schon (1996). With its emphasis on systemic thinking, teamwork and reflective practice, the learning organization seems to offer a vision that is progressive and aligned with the culture and ethos of the caring professions. Finally, knowledge management, a current vogue in human resources and information management theory, indicates a cluster of approaches (not all technology-based) to creating an 'organizational memory' so that expertise can be retained, organized, and made accessible across the organization. Going beyond the concept of the electronic office which mimics the paper-based administrative system, knowledge management seems to capture the potential of the interconnectivity of the Web and intrabased groupware.

It will be argued in the later parts of the chapter that all the models have something to offer in thinking about how information technology can be deployed in human services, but that they all need further elaboration in order to meet concerns about ethical and value-related issues. In particular, we need to give consideration to the relationship between the models and three themes which seem to be recurring in the debates about information technology, information management and professional ethics:

- confidentiality and the giving of informed consent – restricting the sharing of information to those who are authorised

- integrity – ensuring the quality and accuracy of personal data

- availability – the access given to those who are the subjects of data.

Social informatics

During the last ten years there has been a movement towards the development of social informatics as a parallel discipline to that of health informatics, defined in 1988 by the World Health Organization as 'the combination of technology and methodology which makes possible the computer-assisted collection, storage, processing, retrieval, distribution and management of information' (World Health Organization 1988, p.3). Over time health informatics has begun to achieve the kind of 'closure' which characterizes the process by which occupational groups seek to achieve professional status, that is, the development of a body of knowledge, training in universities, etc. (Macdonald 1995). In many ways the professional development of social care, and social work in particular, can be seen as mirroring this process of professionalization, so it is not surprising that we have also seen the emergence of claims for 'social informatics' as a discipline. This has particularly been associated with university-based IT specialists in academic social work departments, but also has champions within service agencies and government departments (some indication of the constituency can be gleaned from Kerslake and Gould 1996 and Gould and Moultrie 1997).

In the title of an edited volume, Jan Steyaert asked 'Information technology and human services, more than computers?' (Steyaert 1996) and this encapsulates the main assertion within the social informatics model, that there are service imperatives which go beyond narrow technical considerations concerning the computerization of services. Steyaert conceptualizes social policy, human services and information technology as independent variables which exert multidirectional influence on one another (Steyaert 1996, p.12). Thus, there is an attempt to steer a course between, on the one hand, a unilinear, causal view which saw policy determining how computers were deployed within agencies and, on the other, a view which saw the social policy agenda, for instance the implementation of care management and charging for services, as facilitated by the information processing capacities which new technology made available (Lewis and Glennerster 1996).

In part this also reflects a historical critique of how different interest groups within the personal social services arena have sought to assert control over the management of information. Kerslake (1996), for instance, has depicted this as the struggle between two factions: the 'enthusiastic amateurs', protagonists from professional social work backgrounds who dabbled in computers and who became champions for the introduction of information technology within their organizations, and 'the programmers who went native', IT professionals seconded from central computing departments or employed from IT backgrounds, who become enthusiasts for developing new technology applications in social service environments (Kerslake 1996, p.7). The implication of Kerslake's argument is that neither the enthusiastic amateur nor the programmer gone native can provide solutions to the problems of information management emerging within the modernization of social services. This, the argument proceeds, requires a particular kind of hybrid specialist who has understanding of the professional and organizational character of social services, but who also has depth of knowledge about information technology:

> If departments try to build client database systems, or indeed any IT systems onto an inadequate analysis and resolution of the information problems then those databases are never likely to succeed. However, for SSDs to change this calls for a senior management that is able to understand the value of information, be able [sic] to implement, cost, and control an information management strategy and be aware of the potentiality of information technology. (Kerslake 1996, p.9)

This quotation encapsulates the essence of the social informatics approach, that this is an emergent area of professional specialism that bridges the professional discipline of social work, and the knowledge and skills of the technician. This perspective has been taken up internationally through networks such as ENITH (European Network of Information Technology in Human Services) and HUSITA (Human Services Information Technology Association). These networks have been significant arenas for the development of a social informatics perspective.

One can extrapolate from this literature a model of social informatics as an approach to understanding a dialectical relationship between social policy, social services organization and practice and information technology. The development of the model is reflected in a series of surveys undertaken from within the European ENITH community in 1992 and 1993 (Colombi, Rafferty and Steyaert 1993; Qvortrup, Glastonbury and De Graaf 1992), which went global in 1996 with an eighteen country survey of how information technology is being implemented in human services (Steyaert, Colombi and Rafferty 1996), and which has continued to be researched and developed (Steyaert and Gould 1999). Across these surveys is a discernable shift of emphasis from the focus on efficiency, to effectiveness, to redesigning care delivery (Steyaert *et al.* 1996, pp.250–255).

Efficiency paradigm
Based on the introduction of word-processing and databases, the initial preoccupation was with increasing the speed of administrative tasks through the 'electronic office'. The assumed impact on service delivery was indirect, that time freed from administration was then available for direct practice with service users.

Effectiveness paradigm
As the agenda of accountability and public sector managerialism became more prominent in the 1980s and early 1990s, primarily making service proiders accountable to funders and politicians rather than service users, so the imperative emerged to implement client and management information systems which could produce data for monitoring and evaluation. 'The focus was on managing budgets, measuring throughput in different categories and quantifying "success" on often rather arbitrary criteria' (Steyaert *et al.* 1996, p.252). This began to shift towards an enlarged conception of effectiveness which included information support for practitioners, such as decision support systems which made evidence available to the practitioner.

Redesigning care delivery paradigm
Steyaert and Gould more recently have written about how, in the European context, core structures of the welfare state have been redrafted, and how these have been supported and facilitated by new technology (Steyaert and Gould 1999). We have tracked four dimensions along which this has taken

place: the retreat of the state from direct provision of services; the separation of purchasing and providing and the introduction of quasi-markets; the reprofessionalization of social work within this market nexus; and the beginnings of user-led service delivery. This combination of linked shifts is contemporaneous with the change in social informatics from the technology of the electronic office to the capabilities for communication and connectedness presented by inter and intranets; a shift from an information to a communication paradigm. This is also a corollary of the organizational transformation of social services, sometimes characterized as a shift to a post-Fordist model (Gould 1996c) or the emergence of the 'network agency'.

Learning organization

Arguably, a more holistic model for locating the contribution of information technology within the caring professions has been that of the learning organization. Although the discourse of organizational learning (how an organization learns) has a longer history, the concept of the learning organization (the characteristics of an organization that learns) began to crystallize from the mid to late 1980s. Under the conditions of a globalizing economy, where competitive edge depends upon maintaining processes of continuous improvement, there has been an emerging view that this depends upon a commitment to continuous learning (Jarvis 1999). In short, the contention is that, although short-term gains might be achieved by 'down-sizing' and other efficiency fixes, the most effective insurance against being left behind by rapid technological change and a volatile economic environment is to embed within the organization processes which facilitate learning in order to keep abreast of change and to innovate (Senge 1990). Hitherto, much of this discourse and practice has emerged from and been confined to management and business theory, and has been exemplified in commercial organizations. However, very recently there has been a growing realization that personal social services are also being caught up in this globalizing world of downward pressure on resources and rapidly changing patterns of social need, where organizational change is not a periodic crisis but a continuous fact of life (Gould 2000; Pugh and Gould 2000; Steyaert and Gould 1999). The linkages between the learning organization, technological innovation and the global economy are quite explicit in the literature:

The growth of the field [learning organizations] can be explained by at least three external factors: the speed of technological change, the advance of globalization; and growing corporate competition. The speed of technological change means that there is continual pressure on firms to reduce the time from conception to launch of new products, and communications innovations such as the Internet mean that companies and knowledge workers within them may have to adapt radically and in unforeseen directions. (Easterby-Smith, Snell and Gherardi 1998, pp.259–260).

The concept of the learning organization reflects many of the preoccupations of globalization theory, particularly those strands which emphasize the impact of new information technologies on organizational life. In turn, this builds on a longer sociological tradition of theorization of the relationship between organizational structure and behaviour. Within classic Weberian theory of the bureaucracy (Weber 1947), learning is strongly associated with traditional notions of professionalization where hierarchical stratification separates the thinkers and deciders from the doers. In later 'scientific' or Taylorist theories of the organization, the emphasis was on the acquisition of technical skills for task efficiency. Individuals were trained to perform a segment of the production process within a highly standardized system. Over time a tension was to emerge between the dehumanizing effects of Taylorism (Beynon 1973) and the human relations movement of the 1960s and 1970s (see for example Maslow 1968) which focused attention on meeting human needs through personal development, job enrichment and the quality of working life.

With globalization this has given way to the view that the achievement of learning for continuous change cannot be located in notions of learning or training that are entirely based on the individual undergoing a discrete training event. Drawing on the action learning theories of Revans (Revans 1980), and later the reflective learning paradigm of Schon (Schon 1983), learning is conceptualized as something which can be promoted through collective problem-based or experiential learning on the job. Associated with this shift is an implied change of metaphor for conceptualizing organizational life, from the dominant Taylorist image of the organization as a machine towards the metaphor of the organization as a system, that has to adapt through learning to the changing demands created by the environment (Senge 1990).

Two fundamental premises lie within this systemic perspective. First, individual learning is a necessary but not sufficient condition for organizational learning. Second, and this has critical implications for the implementation of information technology, the learning experience is more pervasive and distributed than that delivered through the training course or event:

> ...learning incorporates the broad dynamics of adaptation, change and environmental alignment of organisations, takes place across multiple levels within the organisation, and involves the construction and reconstruction of meanings and world views within the organisation. (Gould 2000, p.587)

The theory of the learning organization is essentially a cybernetic or systems theory, and as such it draws energy from the adoption of information technology through distributed systems which disseminate information, elicit feedback and adapt to environmental flux. In a comprehensive review of the literature, Rosengarten (1999) identified one of the core elements of the learning organization as being free vertical and horizontal flow of information. There are now indications that the discourse of the learning organization is seeping into the personal social services as they seek to adapt to many of the same pressures exerted in the global corporate world towards flexibility, accountability and efficiency (Khan and Dominelli 2000). Information management and the use of information technology are key strategies within this development (Gould 2000). A case example is the Children's Society, whose corporate strategy document is permeated with the language of the learning organization. 'We will create a learning environment based on shared access to information and knowledge across the Society, and which acknowledges all experiences as part of the learning process, including failure' (Children's Society 2000 p.9). This is closely, even inextricably, linked with the implementation of an organization-wide, networked database, for collecting and distributing information. 'A corporate strategy on knowledge and information management will be developed' (Children's Society 2000, p.15).

Knowledge management

It is a fairly commonplace observation that the new economy is a knowledge economy; the diffusion of information and communication technologies creates the conditions for an economy based on knowledge (Tapscott 1996).

At the same time, despite initial optimism about the potential of artificial intelligence, there has been a recent recognition that expert knowledge lies in the people within the organization, not the hardware: 'In the new economy the key assets of the organization are intellectual assets, and they focus on the knowledge worker' (Tapscott 1996, p.46).

Part of this realization is that the knowledge worker, or organizational asset, walks out of the office door every night, and if dissatisfied may not return the next morning. This vulnerability extends to the health and social care field, as well as the more obviously commercial sector of the knowledge economy. The UK press recently gave coverage to the example of a consultant neurologist who, for reasons of dissatisfaction with resources, left the National Health Service for the private sector, taking with him his highly specialized sphere of knowledge. One of his particular complaints was the lack of computing facilities:

> Dr Gross, who until last week was chairman of neurosciences at the Royal Surrey county hospital in Guildford, Surrey, wrote in the London Evening Standard that he has never had a computer or easy access to information technology, despite having been in the NHS for 31 years. (Vasagar 2001)

As we have seen, the concept of the learning organization has been one response to the processes and speed of change initiated by the emergence of information technologies. It is also a model of organizational development which utilizes the potential of information technology for the integration and dissemination of information. This can be likened to the creation of an 'organizational memory', a neural-like electronic network which stores the collective experience of the agency, and can be accessed at will (Gould 2000). This notion of an organizational memory prefigures and anticipates a third model, one which at the time of writing has had only marginal impact on the caring professions: knowledge management, or, reduced to the inevitable acronym, KM. Knowledge management recognizes that the basic currency of an IT strategy is knowledge. Complex organizations have a tendency to generate repositories of knowledge, databases and the like, throughout the organization with little co-ordination or oversight of the whole picture. The consequence is that teams or individuals continually and unknowingly re-invent the wheel, or are unable to locate the information they need. A recent report from the Department of Health's Social Services Inspectorate (Social Services Inspectorate and Audit Commission 2001) comments on the finding that sometimes good practice in one area of service was not known to staff working for the council providing it, despite attracting national interest.

There has been a particular concern on the part of commercial organizations that they are increasingly vulnerable to the effects of individuals leaving the company and taking with them their own valuable knowledge, and sometimes their own ability to access idiosyncratic information systems which they have developed. As a response to these problems, knowledge management is seen as a strategy for assembling and disseminating knowledge across the organization, rather than allowing it to reside with individuals or sections of the organization.

In the first 'wave' of knowledge management this has been seen as a technological issue, of creating networked systems which permit the exchange of information. More recently, it has been recognized that this approach overlooks the importance of social capital – networks and relationships – which underpins the motivation and willingness of individuals or teams to pool information. In a culture which may be defensive because of perceived external threats such as merger, rationalization and 'flexibility', the rational response of those with important information will be to hoard it and make themselves indispensable. The concept of knowledge management seems to assume a level of trust which to employees may seem to be at odds with the corporation's overarching imperative to collectivize information because it generates competitive advantages. This realization seems to be producing a shift from viewing knowledge management as a matter of improving integrated systems at the technical level, towards an interest in knowledge as a characteristic of the human relational dimensions of the organization:

> Initially, many companies saw KM as a technical task, and handed it over to their IT people, who went away and created sophisticated IT systems. But it's really a social, not a technological issue. Where it has been effective this has been because more attention was put on the human dimension – the social, emotional and relational context. (Professor Sumantra Ghoshal, quoted in *The Times* (2000)

The discourse of knowledge management is not yet emerging strongly in the human services, but it seems probable that it will, particularly under conditions of high turnover of human resources. In the face of vulnerability to individuals 'defecting' and taking expertise with them, agencies may look to strategies which are defensive and insure the organization against loss of knowledge.

Knowledge, power and professional ethics

Discussions of ethics in relation to professional practice and new technology are often characterized by an assumption that technology has introduced a qualitatively different set of issues to ethical discourse. In fact, it will be argued here, the ethical concerns are those which have been longstanding concerns of professional discourse, although in some respects technologization of practice intensifies some aspects of those concerns.

The concern with confidentiality of information is a consistent feature of treatments of ethical practice which derive principally from a Kantian principle-based approach (Banks 2001). Biestek, the most widely cited exponent of this position within social work, defined confidentiality as the preservation of secret information concerning the service user which is disclosed during the professional relationship (Banks 2001). For Biestek, confidentiality is a basic right of the service user and represents an ethical obligation for the worker. However, and here the problems which have continually beset the tension between the Kantian and utilitarian positions in ethical discourses re-emerge, this 'basic right' can be over-ridden by obligations to the protection of the wider community. Sometimes there is a tendency to take a narrow legalistic approach to discussing the ethics of confidentiality, for instance considering only the content of data protection legislation, rather than focusing on the irreducibly ethical nature of the subject, though this is perhaps more widely recognized in medicine:

> Confidentiality is a fundamental principle of medical ethics. That which passes between the patient and their doctor in the course of a professional relationship is confidential or secret. Its principle as a breach of contract between the parties has not been tested in the courts, so it remains an ethical rather than a legal principle, because there are few rigid rules to apply. (*Croner's Health Service Manager*, June 2000, p.C245)

The presumption of confidentiality has always been attached to keeping paper-based case records, again a longstanding feature of social work as a form of practice. Confidentiality as an issue can be unpacked to reveal an underlying set of questions which relate to privacy and ownership of personal data. In many ways the medium for storing and communicating personal data, be it paper, electronic bytes or oral communication, is secondary to the generic principles which underlie the maintenance of appropriate confidentiality. A useful analysis of these which comes from the field of health informatics but which can be applied to the social care context comes from the Caldicott Committee which in 1997 enunciated a framework of six principles (Department of Health 1997):

- Justify the purpose for using confidential information.

- Use it only when absolutely necessary.

- Use the minimum of information that is needed.

- Provide access only on a strictly need-to-know basis.

- Everyone must understand their responsibilities.

- They must also know the relevant law and act within it.

The dystopian view which sees the computerization of services as a threat to confidentiality rests upon a rather questionable assumption that information is more likely to be breached if stored electronically than if maintained on paper. Because of the power and connectedness of computers it is assumed that the risk of unauthorized access is higher than that which follows from practitioners carrying personal information in notebooks in their briefcase or left in their cars, or stored in filing cabinets. It is interesting to note that in the UK, the sequence of legislating to protect personal data has been to start from a presumption that the need was to protect data in electronic format (the Data Protection Act 1984) and then to enlarge this to incorporate manual records (the Data Protection Act 1998). In other words the legislation has not been reformed to 'catch up' with technological change, rather it has acknowledged the need to equalize the treatment of manual records with that of automated records, recognizing that both can be vulnerable. Thus, under the 1998 Act, and in line with relevant European Directives, health and social care agencies will need to operate within eight principles of data protection:

- the fair and lawful obtaining of personal data

- the holding of personal data for specified and lawful purposes

- that data should be processed within the rights for individuals which are set out under the Act

- that personal data should be adequate, relevant and not excessive in relation to its purpose

- that it should be accurate and up to date

- that it should not be kept for longer than necessary for its purpose

- that it should be safeguarded against loss, damage and unauthorized use

- that personal data should only be disclosed outside the EC if the receiving country itself has appropriate mechanisms for protection of data.

Whichever of the three models discussed above drives the implementation of information technology in social care, be it social informatics, the learning organization or knowledge management, it is the case that all three push towards the greater integration, dissemination and sharing of data. Within organizations concerned with care, this is almost inevitably going to mean co-ordination of sharing of personal data. For instance, the practitioner undertaking a care assessment with a service user in the community may record the assessment on a laptop; periodically this data will be uploaded onto a larger client information system which lies on a networked server; for the purposes of monitoring and strategic planning this data may be aggregated and transformed into statistical reports. As the modernization of health and social care proceed so the likelihood will also develop that some of these processes will take place across organizational boundaries, for instance between health, social care and housing agencies. There is a corollary argument that the relaxation of confidentiality that all this implies will mean a shift of focus to ensuring informed consent by service users to information sharing. This in turn is raising anxieties for some commentators who fear that the protocols that will be required to guarantee that informed consent is given before any service user information is recorded will create conflicts with the objective of delivering timely and effective intervention:

> There will always be significant numbers of people in need of services, often urgently in need, who have not gone through a process of consenting to the use of personal information. What should be the reaction of practitioners? Respect the absence of consent and not give the best service? This would put them in breach of their common law duty of care. Ignore the absence of consent and get on with the job (common practice for many)? There is an information dilemma in need of resolution. (Glastonbury 2001, pp.9–10)

The potential for breach of professional confidentiality within this scenario (which continues to be addressed at a technical level through the continuing development of security protocols such as encryption, firewalls and password management) should not be ignored. However, there is perhaps a danger of becoming preoccupied with the detail of these 'conventional' ethical concerns, without considering the wider political context of information management, and implications for professionals and service users.

At this juncture it will be helpful to consider some of the sociological approaches to understanding the social construction of technology. Sometimes an opposition is drawn between actor network approaches as a form of micro social constructionism (Mackay 1995) and the neo-Marxist approach of writers such as Braverman (1984) which place emphasis on the social-economic forces shaping the implementation of technology. The former, operating at the micro level of analysis, collapses distinctions between technology and the social, so that inanimate objects, as much as individuals, are all actors involved in the implementation of technological systems. Technical objects and people become actors who are enrolled and operate within networks. Such networks exist within uncertain and conflicting processes, such as social work; they enrol and socialize actors within forms of action, disseminate specific forms of rationality, mobilize support for particular approaches or outcomes, and can produce unintended outcomes (Gould 1996b). Neo-Marxism, as exemplified by Braverman, attempts to identify the purposes of technological development as shaped by the interests of capital to extract increased value from the workforce, particularly through the deskilling and exploitation of labour in capitalist economies. As Mackay comments, 'Clearly, it is no great leap for the social shaping of the social technology approach from seeing technology as a social product to seeing it as political' (1995, p.43).

Once we broaden our understanding of technology to include this consideration of the social and political domains, it can be argued that (by and large) these considerations are largely ignored or minimized by the conventional emphasis on privacy and confidentiality as the only ethical or value-based issues raised by the implementation of new technologies in the caring professions.

It is also arguable that the dominant models of technology implementation so far outlined do little to advance a wider political or ethical perspective. Social informatics, learning organization theory and knowledge management all emerge from managerial perspectives which have little to say about how the interests of those who are the recipients of services can exert more control over the technology process, or define the purposes to which it is put.

It has been suggested that learning organization theory is a disciplinary discourse which is 'suspected of colluding with the ruling courts which govern organizations and of employing, in an ideological manner, a discourse of democracy and liberation' (Gherardi 1999, p.105). This might also be suggested in relation to social informatics and knowledge management. In other words, the humanistic claims for these models (Dovey 1997), that they are empowering and participatory, are contradicted by their actual, strategic function of mobilizing consent and compliance around top-down managerial agendas. They are also models which are silent on the issue of service user access to, and control of, information. There is growing research evidence that the 'digital divide' reinforces the traditional fault lines of social exclusion; as Blackler, Crump and McDonald (1998) have commented, information and knowledge are culturally situated, technologically mediated and socially distributed. Service users have little serious purchase on shaping new technology to provide more responsive services (Fabian Society 2001).

I began this chapter by considering how technological innovation and human services practice had interacted dialectically as mainframe computers gave way to PC-based databases and, most recently, mobile telephony. The technology exists for social services to continue becoming 'intelligent organizations' with hierarchical systems which not only provide routine administrative support, and generate indicators of organizational performance, but also provide global access through the Internet to complex expertise and knowledge. But, thankfully, the ethical and political spaces which give practice its critical dimension are not replaced by such technology.

References

Argyris, C. and Schon, D. (1996) *Organizational Learning II: Theory, Method and Practice.* Reading, MA: Addison-Wesley.

Banks, S. (2001) *Ethics and Values in Social Work.* Basingstoke: Macmillan.

Beynon, H. (1973) *Working For Ford.* London: Penguin.

Blackler, F., Crump, N. and McDonald, S. (1998) 'Knowledge, organizations and competition.' In G. von Krogh, J. Roos and D. Kleine (eds) *Knowing in Firms: Understanding, Managing and Measuring Knowledge.* London: Sage Publications.

Braverman, H. (1984) *Labour and Monopoly Capital: The Degradation of Work in the Twentieth Century.* London: Monthly Review Press.

Children's Society (2000) The Corporate plan 2000–02. London: The Children's Society.

Colombi, D., Rafferty, J. and Steyaert, J. (eds) (1993) *Human Services and Information Technology: A European Perspective.* Antwerp: European Network for Information Technology.

Croners Health Service Manager, June 2000. Kingston upon Thames: Croner.CCH.

Department of Health (1997) *The Caldicott Committee: A Report on the Review of Patient-identifiable Information.* London: Department of Health.

Department of Health (2000) *Information For Social Care: A Framework for Improving Quality in Social Care through Better Use of Information and Information Technology.* London: Department of Health.

Dovey, K. (1997) 'The learning organization and the organization of learning: power, transformation and the search for form in learning organizations.' *Management Learning* 29, 3, 331–349.

Easterby-Smith, M., Snell, R. and Gherardi, S. (1998) 'Organizational learning: diverging communities of practice?' *Management Learning 29*, 3, 259–72.

Fabian Society (2001) *Beyond Access: ICT and Social Exclusion.* London: Fabian Society.

Gherardi, S. (1999) 'Learning as problem-driven or learning in the face of mystery.' *Organization Studies 20*, 1, 101–24.

Glastonbury, B. (2001) 'Calling the tune in social care information.' *New Technology in the Human Services 13*, 3 and 4, 1–10.

Gould, N. (1996a) 'Introduction.' In A. Kerslake and N. Gould (eds) *Information Management in Social Services.* Aldershot: Avebury.

Gould, N. (1996b) 'Care management and information technology: science or reading the tea-leaves?' In J. Steyaert (ed) *Information Technology and Computers: More Than Computers?* Utrecht: Netherlands Institute for Care and Welfare.

Gould, N. (1996c) 'Social work, information technology and the post-Fordist welfare state.' In B. Glastonbury (ed) *Dreams and Realities: Information Technology in the Human Services.* Helsinki: STAKES.

Gould, N. (2000) 'Becoming a learning organisation: a social work example.' *Social Work Education 19*, 6, 585–596.

Gould, N. and Moultrie, K. (eds) (1997) *Information Management and Social Services: Effective Policy, Planning and Implementation.* Aldershot: Ashgate.

Griffiths, R. (1988) *Community Care: Agenda for Action.* London: The Children's Society.

James, A. (1994) *Managing To Care.* Harlow: Longman.

Jarvis, P. (1999) *The Practitioner Researcher: Developing Theory from Practice.* San Francisco: Jossey-Bass.

Kerslake, A. (1996) 'Information management: beyond information technology.' In A. Kerslake and N. Gould (eds) *Information Management in Social Services.* Aldershot: Avebury.

Kerslake, A. and Gould, N. (eds) (1996) *Information Management in Social Services.* Aldershot: Avebury.

Khan, P. and Dominelli, L. (2000) 'The impact of globalization on social work in the UK.' *European Journal of Social Work 3*, 2, 95–108.

Lewis, J. and Glennerster, H. (1996) *Implementing the New Community Care.* Buckingham: Open University Press.

Macdonald, K. (1995) *The Sociology of the Professions.* London: Sage.

Mackay, H. (1995) 'Theorising the IT/society relationship.' In N. Heap, R. Thomas, G. Einon, R. Mason and H. Mackay (eds) *Information Technology and Society.* London: Sage Publications.

Maslow, A. (1968) *Towards a Psychology of Being.* New York: Van Nostrand.

Pugh, R. and Gould, N. (2000) 'Globalization, social work and social welfare.' *European Journal of Social Work 3*, 2, 123–138.

Qvortrup, L., Glastonbury, B. and de Graaf, H. (1992) *European Resource Book: Information Technology and Human Services.* Utrecht: ENITH/NIZW.

Revans, R. (1980) *Action Learning.* London: Blond and Biggs.

Riley, L. and Smith, G. (1997) 'Developing and implementing IS: a case study analysis in social services.' *Journal of Information Technology 12*, 4, 305–21.

Rosengarten, P. (1999) *The Characteristics, Outcomes and Sources of the Learning Organization: The Case of Car Component Suppliers in Britain.* Unpublished MPhil thesis, London School of Economics.

Schon, D. (1983) *The Reflective Practitioner.* New York: Basic Books.

Senge, P. (1990) *The Fifth Discipline.* London: Random Century.

Social Services Inspectorate and Audit Commission (2001) *Delivering Results: Joint Review Team Fifth Annual Report 2000/1.* London: Department of Health.

Steyaert, J. (1996) 'Information technology and human services, more than computers?' In J. Steyaert, (ed) *Information Technology and Human Services, More than Computers? Utrecht: Netherlands Institute for Care and Welfare.*

Steyaert, J., Colombi, D. and Rafferty, J. (eds) (1996) *Human Services and Information Technology: An International Perspective.* Aldershot: Ashgate.

Steyaert, J. and Gould, N. (1999) 'Social services, social work and information management: some European perspectives.' *European Journal of Social Work 2*, 2, 165–75.

Tapscott, D. (1996) *The Digital Economy: Promise and Peril in the Age of Networked Intelligence.* New York: McGraw-Hill.

Times, The (2000) 'A lesson in the way to make knowledge pay.' *Delivering Results: Joint Review Team Fifth Anual Report 2000/1.* London: Department of Health.

Vasagar, J. (2001) 'NHS in chaos from top down, says consultant.' *The Guardian,* 5 July, p.5.

Weber, M. (1947) *Theory of Social and Economic Organizations.* New York: Free Press.

World Health Organization (1988) *Informatics and Telematics in Health: Present and Potential Uses.* World Health Organization: Geneva.

CHAPTER 2

Using the Internet for Evidence-based Practice

Mark Watson

This chapter examines the extent to which libraries and related services have historically provided social work practitioners and their managers with knowledge relevant to their task. The potential of the Internet to provide access to library resources is then reviewed, and the chapter concludes with the identification of obstacles preventing social care from benefiting fully from the potential the Internet offers in this respect.

The focus on evidence-based practice in social care in the UK followed the publication of *A Wider Strategy for Research and Development Relating to Personal Social Services* (Department of Health 1994). One of the outcomes of this report was the establishment of a pilot project in the south west of England, funded for three years by the Department of Health and the Association of Directors of Social Services. Whilst the initial aim of the project was to disseminate research findings, it was launched with a more specific name – the Centre for Evidence Based Social Services (CEBSS) (http://www.exeter.ac.uk/cebss). Led by Professor Brian Sheldon, who had been actively promoting the 'effectiveness' debate since the late 1970s (see Sheldon 1979), the focus on evidence-based practice was very timely. It coincided with the government's and health sector's interest in this topic. However, concern over a perceived dominant focus on 'randomized controlled trials' as the 'gold standard' within CEBSS has led to a vigorous academic debate about what constitutes evidence (see Fisher 1997) and more fundamentally about the validity of evidence-based practice itself (see Webb 2001). This chapter will take a pragmatic approach and attempt to cover the widest spectrum of 'evidence' and 'knowledge', without venturing into this debate. The chapter will concentrate primarily on developments in England.

Access to knowledge prior to the Internet

The current interest in 'evidence-based practice' in social care comes some 75 years after the issue of social workers' use of literature was first raised. In an editorial in the *Journal of Social Forces* entitled 'The reading habits of the social worker' Jesse F. Steiner bemoaned the poor reading habits of the social worker and promoted reading for the enrichment of cultural life:

> The very nature of the task of social work makes inevitable heavy spiritual drains. Daily contact with distressing conditions and the burden of responsibility for their alleviation tend to develop a warped view of life in which pessimism and discontent and ugliness and suffering and injustice play too prominent a part…the social worker above all people needs the stimulus of quiet hours with the master minds of literature, the poets and philosophers who have thought deeply and spoken wisely about the mysteries of life. (Steiner 1923, p.477)

Whilst the nature of the social work task may have changed little since then, the focus on the means to support the social worker has moved on somewhat. It is significant that social work has moved on to a more scientific, rather than philosophical, basis for practice – unless those undertaking research see themselves as being master minds of literature, poetry and philosophy! Some half a century after these comments, the need for access to literature was still an issue:

> As professional development should be seen as a continuing process, however, one would hope that many more employers would be encouraged to see the value of making adequate social work literature of all forms more readily available to their staff. (McCulloch and Brown 1968, p.570)

The reluctance of social work practitioners to make use of libraries was later identified during a project funded by the Office of Scientific and Technical Information. Their report entitled *The Information Needs of Social Workers* (see Line, Brittain and Cranmer 1971) highlighted the informal nature of social workers' attempts to keep up to date with developments in the field – and the fact that they often preferred to do this through personal contact rather than through the literature. This preference was echoed the following year:

> I believe that every practitioner and fieldworker needs a telephone number – and preferably a known person – to ring which will be the gate into the vast existing resources of information. (Grose 1974, p.22)

In 1977 the National Institute for Social Work (NISW) published a report which highlighted the difficulties in keeping track of the increasing volume of literature and research findings (see Webley 1977). It looked forward to the further development of the mooted Department of Health and Social Security (DHSS) Library publication *Social Services Abstracts*. The report cited 12 key social work journals – a very small number by comparison to the situation today. In 1975 Project INISS (Information Needs and Information Services in Social Services) was established. Funded at first by the British Library, and later by the DHSS, this major study lasted over five years and had the potential to be a seminal piece of research. However, in retrospect, the impact of the research was not as great as it could have been. The authors of the research found that information was 'taken for granted' in social services departments (SSDs). Furthermore, there was little effort to ensure that the communication of information took place, and there was no sense of information as a resource to be managed. They argued strongly for the need for social services departments to establish information policies. This report should have laid the foundation for the establishment of a robust, strategic infrastructure for social care information.

Over the following years, effort was made to maintain the momentum of the INISS work. During 1983 and 1984 NISW hosted a series of seminars as part of its Practice and Development Exchange, which was investigating the dissemination of practice innovation in the social work field. These seminars resulted in the publication of a report which concluded that, whilst the volume of available information was increasing, it was not necessarily finding its way to social workers – hence the title *Information Exchange: Swamp or Desert?* (Smale 1984). This report promoted the need for 'switchboards' linking practitioners to information, echoing the call made by Grose a decade earlier. SSDs were encouraged to appoint information officers, and it was an indication of the project's success that, in at least one local authority, this occurred. A new post was created and the post-holder attended one of the later seminars.

A small number of SSDs had established libraries, with notable forerunners Kent and Essex employing qualified librarians. A successful argument was made for a well-resourced library service within Hampshire SSD (Francis 1986). That library resource still exists today, but remains the exception, rather than the rule. The limited number of libraries in SSDs can perhaps be seen as an unintended consequence of the development work undertaken by the NISW Practice and Development Exchange. The NISW Information Service (NISWIS) was initially funded by the Joseph Rowntree Memorial Trust. This service made the NISW Library available to subscribing agencies. It provided postal book loans, photocopy services, library tickets for those authorities within visiting distance, and a literature search facility. This latter service was initially based on physically scanning library shelves for likely material.

It is worth noting the vision shown by Professor Roy Parker in 1983, when he suggested that information technology could eventually provide easy 'on-line' access for practitioners, for the purposes of predicting, checklisting and abstracting (see Dartington Social Research Unit 1983). The extent to which his vision has been realized will be returned to at the end of this chapter. Whilst access to literature was becoming more readily available, inherent problems were identified in terms of social workers' reliance on personal contact in preference to paper-based information systems to provide the information they required to do their jobs:

> Our findings concur with the conclusions of the [NISW] Practice and Development Exchange, that there is at one and the same time a flood and drought of information. Social workers are not skilled information seekers and the pressures of their job leave them little time to search through information which is often uncoordinated and difficult to access in order to find an answer to an immediate problem. (Forrest and Williams 1987, p.81)

In July 1994 the Department of Health published *A Wider Strategy for Research and Development Relating to Personal Social Services* which concluded that the social services did not lack a research culture, nor the motivation to use research, but that access was the problem. It argued that access to and use of research findings require attention to be paid to process as well as outcome (see Department of Health 1994), and in due course the establishment of the Centre for Evidence Based Social Services followed.

Considering that the report focused on dissemination, it did signally fail in interviewing no respondents other than academic researchers, thus ignoring the experience of an increasing number of services providing access to research findings. In addition to NISW, an increasing number of social welfare organizations were providing information services to the field. This included the National Children's Bureau which provided the two-page A4 'Highlights' series that identified key research on individual topics. The report also suffered by being published just as social welfare libraries were taking advantage of new technologies, and moving from paper-based current awareness services, to the new medium of CD-ROM. The NISW monthly current awareness bulletin 'Social Care Update' became available as the cumulated database 'Caredata'. The National Children's Bureau library database became the 'ChildData' database, and the Centre for Policy on Ageing's 'New Literature on Old Age' transformed into the more succinctly, if somewhat less clearly, named database, 'AgeInfo'. These initiatives followed the pioneering launch of the 'Volnet' CD-ROM database by Kevin Harris at the Community Development Foundation.

Whether paper-based current awareness services, or CD-ROM databases, the key difficulty for practitioners was obtaining access to those services, and obtaining access to literature which they referenced. By a combination of subscriptions to the NISW Information Service and the NISW Caredata database, local authorities were able to have a reasonably integrated service, albeit at arm's length. A telephone call from a busy practitioner to an information specialist would result in a literature search being carried out. A list of appropriate references could be posted, faxed or (later) emailed. The practitioner could then choose which books or articles appeared to be most relevant to their needs, and, postal service notwithstanding, would receive those items in due course. In 2001 this service was a casualty of the establishment of the Social Care Institute for Excellence (SCIE), in that there was to be no place in SCIE for the NISW Library, upon which this service was reliant. Part of the rationale for this decision was that the Internet was seen as making a traditional library service a thing of the past. These electronic developments are the focus of attention in the next part of this chapter.

Access to knowledge through the Internet

The last five years have seen the World Wide Web radically redefine the means by which computers can be used to provide and retrieve information.

As high-speed connectivity becomes more commonplace, access extends beyond the home PC through the television, but also via public libraries and Internet cafés. The potential to establish a radically new form of knowledge exchange and provision has become available. There are a small number of Internet success stories such as the FriendsReunited website (www.friends reunited.co.uk), which has attracted a large amount of both media interest and visitors on the site. In addition, the overwhelming demand for access to the on-line 1901 UK Census caught out those who had been promoting the web resource. In consequence, due to the excessive demand, the service had to be withdrawn. In general, however, potential remains unfulfilled (except in the less salubrious side of the Internet).

Whilst the Internet can be seen as a recent phenomenon, electronic access to social work databases by modem was established as far back as the early 1980s, and electronic networking amongst social workers was similarly common at that time. During the same period, on-line 'hosts' such as Data-Star and Dialog facilitated the DHSS-DATA and Social Work Abstracts databases, that were produced by the DHSS Library, and the National Association of Social Workers (based in Washington DC) respectively. This author was one of the early adopters who struggled with a slow data connection, cumbersome searching syntaxes, and printouts being delivered from Switzerland (Watson 1996). Such problems made practitioner access inappropriate. The later development of CD-ROM appeared to offer the chance of providing more widespread access. Certainly, the availability of CD-ROM databases, such as Caredata (NISW), AgeInfo (Centre for Policy on Ageing), ChildData (National Children's Bureau), and Volnet (Community Development Foundation and partners) during 1994 and 1995, enabled access by a much wider range of users. The search interfaces were generally more user-friendly and, other than the annual subscription, there were no on-line charges to worry the searcher.

For the more advanced searcher, particularly those wishing to carry out systematic reviews of the literature, there are a wealth of databases available on CD-ROM and the web, primarily on a subscription basis (see Watson 2001). In addition to web versions of the major subscription-based social science and social care databases, the advent of cheaper connection to the web has allowed a number of social welfare libraries to make their databases available – including Alcohol Concern, Drugscope and the NSPCC. However, to the individual practitioner, a wide range of databases with their own search interfaces and keywording systems, all leading to abstracts of printed materials (the vast majority of which are not readily available), remains some way short of providing support with an urgent practice problem. This is in contrast with the health sector, where a much larger proportion of the workforce has greater access to local libraries. In this situation, finding a reference to an article or report and obtaining a copy to read is a much simpler task.

In the absence of local social work libraries, electronic access to journals is one way forward. In the UK academic sector, the Ingenta (www.ingenta.ac.uk) initiative has pioneered access to the electronic full text of journals. It now provides the academic sector with several hundred journals in that format, primarily from major academic and scientific publishers. These include a significant proportion of the major academic social care journals. In addition to other 'intermediaries' that provide electronic access to journal content, many publishers also make their journals available to subscribers through their own websites. Unfortunately, the databases previously mentioned, which can identify relevant articles, are not linked directly to the electronic format. In consequence, a social work academic or student can identify a potentially useful journal article from a database (such as Caredata, ChildData or AgeInfo) but be unaware that the journals are available through the university network. However, a more serious obstacle to the use of electronic journals in social care is that those in practice settings will not typically have access. Again, this is in contrast with the health sector, where regional libraries typically have electronic access arrangements with a variety of e-journal providers.

The majority of major journals are now published in electronic format and are available (sometimes at extra cost) alongside printed subscriptions. There are few exceptions in terms of providing free access. One of the leading free e-journals is the British Medical Journal (known as the eBMJ). The eBMJ is fully on-line (http://www.bmj.com) and has additional functionality to the printed version. It offers links to the Medline database, email alerts when an article appears citing a topic in which you are interested, and on-line discussions enabling immediate feedback to authors. The eBMJ has the distinct benefit of being part of a very large publishing empire, which can evidently afford to make its content freely available.

In the social care field, there are a number of websites that provide access to content of interest to practitioners. The *Guardian* newspaper's Society supplement has an electronic version (http://www.societyguardian.co.uk), and the ubiquitous *Community Care* magazine's second attempt at a web presence (http://www.community-care.co.uk) has been more successful than its first, subscription-based attempt. However, rather than offering journal articles, their content is news-oriented, and *Community Care's* more research-based 'Research Matters' remains a subscription-based service. The one freely accessible academic journal on social care is Research Policy and Planning. Provided by the Social Services Research Group through the electronic Library for Social Care (http://www.elsc.org.uk), it has three years of content available in web format, and an archive of all articles dating back to 1986 in a more basic format.

A further gap in supporting the development of evidence-based practice is the relative inaccessibility of information on current research. For policy makers commissioning new research as well as practitioners and managers, reliance on journals can be inadequate because of the time it takes for material to be published. There are two major national information resources in health and social care: both are Department of Health databases. The National Research Register (http://www.update-software.com/National/) covers several health databases. However, its usefulness to social care is reduced not only by the limited social care content, but also by the fact that medical subject headings are used for keyword retrieval. The main database covers only research funded by the Department of Health. The Research Findings Electronic Register poses similar difficulties for those in social care, with a display presentation that does little to encourage the searcher to persevere.

An example of a user-friendly Internet database of ongoing research is that of the Joseph Rowntree Foundation (www.jrf.org.uk). The Joseph Rowntree Foundation was an early pioneer in making their short 'Findings' available on the web. It has been a model of good practice in enabling visitors to the site to find out what research is being commissioned, what research is in progress, and what projects have concluded. The Economic and Social Research Council (ESRC) REGARD database (http://www.regard.ac.uk), developed by the Institute for Learning and Research Technology (ILRT) at the University of Bristol, is also well designed, easy to use and content rich. Whilst the functionality of such databases is a significant element in making retrieval of current research information available, the content itself is of course of primary importance. Ensuring that information about research appears on a database is no easy matter.

Despite the pervasiveness of the Internet, the availability of information on research is less satisfactory than it was over a decade ago. At its peak in the mid 1980s, the printed *Register of Social Care Research* (published through the Clearing House for Local Authority Social Services Research) contained several hundred descriptions of research projects, and had a degree of comprehensiveness which made it an invaluable tool. Sadly, over a period of time, the number of records in each annual collection began to dwindle. The journal, renamed *Social Services Research*, ceased publication just a couple of years before the central government Best Value initiative placed requirements on authorities to evaluate their service provision against specific standards. Those who had changed from being researchers, to administrators of performance measurement, had to return to their roots. A research database established by NISW and the Social Services Research Group was slow to develop. Despite being one of the most popular parts of the NISW website, with many visitors searching the database, it has been less successful in encouraging those carrying out research to enter details therein.

The previously described resources are concerned with the provision of access to primary research and literature. Social work literature is aimed at several audiences – the researcher, the teacher, the student, the service planner or the casual reader. Identifying and gaining access to materials that would help with an immediate practice problem is not always straightforward. Whilst research and literature reviews, as well as systematic reviews, have been used extensively in health and increasingly in social care to establish 'what works', there has been little investment in incorporating the knowledge base into 'decision support' or 'expert systems'. Professor Dick Schoech at the University of Texas in Arlington, has carried out innovative social work developments in this area. One particularly innovative use of multimedia was the 'Keisha' child protection module (http://www2.uta.edu/cussn/keisha/default.htm) developed during the early part of the last decade. A simulation which enabled social work students to investigate a child protection allegation through obtaining information and evidence from files, telephone messages and interviews, the software made the most of the limited multimedia capabilities of the time to provide a reasonable semblance of the reality of complex practice situations. More recently, Schoech has also developed a Worker Safety Advisor resource (http://www2.uta.edu/cussn/wsa/default.htm) which assists the social worker in identifying the likelihood of violence in social work situations. Whilst the focus is on the prevention of violence to the social worker, the final screen offering advice and guidance states in large letters 'Remember –

protect the child!' This latter resource can be freely accessed and run on the Internet.

In the UK, multimedia CD-ROMs developed by social work practitioner Tarsem Singh Cooner show how the attention of social workers can be drawn in a more interactive way to practice issues. His 'Race and Social Work' multimedia package includes video clips of social work interventions (enacted by colleagues of Cooner) which are used to illustrate 'bad practice'. The person using the training resource is required to identify the bad practice, as it is presented on-screen, and the programme is able to offer feedback on how successful the user has been. The 'research in practice' initiative led by Celia Atherton and based at the Dartington Social Research Unit has been innovative in exploring different means by which research can support practice (see Atherton 1999). Their use of audio tapes, and their Internet-based Evidence Bank structured to support decision making, is supplemented by work on evidence-based team working learning modules, and input into a 'Research Mindedness' web module which is discussed later in this chapter.

The focus of the chapter up to now has been on practitioners accessing published and ongoing research, and for the most part being passive recipients of information and knowledge. The potential for the Internet to enable networking amongst practitioners to exchange their knowledge should not be underestimated. However, this potential remains largely unfulfilled. Whilst concern with the Internet in recent years has primarily focused on the World Wide Web, the Internet was originally built on email networking during the 1970s and 1980s. The Internet was based on the linking of existing computer networks, such as the academic network JANET in the UK, and BITnet in the US and elsewhere. For those not able to participate in academic networks 'bulletin boards' were popular. Bulletin boards allowed other PC users with modems to exchange messages and files. Primarily hobbyist, there was some international networking through the 'Fidonet'. One relevant example was Cussnet (Computer Users in Social Services Network) which was most active during the 1980s (http://www2.uta.edu/cussn/cussn.html). Fifteen years ago Forrest and Williams (1987) suggested that the gap between 'serious' use of bulletin boards and their use by dedicated enthusiasts burning the midnight oil was narrowing. There is little evidence that we have moved very far from this point. Personal experience of a number of mailing lists and message areas on websites suggests that there has been relatively little new uptake of this technology. Those early adopters of the Internet in the 1990s were typically committed networkers, for whom the numerous email 'listservs' offered exciting new opportunities for the exchange of knowledge. Berman (1996) investigated three such lists, and found that whilst there were a lot of messages providing information about events, publications and so forth (information transfer), there was little in the way of knowledge exchange.

One simple example of facilitating knowledge exchange was the 'Theorizing Social Work Education' seminar series (http://www.nisw. org.uk/tswr) organized by Joint University Council – Social Work Education Committee, as part of an ESRC-funded programme. Papers were published on the Internet some days prior to seminar, enabling participants to read the papers in advance. At the seminar itself, authors of a paper would spend a short time summarizing it, allowing more time to be spent on discussion. The loading of papers onto the web was not problematic, however, getting academics to make use of the electronic messaging option was not as successful.

In addition to providing access to the aforementioned information resources and opportunities for the exchange of knowledge, it is essential to ensure that those who may need to use the resources have the skills to do so. 'Use of the Internet' is one of the modules in the 'European Computer Driving Licence'. This course is increasingly being used by health and social care organizations to ensure that employees are equipped with the basic competencies in standard software packages. The application of this basic knowledge to a social care setting is helped through resources such as the 'Internet Tutorial for Social Workers' (http://www.vts.rdn.ac.uk/). One of a range of subject-specific modules, it was developed by the Resource Discovery Network (http://www.rdn.ac.uk) and built on earlier work, including that of a learning module entitled the 'Internet Detective'. The social worker tutorial guides newcomers through a range of social care websites, importantly stressing how such resources should be seen in the context of a range of other resources. Additionally, a critical perspective is promoted by recommending that when visiting a website, the user should assess it with regard to the quality of information being provided – particularly in terms of authority, relevance and currency.

This addresses one of the main concerns in information-seeking behaviour: that is, the tendency for users to seek only as long as it takes to find something apparently relevant. There is a major problem concerning the quality of information on the Internet, especially when a majority of users will not be skilled in evaluating the currency or quality of information they find. The concern is that the inexperienced Internet user will come across examples of websites which flatter to deceive, such as www.socialworksearch.com and www.childwelfare.com which have 'top-level' domain names but content that is far from top-level. One excellent example of a web-based resource that will provide information on research and its use in practice, is the 'Research Mindedness' module funded by the Department of Health and developed by the Centre for Human Services Technology at the University of Southampton (http://www.sws.soton.ac.uk/rminded/). The module has input from Celia Atherton from the 'research in practice' initiative, and from the late Gerry Smale of NISW, on managing change. The module has a range of sections that can be navigated as desired – there is no linear path to be taken through the module. This has the benefit of enabling users to pursue their own needs rather than following a set path. A related development in health is the Critical Appraisal Skills Programme (http://www.phru.org.uk/~casp/ index.htm). This has been translated into social care through work commissioned by the Centre for Evidence Based Social Services. It is a rigorous programme aiming to assist practitioners to evaluate critically the quality of published research. However, it does rather raise the question of why a social care workforce of over one million should be required to do this – surely the quality of the research should be ensured through editorial boards, peer review, ethics committees and so forth?

In addition to using resources described above for the purposes of creating a personal 'virtual library' (Watson 1996), there have also been a range of digital/electronic developments in the academic and practice settings. The main development in the social sector has been the electronic Library for Social Care (eLSC) (http://www.elsc.org.uk). Funded by the Department of Health, it has been set up to work alongside the National electronic Library for Health (NeLH) (http://www.nelh.nhs.uk). The NeLH was proposed in the comprehensive 'Information for Health Strategy' and since then the main NeLH (as well as a number of 'virtual branch libraries' and 'professional portals') has been taken forward in a pilot phase. The completion date for that phase has, however, been continually delayed. There have been a number of different approaches within the virtual branch libraries. Some have been able to build on an existing national centre, for example, the National Electronic Library for Mental Health. Others, such as the National Electronic Library for Learning Disability, have been hamstrung by lack of funding and infrastructure within that sector. The British Institute for Learning Disabilities is reliant on income from charging for its information services. In social care, the electronic Library for Social Care has to date made a couple of notable achievements – that of making the NISW 'Caredata' database free of charge, and making the Social Services Research Group's *Research Policy and Planning* journal similarly freely available. To be ultimately successful, it needs to become more than simply another information provider, in the same way that SCIE needs to become more than simply another source of evidence about 'what works'. Are the resources available for this to happen?

Conclusion

The presence of a chapter on the National electronic Library for Health in the NHS Information Strategy (Department of Health 1998) is testament to the importance of evidence in medicine and health care. The existence of a well-established network of traditional libraries in the NHS is a foundation upon which the NeLH can build. The size of that foundation may not be apparent to those in social care. Some indication of the size of the NHS library network can be seen in the opening paragraph of a recent NHS Executive London report:

> In 1999/2000 over £6.73 million was invested in library and information services across the London Region and a further £1m in 24-hour knowledge access services and in innovative projects to support NHS staff in the workplace and at the interface of care delivery. (NHS Executive London 2001, p.6)

For social care there is good news in that their responsibility to provide library services is now extended to cover health 'and social care'. The numbers of librarians working in the NHS is in excess of 1000, and a total spend of over £60 million in health library services was quoted in 'Information for Health' (see Department of Health 1998). The establishment of the post of NHS Library Advisor several years ago ensured that the role of libraries and related services was being promoted within central government at the highest political level. Responsibility for the library function within the NHS transferred to the newly established Workforce Development Confederation structure in 2001. For social care there is good news in that 'and social care' has been added to the responsibility to provide library services. There is concern, however, that social care will hang on the NHS coat tails and rely on local developments. In consequence, it may fail to provide a consistently top quality service across England, that is nationally co-ordinated and social care led. This is due not to failings of the library providers, but to the lack of a lead in social care.

The Department of Health's *Quality Strategy for Social Care* placed a requirement on social care organizations to become 'learning organizations' (Department of Health 2000a). Continuing professional development will be a key element in the re-registration of professionals with the General Social Care Council. Standards are being produced which require practitioners to base their practice on evidence. However, the means by which this can be achieved are less clear. The Department of Health's *Information for Social Care* (Department of Health 2000b) strategy covered evidence-based practice only in passing, as its primary purpose was to set in place a strategic agenda for the collection of performance management data. The absence of a national strategy for the dissemination of research findings that will inform practice has led to a range of developments discussed in this chapter. Some of these are complementary and some overlap. It has been left to the local authority to decide to which, if any, of the services it will subscribe. At one extreme there was one authority that belonged to CEBSS, 'research in practice', subscribed to Caredata and NISWIS, and provided its own comprehensive library services. At the other extreme were authorities that did not provide access to any of these services. The fact that the NISW library, the one major social care collection of its kind, did not transfer from NISW to the Social Care Institute for Excellence, is worrying. What should be a key element of evidence-based practice is not yet on the social care agenda.

There needs to be a national strategic lead in establishing a 'knowledge infrastructure' for social care. The NeLH can purchase national licences to information resources to make them available throughout the centralized NHS. As social care is delivered by local government, this is far more problematic. However, a CEBSS/NISW initiative provided CEBSS partner agencies access to the NISWIS enquiry service, article photocopy service, and free access to the Caredata database, which shows that it can be done. Without such a strategic lead, the access of social care staff to the knowledge resources mentioned in this chapter will be subject to the postcode lottery. Glastonbury (2001) has argued strongly that social care has been following health and failing to set its own agenda. As a consequence, health has been the driver of information developments in the care sector, and where the

NHS goes social services has to follow. The NHS Information Authority has a wide brief which covers all types of information, and the absence of a comparable body in social care remains problematic. The NHS has invested responsibility for libraries within its Workforce Development Confederation. In social care the Training Organization for Personal Social Services should be addressing this agenda. It should be doing much more than simply setting standards requiring practice to be based on evidence.

At a local level, there is a need for access to libraries, and, importantly, librarians. Librarians could support practitioners in accessing the wealth of non-Internet information resources (see Upton and Watson 2001). Additionally, staff should have access, both at work and at home, to the Internet. This would facilitate the use of electronic databases, journals and decision support tools. Employers need to encourage organizational cultures that genuinely support staff in learning: 'learning organizations' should become the reality not just the rhetoric. Organizations need processes and tools to ensure full exploitation of knowledge resources that lie both inside and outside the organization's boundaries.

Students on social work courses will require access to electronic databases and electronic journals. Additionally, e-learning of various kinds should be embraced by programmes, as should a focus on developing evidence-based practice skills. The use of ICT in social work education would appear to be very much dependent upon the presence or otherwise of an 'IT enthusiast' amongst the staff. Worryingly for the social care sector, the number of such enthusiasts does not appear to be increasing. The strategic and skills gap in social care means that benefits from linkage to electronic initiatives in academia are not being realized. A challenge for social work education is to ensure that students, once qualified, continue to use electronic journals and databases. Otherwise:

> The [social worker's] graduation from school or college is looked upon as an emancipation from books, and they turn with a feeling of relief to what seems a more attractive educational discipline – practical experience in a world of affairs. (Steiner 1923, p.478)

Finally, it has to be acknowledged that a lack of resources is a major obstacle to these developments. Resources have to be substantial enough to provide an infrastructure that enables social care organizations to build on the piecemeal, albeit high quality, work in this area, which has primarily been funded by subscription revenues rather than central government. If the NHS can spend £6 million per annum on library and knowledge services in London alone, how can social care organizations begin to address the evidence-based practice agenda, on a fraction of this amount?

References

Atherton, C. (1999) 'Getting a grip.' *Research Policy and Planning 17*, 1, 1–4.

Berman, Y. (1996) 'Discussion groups on the Internet as sources of information: the case of social work.' *ASLIB Proceedings 48*, 2, 31–36.

Dartington Social Research Unit (1983) *The Dissemination of Research Findings in Social Work: Report of a Seminar held at Dartington Hall, January 27th and 28th, 1983.* Dartington: Dartington Social Research Unit.

Department of Health (1994) *A Wider Strategy for Research and Development Relating to Personal Social Services.* London: Department of Health.

Department of Health (1998) *An Information Strategy for the Modern NHS 1998–2005: a National Strategy for Local Implementation.* London: Department of Health.

Department of Health (2000a) *A Quality Strategy for Social Care.* London: Department of Health.

Department of Health (2000b) *Information for Social Care: A Framework for Improving Quality in Social Care through Better Use of Information and Information Technology.* London: Department of Health.

Fisher, M. (1997) 'Research, knowledge and practice in community care.' *Issues in Social Work Education 17*, 2, 17–30.

Forrest, J. and Williams, S. (1987) *New Technology and Information Exchange in Social Services.* London: Policy Studies Institute.

Francis, J. (1986) *Strategy for the Achievement of a Departmental Library Service.* Winchester: Hampshire Social Services Department.

Glastonbury, B. (2001) 'Calling the tune in social care information.' *New Technology in the Human Services 13*, 3/4, 1–10.

Grose, D. (1974) 'Some deprived information users.' *ASLIB Proceedings 26*, 1, 9–27.

Line, M. B., Brittain, J. M. and Cranmer, F. A. (1971) *The Information Needs of Social Workers.* Bath: Bath University.

McCulloch, J. W. and Brown, M. J. (1968) 'What do social workers read?' *New Society*, 17 October, 570–571.

NHS Executive London (2001) *The Library is Open: Building the Future of Library Services for Health and Social Care in London.* London: NHS Executive London.

Sheldon, B. (1979) 'Theory and practice in social work: a re-examination of a tenuous relationship.' *British Journal of Social Work 8*, 1, 1–22.

Smale, G. (1984) *Information Exchange: Swamp or Desert?* London: National Institute for Social Work.

Steiner, J. F. (1923) 'The reading habits of the social worker.' *Journal of Social Forces 1*, 4, 477–484.

Upton, A. and Watson, M. (2001) 'Human services.' In D. Fisher, S. P. Price and T. Hanstock (eds) *Information Sources in the Social Sciences*. Munich: K.G. Saur.

Watson, M. (1996) 'The Internet as a virtual social work library.' *New Technology in the Human Services 9*, 4, 28–32.

Watson, M. (2001) 'Social and behavioural sciences.' In C. J. Armstrong and A. Large (eds) *Manual of Online Search Strategies, Volume III*. Hampshire: Gower.

Webb, S.A. (2001) 'Some considerations on the validity of evidence-based practice in social work.' *British Journal of Social Work 3*, 1, 57–59.

Webley, M. (1977) *Information Needs in Social Welfare: a Survey of Resources*. London: National Institute for Social Work.

Further Reading

Sharkey, P. (2000) 'Running hard to stand still: communication and information technology within social work training.' *Social Work Education 19*, 5, 513–520.

Sheldon, B. and Chilvers, R. (2000) *Evidence-based Social Care: A Study of Prospects and Problems*. Lyme Regis: Russell House Publishing.

Streatfield, D. R. and Wilson, T. D. (1980) *The Vital Link: Information in Social Services Departments*. Community Care/Joint Unit for Social Services Research.

CHAPTER 3

Real Records, Virtual Clients

Annie Huntington and Bob Sapey

In recent years it has become apparent that within social services, assessment has come to dominate the social work task. At the same time, there appears to have been a reduction in the provision of services to social work clients, at least relative to demand. These seem to be contradictory trends, in that welfare agencies are able to find the resources to increase the quantity and sophistication of assessment whilst simultaneously failing to find the resources to maintain service delivery. There have been different explanations of these trends:

1. The widespread application of an incremental approach to management often results in an uncritical acceptance of the need for greater monitoring of risk, with an assumption that the state cannot be solely responsible for meeting the increases in need that are caused by demographic change. Indeed, the House of Lords have declared in R versus Gloucestershire County Council (Coren 1998) that needs which the state cannot afford to meet are not unmet, rather they do not exist.

2. Alternatively, some critical analysts, for example Holman (1993), might account for these changes with reference to the ideological shift towards a more individualistic or neo-liberal approach to social policy. Within this framework, it is independence, not interdependence, that defines relationships between citizens and the state. The state, therefore, discharges its responsibilities by assessing need without any assumption that the need will be met. Instead, assessments enable the state to monitor the behaviour of individuals.

3.   Others might argue that these developments are the result of power struggles between managerialism and professionalism in which, through processes of managerial accountability, the former is seeking to control the latter (Clarke 1995).

Our reflections on the changing nature of social work intervention lead us to consider another possibility, that a paradigm shift is occurring, wherein the outputs of social work are measured in terms of information known about social services' clients, rather than the material services provided to them. Significantly, this would imply a fundamental change in the relationship between welfare providers and welfare recipients. Rather than the former providing services to the latter, the position is reversed so that clients provide social workers with the data they require to meet their output measures. In this scenario, records gain a new status and become the real output of the organisation, whilst the more limited role of data provider, rather than service recipient, renders the client virtual, in very much the same way as the House of Lords have managed to virtualise unmet need.

This observation is based upon an historical materialist analysis of the economy. Specifically, our explanation of the events occurring within social work is informed by part of Manuel Castells' thesis. According to Castells (1996) we are in the midst of an informational revolution on the scale of the industrial revolution of the nineteenth century. In this chapter we aim to use Castells' work to analyse the process of assessment in social work, and to argue that emphasising information over material products will undermine both social work practitioners and clients. To begin, we shall examine certain aspects of the informational thesis and then move on to reviewing recent trends in assessment.

The informational age

Adopting this approach to analysing issues in the social welfare field is not new and has, for example, proved to be particularly powerful in the case of the social model of disability (Oliver 1990). Any failure to acknowledge the importance of macro-economic issues results in a decontextualised analysis of welfare and, as we shall argue, it is only through understanding the nature of the informational revolution that we can fully comprehend contemporary trends in social work practice.

Castells uses the term 'informational age' quite deliberately in order to distinguish it from the more commonly used phrase 'information age'. He argues that:

> ...information, in its broadest sense, e.g. as communication of knowledge, has been critical in all societies, including medieval Europe which was culturally structured, and to some extent unified, around scholasticism, that is, by and large an intellectual framework. (Castells 1996, p.21)

However, in the informational age, the production, processing and distribution of information have become the principal part of a new globalised economy, which challenges the dominance of industrial and agricultural production. The influence of informationalisation is not limited to economic areas of life, just as the impact of industrialisation was not so limited either:

> An industrial society (a usual notion in the sociological tradition) is not just a society where there is industry, but a society where the social and technological forms of industrialization permeate all spheres of activity, starting with the dominant activities, located in the economic system and in military technology, and reaching the objects and habits of everyday life. My use of the terms informational society and informational economy attempts a more precise characterization of current transformations, beyond the commonsense observation that information and knowledge are important to our societies. (Castells 1996, p.21)

Castells has assembled a considerable mass of data from around the world to support the view that an informational economy is developing and competing in terms of size and importance with the industrial economy. Furthermore, it is particularly in the US and the UK that these developments are most advanced. These changes are far more significant than might be suggested if we simply viewed them as an extension of the industrial economy, for as Jonscher (1999) says:

> Deep down, the information revolution is not about technology working with data but about people working with knowledge. It is a comprehensive shift of mankind's efforts from the creation of physical goods to the creation of ideas, images and insights – data, information and knowledge of every kind. (p. 26)

Within social work there have been several critical voices regarding the introduction of new technologies. For example Sapey (1997) identified how, at an institutional level, technology might change the nature of practice and has warned of the dangers of treating computers simply as tools. Nellis (1991) and Whitfield (1998) have both emphasised the need to critically analyse the use of electronic monitoring of offenders and Thornton (1993) argues for a similar approach to evaluating the power relationships that control the provision of electronic communication systems to older people. However, our focus here is wider than the impact of particular technological innovations. Rather, we are concerned with the extent to which the economic changes that have been made possible by technology, particularly the valuing of information itself as a product, may cause profound changes in the nature of social welfare and of social work practice. Whilst we might argue that social work has inevitably been an occupation involved in ongoing evolutionary change, recent developments around the issue of assessment can be viewed as reflecting a revolutionary transformation in its purpose and practice. This, in turn, requires a paradigm shift in the way social workers view their role and task.

Assessment in social work: models and arguments

Assessment is not new to social work practice as it has always been integral to informed intervention, but in the recent past what we have seen is its separation and reification as an outcome. This development reflects an instrumental approach to the management of welfare (Blaug 1995). It can be seen most clearly in the Social Services Inspectorate's guidance on care management (Department of Health and Scottish Office 1991a, 1991b) and within the requirements laid down by the Central Council for Education and Training in Social Work (CCETSW 1989) for the Diploma in Social Work (DipSW). There is recent evidence of it in the single assessment process (Department of Health 2001).

This trend is not limited to community care, but is evident across all service sectors and operates when any prospective client engages with their local social services department. In children and families work the Department of Health (2000a) has not only emphasised the importance of assessment, but has also prescribed in great detail the way in which agencies must respond when a family seeks support. This requirement is replicated throughout the client's career as a service user, at each and every point when new services are introduced (Bannister 1997). This is unsurprising when we consider that the government places assessment (Goodinge 2000) and information (Department of Health 2000b) at the centre of its policy on service delivery.

Ostensibly, the centrality of assessment links to the desire to provide good quality services that are based on an identification of needs. This identification should involve a partnership between professionals and clients (Department of Health 2000b, 2000c). Individualised assessments then sit within a wider framework structured by government modernisation initiatives designed to improve the consistency of service responses (Department of Health 1998). Eligibility criteria are thus articulated as a mechanism to ensure parity of service responses, not as a primary route to gatekeeping scarce resources. Within this framework, social workers are to be afforded recognition for their skill, as they are required to make judgements in complex and often unpredictable situations. In the child care arena, for example, there is some acknowledgement that assessment practices require professional skills (Department of Health, Home Office and Department for Education and Employment 1999). Further, clients are expected to be treated as citizen consumers with rights and responsibilities that should be met in ways that lead to them feeling empowered, rather than disempowered by their contact with public service agencies.

The extent to which such a perfect distribution of information and communication is operationalised is open to question. There is clear evidence (for example, Ellis 1993) that social services' assessments need to change quite radically if empowerment is ever to become a reality for clients. Smale *et al.* (1993) identified three distinct models of assessment: procedural; questioning; and exchange. Using this typology, it is clear that an exchange model, which has more reciprocity than the questioning approach, may have an empowering potential. Procedural approaches to assessment, which are favoured by the Department of Health and which appear to be primarily designed to gain quantifiable, comparative data, are likely to have the opposite result (Ross 1997). Differing approaches to assessment either undermine or facilitate the path to empowerment (Barnes and Warren 1999). Certainly, assessment as understood within the Diploma in Social Work is based on a technical–rational model, and is inadequate for the development of effective empowering social work practice (Froggett and Sapey 1997). It is only through a return to communicative practices that anti-discriminatory social work, which has been so central to CCETSW requirements for professional practice, can be realised.

In practice, evidence is available to suggest that clients and social workers are struggling with the dissonance created by the necessity for an exchange model in order to achieve empowerment, whilst much of the guidance on assessment relies on the use of a procedural approach to meet organisational agendas. Huntington's (2000) study of one children and families service confirmed this struggle and also found numerous and varied incidents of practitioners and managers who were frustrated with the requirement to carry out procedurally driven assessments when no services were actually available. This emphasis on assessment of need as opposed to the delivery of service has become the central principle of social work policy. It is evident in practice with both children and adults. Although this shift can be viewed as a positive attempt to improve the process of assessment by reducing bureaucratic rigidity, there have been many negative effects for service users. Against this managerialist backdrop, it is extremely unlikely that the aim of empowerment will be achieved.

The failure to use an exchange model also undermines claims to value the skills of social workers. In the development of procedural approaches, what we have seen is an increasing move to the use of new technologies that purport to offer an equitable and more rational method of assessment. However, there are real problems with trying to practise social work via checklists and computer programmes (Corner 1997). Inferential decision-making processes, which are essential to social work and other professions, cannot be replaced by the algorithmic logic of microprocessors (Ravetz 1993). However, there are those who argue that more mechanistic methods can enhance social work practice (see Ypren 1996 and Manning 2000). Such approaches have been challenged as pathologising individuals rather than recognising the ways in which certain social groups are oppressed. According to Sapey (1996) Ypren's choice of the International Classification of Diseases as the basis of an assessment tool was simply convenient to the numerical preference of new technology. The approach fails to take into account the criticisms made by social model theorists concerning the assumption of causal relationships between medical diagnosis and social need.

Approaches to welfare therefore inform and shape models of provision, which in turn influence the construction and application of assessment models for practice (Cooper 1993). Consequently, any assumption that assessment protocols or practices are neutral expressions of good sense are rendered problematic. Moreover, analysis that highlights the ways in which facts are socially constructed undermines any assertion that assessments are solely rational, technical undertakings that require instrumental approaches (Milne and O'Bryne 1998; Taylor and White 2000). Rather, the development of instrumental approaches to assessment reflects the need of managers and politicians to control professionals, not to value them.

Furthermore, it is our contention that despite the rhetoric of a needs-led assessment, the planning stage of the care management process adopted by both government and the social work profession actually acts as a means of ensuring any provision is resource-constrained. This means that assessment is concerned with gatekeeping and that claims to equity are not valid. It is our view that in order to manage the consequences of a resource-led service within a needs-led rhetoric, agencies have increasingly focused on risk. This can have considerable resource implications. For example, an MBA student undertaking a project within a local voluntary agency reported that in order to organise an evening outing to the pub for a group of adult clients with learning difficulties, it took staff seven days to undertake the required risk assessments and attendant paperwork. In this case, the recording clearly has an importance that is not congruent with the extent of the service delivered.

This approach is in line with the development of a culture of accountability throughout the public sector, for example government agendas aim to transform children's services through written plans, specified bench marks, audits and assessed outcomes (Department of Health 1998, 1999, 2000d). However, there is an inherent contradiction in policies that demand more time to be spent on the gathering and recording of data, when service provision is declining, at least in relation to demand. In this situation, recording as a system of accountability takes on a new meaning. Whilst the government might appreciate the limitations of focusing on risk, its analysis nevertheless places the responsibility for assessing and managing risk on professionals and managers (for example Department of Health 1995). It also fails to recognise the global preoccupation with risk, which in turn is influencing the structure of local social services agencies. Froggett (2002) argues that the reorientation of professionals towards the assessment and management of risk is more than a pragmatic response to local events, rather it is part of the rise of a global actuarial consciousness. Could the preoccupation with risk be encouraging the informational revolution? This preoccupation with risk is encouraging the information revolution and as such fits into the cycle of technological innovation and application leading to further innovation, described by Castells (1996) as central to the changes at this point in history.

Assessment in social work: informationalisation

It is our contention that by viewing these changes as a reflection of the wider economic revolution of informationalisation (Castells 1996), it is possible to explain some of these contradictions. Recording has always been important to social work practice, but our concern is that the collection and collation of assessment data has become an outcome in its own right. Gomm (2000) maintains that records are kept for two main purposes, as case or management decision support systems. Traditionally, individuals' records have been used for the former whilst records concerning resources have been used for the latter. However, as a result of technical possibility, welfare organisations are attempting to use individuals' case records as the basis of management systems. The strategic management of community care has been developed in this way (see Sapey 1995). According to Sapey, this management system has influenced the nature of practice: social workers have become more concerned with data input than casework.

Concerns about the impact of informationalisation within the welfare field are not just the province of social workers. As Yalom states:

> The contemporary managed care movement in health care poses a deadly threat to the field of psychotherapy... The profit hungry health care executives and their misguided professional advisors assume that successful therapy is a function of information obtained or dispensed rather than the result of the relationship between patient and therapist. (Yalom 2000, p.152)

Although Yalom is discussing work as a psychotherapist within the American context, his words are useful for our purposes here. Embedded within his complaint is an indication of the extent to which psychotherapy is reduced to a sort of data-bank activity. Information deposits and withdrawals become the currency of interactions, which are largely organised around instrumental agendas dictated by others, whose priorities professionals may not share but have to comply with. This information processing approach is, in Yalom's terms, de-humanising and antithetical to his understanding of the core role of relationships and service within therapeutic encounters. We are arguing that a measurable outcome of social work has become the recording of assessments of need, rather than the delivery of material services. Yalom's point about psychotherapy also applies to social work practice, in that we are also witnessing a move away from the idea of the social worker providing a therapeutic service, to the idea of the social worker fulfilling a data collection and processing function. Therefore, records become the valued output of the agency and clients become the providers of their content.

It has been common over the last decade for social service agencies to undertake wide-scale reviews of their community care clients' needs, not in order to provide services, but to justify their withdrawal. Some practice teachers now describe the learning opportunities in adult services as being to undertake assessment and to practise saying no to the provision of a service. This trend is also evident in child care services, for example where the specification and re-specification of threshold criteria for service delivery leads to the refusal or withdrawal of services. Assessment and reassessment then become the norm for many children and their families as they seek to access services. Increasingly, social work practitioners are required to meet performance criteria that are demonstrated through the completion and recording of assessments and reviews to specified organisational standards (Huntington 2000). The trend has also been identified by social work academics, for example Clough (1990) suggests that saying no, nicely, is an integral part of the social work role.

The evaluation of services often focuses on the quantifiable aspects of the service and on fairly simple notions of whether people are happy or not with particular features of the agency. Methodologically, such approaches have been criticised for their failure to access the experiences of service users and their denial of the powerlessness of respondents to be honest (Wilson 1993). However, where such issues have been taken into account, research findings suggest that clients are more concerned with issues to do with the quality of relationships and task completion, than with information and management (Willis 1995). According to one client commenting on her social work assessment, 'they really did make me feel as if I was, well not important, but they really make you feel that you were worth helping' (Sapey et al. 1996, p.20). Whilst the evidence therefore suggests that the quality of relationship-based activities and service delivery should be the main concern, agencies continue to focus their attention on the instrumental aspects of the work.

As indicated above, these trends may constitute attempts to improve the delivery of services, or indeed the reliability of assessment and evaluation

(Woolham 1996). However, this approach denies the influence of macro-economic factors. Castells' point that informationalisation will 'permeate all spheres of activity...reaching the objects and habits of everyday life' must be considered when explaining the emphasis on the collection and collation of client data. According to Castells, information has gained a new and different value. Therefore, what we may be witnessing is a process of agencies collecting resources that increase their assets, which in the commercial sector would have an economic value. Clearly there are structural and cultural barriers to exploiting this value in the public sector, but in such circumstances, it would be folly for any senior manager to reject the opportunity of balancing the books by refusing to be part of this new economic system.

It has been argued that clients have a new role in providing data to meet the agency aims of increasing its own worth. However, if the records, which are often maintained in the virtual environment of a database, become the valued output of this intervention, then they take on a new reality. Simultaneously, the client, who provides the data but is less likely to receive a material service, begins to take on a more virtual existence within this relationship.

The new emphasis on the client as provider and agency as data consumer has altered the nature of the social work relationship. Traditionally, this relationship had a therapeutic role not in the clinical sense of therapy, but by providing very marginalised people with a positive experience of the state. Humanistic and person-centred approaches to practice have dominated social casework, not simply because of their effectiveness in helping people to understand their needs, but because they fit in with the aim of social work to humanise the delivery of care. The scenario described in this chapter suggests that the therapeutic value of social work has been lost.

Concluding comments

It has often been through the provision of relationship-based activities and the construction of social work as a service itself, that the needs of many marginalised people have been met. Informationalisation of social work can thus be seen to undermine two important social work traditions – the maintenance and therapeutic approaches – whilst creating a new arena for the attention of radical thought.

Many groups of people do not have access to or an interest in using new technologies (Morrison and Svennevig 2001). Clearly this is true for a significant proportion of those who seek help from social work agencies, largely due to their lack of material and cultural advantage. However, while Morrison and Svennevig view people as actively opting out of using information and communications technology, what we are witnessing in the current changes is a developing pattern of action from social welfare organisations, which not only ignores their structural disadvantage, but imposes informational responses on them. Thus, people who apply for material help may have such requests refused, but nevertheless are given a full assessment of what the state considers they need, and because they are then felt to have been informed, they are made responsible for their own circumstances. Furthermore, whilst the state often refuses its citizens the help they seek, these citizens provide the state with a valued commodity – information. This constitutes a reversal of earlier welfare relationships in which the citizen in need became the recipient, whilst the state was the provider.

It would be erroneous to think of informationalisation as arising through some form of technological determinism, as it is only through the interaction of political and social forces with the new technological processes that such changes can occur. So, while technology may be strongly influencing its application, its application is also due to our actions. Analysis therefore needs to extend beyond technical usage (McCurry 1999) to include its impact on social orders (Couch 1996). This is not to argue that more localised analysis of the impact of ICT practices is redundant. Rather, we believe that we need to situate specific discussions around the use of technology in a wider framework that takes account of structural concerns. For example, although the government asserts that the technology of the information age 'will be used to meet the needs of citizens and business' (Department of the Environment, Transport and the Regions 1998, p.5), we need to ask which citizens are most likely to benefit and in which ways. There is compelling evidence, for example, that despite the promise that new technologies would herald the end of disability as an oppression (Finkelstein 1980), disabled people are far more likely to be found working in the agricultural sector than in the informational sector (Sapey 2000). Although some writers (for example Bates 1995) discuss the potential for empowerment through the use of ICTs, we must also consider the extent to which technological innovation has the ability to disempower and exclude as well as empower and include (Anderson et al. 1995; Regan-Shade 1998; Thornton 1993).

Social workers can use their knowledge of organisations to ensure technological developments reflect social work values and understanding (Sapey 1997). For this to occur they need to critically analyse technological innovations, as advances can be used in ways that increase the control functions of the welfare system rather than the empowerment of citizens. The informationalisation thesis also suggests that 'the information revolution is not about technology working with data but about people working with knowledge'. In consequence, the impact will be on the purpose of social work. Therefore, social workers need to consider the ways in which macro-economic changes affect their functions. Our opinion is that these are fundamentally changing as is the general output of welfare organisations. At the same time, specific technologies continue to alter organisational structures and processes.

Informationalisation may be driving a process of change within welfare agencies that is anything but liberating or empowering for the citizen consumer. Clients are becoming increasingly virtual within this environment as they exist as a source of information for organisations and professionals, which are largely incapable of offering service responses following assessment. Within this context it is increasingly the records that are real. These records exist as the legitimate products of systems established within an informational age. We have spent time here deconstructing the potential impact of informationalisation for social welfare recipients and providers. Outcomes are not assured; the use of technology can have differing consequences. Consequences will vary given that social structures of inequality remain. As Burnes, Knights and Willmot (1988) have argued, we need to question and challenge the view that all technologies are progressive. Such a critical stance is needed if we are committed to resisting the futuristic fatalism that can be said to have accompanied the informational revolution.

References

Anderson, R., Bikson, T., Law, S. and Bridger, M. (1995) *Universal Access to E-Mail: Feasibility and Societal Implications.* Santa Monica: Rand.

Bannister, A. (1997) *The Healing Drama: Psychodrama and Dramatherapy with Abused Children.* Chadlington: FAB.

Barnes, M. and Warren, L. (1999) *Paths to Empowerment.* Bristol: The Policy Press.

Bates, J. (1995) 'An evaluation of the use of information technology in child care services and its implications for the education and training of social workers.' *Social Work Education 14*, 1, 60–76.

Blaug, R. (1995) 'Distortion of the face to face: communicative reason and social work practice.' *British Journal of Social Work 25*, 4, 423–439.

Burnes, B., Knights, D. and Willmot, H. (1988) *New Technology and the Labour Process.* Basingstoke: Macmillan.

Castells, M. (1996) *The Information Age: Economy, Society and Culture: Volume 1 – The Rise of the Network Society.* Massachusetts: Blackwell Publishers Inc.

Central Council for Education and Training in Social Work (1989) *Requirements and Regulations for the Diploma in Social Work.* London: CCETSW.

Clarke, J. (1995) *Doing the Right Thing? Managerialism and Social Welfare.* Paper for ESRC Professionals in Late Modernity seminar, Imperial College, 26 June.

Clough, R. (1990) *Practice, Politics and Power in Social Services Departments.* Aldershot: Avebury.

Cooper, D. (1993) *Child Abuse Revisited: Children, Society and Social Work.* Buckingham: Open University Press.

Coren, E. (1998) 'Unmet needs – a contradiction in terms?' *Social Services Research 1*, 1–13.

Corner, R. (1997) *Pre-birth Risk Assessment in Child Protection.* Norwich: Social Work Monographs.

Couch, C. (1996) *Information Technologies and Social Orders.* New York: Aldine.

Department of the Environment, Transport and the Regions (1998) *Modern Local Government In Touch with the People.* London: DETR. http://www.local-regions.detr .gov.uk/lgwp/index.htm (accessed January 1999).

Department of Health (1995) *Child Protection: Messages from Research.* London: HMSO.

Department of Health (1998) *Modernising Social Services: Promoting Independence, Improving Protection, Raising Standards.* London: The Stationery Office.

Department of Health (1999) *The Government's Objectives for Children's Services.* London: Department of Health.

Department of Health (2000a) *Framework for the Assessment of Children in Need and their Families.* London: The Stationery Office.

Department of Health (2000b) *A Quality Strategy for Social Care.* London: Department of Health.

Department of Health (2000c) *Undertaking Assessments of Children and Families: A Directory of Training Materials, Courses and Key Texts.* London: Department of Health. http://www.Department of Health.gov.uk/quality3.htm (accessed June 2000).

Department of Health (2000d) *The Children Act Report 1995–1999.* London: Department of Health.

Department of Health (2001) *The Single Assessment Process: Guidance for Local Implementation.* London: Department of Health. http://www.Department of Health.gov.uk/scg/ sap/locimp.htm (accessed January 2002).

Department of Health, Home Office and Department for Education and Employment (1999) *Working Together to Safeguard Children: A guide to Inter-agency Working to Safeguard and Promote the Welfare of Children.* London: The Stationery Office.

Department of Health and Scottish Office (1991a) *Care Management and Assessment: Practitioners' Guide.* London: HMSO.

Department of Health and Scottish Office (1991b) *Care Management and Assessment: Managers' Guide.* London: HMSO.

Ellis, K. (1993) *Squaring the Circle: User and Carer Participation in Needs Assessment.* York: Joseph Rowntree Foundation.

Finkelstein, V. (1980) *Attitudes and Disabled People: Issues for Discussion.* New York: World Rehabilitation Fund.

Froggett, L. (2002) *Love, Hate and Welfare.* Bristol: The Policy Press.

Froggett, L. and Sapey, B. (1997) 'Communication, culture and competence in social work education.' *Social Work Education 16*, 1, 41–53.

Gomm, R. (2000) 'Agency information for better practice.' In R. Gomm and C. Davies (eds) *Using Evidence in Health and Social Care.* London: Sage.

Goodinge, S. (2000) *A Jigsaw of Services: Inspection to Support Disabled Parents in their Parenting Role.* London: Department of Health.

Holman, B. (1993) *A New Deal for Social Welfare.* Oxford: Lion.

Huntington, A. (2000) *Differing Perceptions of Legislative and Policy Change in Children and Families Services: A Vertical Analysis.* PhD Thesis, University of Central Lancashire.

Jonscher, C. (1999) *Wiredlife: Who Are We in the Digital Age?* London: Anchor.

Manning, B. (2000) 'Psyco-social needs classification: an aid to identifying best practice.' *New Technology in the Human Services 13*, 1/2, 18–26.

McCurry, P. (1999) 'Wired for work.' *Community Care.* 14–20 January, 18–20.

Milne, J. and O'Bryne, P. (1998) *Assessment in Social Work.* Basingstoke: Macmillan.

Morrison, D. and Svennevig, M. (2001) 'The process of change: an empirical examination of the uptake and impact of technology.' In S. Lax (ed) *Access Denied in the Information Age.* Basingstoke: Palgrave.

Nellis, M. (1991) 'The electronic monitoring of offenders in England and Wales: recent developments and future prospects.' *British Journal of Criminology 31*, 2, 165–185.

Oliver, M. (1990) *The Politics of Disablement.* Basingstoke: Macmillan.

Ravetz, J. (1993) 'Information technology support systems in the human services.' In B. Glastonbury (ed) *Human Welfare and Technology: Papers from the HUSITA 3 Conference on IT and the Quality of Life and Services.* Assen: Van Gorcum and Comp.

Regan-Shade, L. (1998) 'A gendered perspective on access to the information infrastructure.' *The Information Society 14*, 1, 33–44.

Ross, L. (1997) 'What is an assessment? Services users, their carers and the community care assessment visit.' *Social Services Research 4*, 26–38.

Sapey, B. (1995) 'Social services and communication technology: a user perspective of the implementation of a care management system in a social services department.' *New Technology in the Human Services 8*, 1, 2–9.

Sapey, B. (1996) 'Coding and classification – two problems in social welfare.' *New Technology in Human Services 9*, 4, 25–27.

Sapey, B. (1997) 'Social work tomorrow: towards a critical understanding of technology in social work.' *British Journal of Social Work 27*, 6, 803–814.

Sapey, B. (2000) 'Disablement in the informational age.' *Disability and Society 15*, 4, 619–636.

Sapey, B., Pashley, G., Burchell, D. and Sherman, C. (1996) 'An investigation into the appropriate means of assuring quality in the delivery of social work services.' *Social Services Research 1*, 15–23.

Smale, G. and Tuson, G. with Biehal, N. and Marsh, P. (1993) *Empowerment, Assessment and the Skilled Worker.* London: HMSO.

Taylor, C. and White, S. (2000) *Practising Reflexivity in Health and Social Welfare: Making Knowledge.* Buckingham: Open University Press.

Thornton, P. (1993) 'Communications technology – empowerment or disempowerment?' *Disability, Handicap and Society 8*, 4, 339–349.

Whitfield, D. (1998) 'The magic bracelet.' *Criminal Justice Matters 31*, 18–19.

Willis, M. (1995) 'Customer expectations of service quality at community team offices.' *Social Services Research 4*, 57–67.

Wilson, G. (1993) 'Users and providers: different perspectives on community care services.' *Journal of Social Policy 22*, 4, 507–526.

Woolham, J. (1996) 'The effectiveness of assessment and care planning in a care at home service: a plea for reliability in social work assessments to improve equity in provision.' *Social Services Research 4*, 8–28.

Yalom, I. (2000) *Momma and the Meaning of Life: Tales from Psychotherapy.* London: Piatkus.

Ypren, T. A. van (1996) 'On coding and classification in social welfare.' *New Technology in the Human Services 9*, 3, 3–10.

CHAPTER 4

Technology and Systems of Referral Taking in Social Services

From Narrative to Code

Suzanne Regan

Centralized, 'one stop shops, 'customer services', 'central duty teams' and 'access points' have become conspicuous features of service development in social services agencies since the early 1990s when former beneficiaries of the welfare state became its customers and consumers. However, with the advent of the Blair government's agenda for modernization and its strategy for 'information age' government they have been given a new emphasis.

This chapter draws on focused ethnographic research undertaken in 59 referral-taking settings across 13 local authority social services agencies to consider aspects of these developments as they relate to settings where referrals are taken at a central site and then transferred to local specialist social work teams via computer technology. Thirty of the fifty-nine settings studied fell into this category. Particular attention is paid to referral taking in settings where referrers are reporting their concerns over the care of children. These settings best illustrate the lacuna between the persuasive rhetoric surrounding the modernization agenda and the realities of everyday, situated social work practices. Underpinning this investigation is the belief that referral taking in social work organizations is a specialist task requiring local knowledge, casework experience and skill in the interpretation and categorization of narratives. The transfer of this task to workers who operate at a distance from the local fieldwork office has only been made possible through the deployment of information technology which facilitates a computer-based link between dispersed sites.

The first part of the chapter briefly examines the assumptions made about the transformative capacities of technology and compares them to similar claims made about the capacity of the market to improve services for consumers of social services. The comparison reveals a degree of continuity in modes of reform which tightly couple the rhetoric of reform to prescriptive models of organization and practice. The establishment of centralized customer services sites, like the purchaser/provider organizational arrangements, have become uniform, visible and measurable indicators of progress.

The second part of the chapter begins with a discussion of the background to the research and describes the various organizational arrangements across the 59 sites. In assessing the particular contribution of information technology to improving systems of service delivery, the interactions between workers, computers and other technologies in their everyday settings were video-taped. The analysis of the data identifies some fundamental mismatches between the claims made for technology-led improvements and features of referral taking in specialist fields of social work. The evidence suggests that when referral taking is mediated by customer services workers a number of things can happen. Callers can receive helpful and timely information in response to their enquiry. Sometimes the right sort of information is not being elicited and referrers are re-contacted by workers at the fieldwork site. Often the requirement for all new referrals to be logged on at customer services creates a superfluous loop in a chain of communication. On other occasions a referral can be coded inappropriately and as a result more work not less is generated for workers at the fieldwork site. This sometimes happens because the work routines of customer services workers do not involve the accessing of narrative information from case-files. Examples of all of these outcomes are given later in this chapter. In the final analysis the mismatches are seen to emerge from the imposition of social policy reforms which are orientated towards the implementation of fantasies of an ideal world rather than measures which are capable of addressing the complexities and vicissitudes of the lifeworld, that is to say the world as it is experienced by ordinary men, women and children (Abercrombie, Hill and Turner 1988).

Technology: strengthening the control of the code

Many of the government's policy initiatives to modernize services and to improve quality through the use of information technology embody unarticulated assumptions about the transformative capacities of technology. For example, under the broad framework of the policy initiative, *Information for Social Care*, information technology is considered as essential both to improving the quality of social care and to meeting the e-government agenda (Department of Health 2001).

Increasing access to information via communication and digital technology forms another key plank in the government's drive to have all services on-line by 2005. In launching the 'e-government Interoperability Framework', which sets out the government's technical policies and standards for achieving interoperability and information systems coherence across the public sector, Cabinet Office Minister Ian McCartney stated that the framework will 'help workers to do more of their work in simple electronic ways. And by tearing through the paper-trails created by routine transactions, we can free up frontline workers to provide a better service to the public' (db@socialworkalliance.net October 2001).

In a launch of yet another national strategy for 'transforming public services – local e-government', Local Government Minister Mr Nick Raynsford said that e-government is central to putting 'citizens and customers at the heart of everything councils do', 'to transforming the way services are delivered' and to 're-engaging their communities' so that by 2005 all local services will be 'joined up in ways that make sense to the customer; are accessible at all times and places most convenient to the customer and are delivered seamlessly' (db@socialworkalliance.net April 2002).

A form of technological determinism (Woolgar and Grint 1997) informs these initiatives in their presumption that a linear relationship exists between technology, the management of information and the desired outcomes of 'citizen focus, accessibility, inclusiveness and accountability' and so on (Department of Health 2001). From another perspective Flynn (2002) considers that the modernization agenda is illustrative of the Labour government's tendency to impose arbitrary targets for reforms without attending to important details.

Not surprisingly commercial companies set to profit from the growth of 'e-government business' and information technology are even more enthusiastic in their portrayals of the innate capacities of information technologies. In one company's widely circulated quarterly bulletin, a consultant claims that 'citizens who are concerned about the safety of a person in the home, e.g. older person, persons with a chaotic lifestyle due to drugs, alcohol, or mental health issue,' could (potentially) access a 24 hour website facility for advice, using keyword searches such as 'risk', 'safety', 'mental health', 'violence', 'abuse' etc. The ultimate aim of on-line access is the 'provision of direct links with service providers and linkages across agencies' (Smith 2001, p.17).

There is much to consider here. While not denying what Castells (2000) refers to as the 'truly fundamental significance of the information technology revolution', any professional with experience of implementing new technology in their workplace would recognise 'prophetic hype and ideological manipulation' at work (p.29). Reports from the call centre industry point to 'a wide gap between declared aspirations and the current reality' with regard to web-integrated call centres. Fewer than one in ten centres have the facility to link consumers to staff in a call centre via a website (IDS 2000, p.17).

Kling (1992) observes that commercial and government organizations have a stake in shaping public discourses about computerization. In doing so they 'establish links between social advantage and technological innovation' (p.351). In other words technology is not a politically or morally neutral factor in the implementation of social policy.

Woolgar and Grint (1997) make a particularly strong case for the adoption of an 'anti-essentialist' stance in relation to the interpretation of the 'effects' of technology. They make the point that technologies do not embody 'essences' which are separate from the contexts in which they emerge. In their view technologies would be most fruitfully understood as 'texts that are embedded in, and at the same time constitute their interpretative contexts' (p.32).

In considering this stance in relation to the development of on-line access to information, an experienced professional might also note the way in which potentially complex social interactions are reduced to the binary coded categories of 'risk', 'safety', 'violence', 'abuse' and so on. Woolgar and Grint's argument suggests that the adoption of these particular codes or keywords reflects the form of representation which is already embedded in the constitutive discourses of everyday practice. In this view, any further development of information technology would not necessarily be innovative in practice terms but would simply result in the transfer of the existing forms of representation to computerized and possibly networked versions of the same thing.

In an era when social policy is consumed by the protection of the public from risk (Adam, Beck and Van Loon 2000; Beck 1992), the extension of the risk agenda to incorporate, via an interoperable information system, the investigation of more forms of publicly reported deviance is perhaps not as fanciful as it first appears. In local authority families and children services, where an anonymous telephone call can trigger a joint police and social work child protection investigation, it would make little difference if the communication were to arrive via an email link from a website. An information system which co-ordinated these already proceduralized inter-agency responses to reports of suspected 'domestic violence', 'risk' or 'abuse' would reduce somewhat the oxymoronic overtones of the term 'interoperability'.

The connections being made here between the visions articulated by government for the development of technology, binary codes and proceduralized practices underscore the central concerns of this chapter. The interpretation given to the term 'code' is particularly important to understanding the argument which is developing. In the Collins English Dictionary (1986, second edition) the word 'code' is defined as 'a system of letters or symbols and rules for their association by means of which information can be represented or communicated for reasons of secrecy or brevity etc.; binary code; morse code; genetic code; a message in a code; symbol used in code; conventionalized set of principles'. The contemporary usage of the term in social theory originated with the French social theorist Jean Baudrillard whose theories of society are often said to be characterized by 'brilliant aphoristic statements rather than by consistent argument' (Cubbitt 2001, p. 45). Nonetheless, his descriptions of how codes operate to reduce complex social systems of communication, meaning and value to the level of a 'binary signalling system: a perpetual test' shed a bright light on otherwise opaque aspects of culture and systems of production and consumption in consumer capitalist societies (Baudrillard 1988, p.142).

For Baudrillard, 'the code' refers to the collective language of commodity culture. The linguistic practices governed by the code are not meant to represent the real world but rather their purpose is to construct for us an imaginary world through the arbitrary and unconventional juxtapositioning of signifiers and meanings (Simpson 1995). From this standpoint a world thus made is what Baudrillard (1981) refers to as 'hyper-real'. Jackson and Carter (2000) usefully observe that hyperreality is the concept used to describe the condition which occurs when the real and the imaginary become confused and the symbol or sign comes to be 'more real' than its meaning. They use the example of television programmes in which viewers respond to events in television soap operas by sending congratulations or condolences (p.25).

In his essay on 'Consumer society' Baudrillard (1970) observes the proliferation of (brand) signs as forms of communication in which corporations use their logos as codes which simultaneously embody meaning and interpretation. This process he referred to as branding. The McDonald's corporation's globally distinctive, trademarked 'M' sign is a useful example of the way in which a meaningless sign advertises particular features of the McDonald's corporation and hamburgers. Through highly selective and well-targeted advertising and marketing campaigns the 'M' signifier now circulates as an instantly recognizable code which communicates an association with the McDonald's corporation, food and the desire (for some) for a McDonald's product. In doing so it operates as a self-referential, binary signalling system which, according to Denzin (1992), 'excludes all communicators except those frozen within the communicative frame itself' (p.80).

The mediation of a virtuous circle of a human need, desire and satisfaction by a commercial signifier is also indicative of a new mode of production in consumer capitalist societies. Denzin (1992) considers that in 'each epistemic phase capitalism has called forth and produced particular consumer ideologies' (p.78). Ideology has shifted away from consumers utilizing commodities within a fixed system of need to a situation where commodities are consumed for their symbolic or sign value. In this sense therefore the symbolic value of an object is worth more (in terms of exchange) than its actual use value. In an era of consumption where goods are to 'think with' and carry social meanings (Douglas and Isherwood 1979), the needs and desires of individuals have become the new forces of production (Baudrillard 1970). Therefore, they have become the prime target of corporations, in their anxiety to code and thereby control the meaning consumers associate with their brand. These last observations are important to understanding the nature of social policy reform in the social services.

The introduction of the National Health Service and Community Care Act (1990) represented something of a watershed in the history of welfare reform. These reforms dramatically changed the role of the state in the production and consumption of health and social services. In addition it signalled a discontinuity with the anti-poverty measures of previous state interventions dating from the Poor Laws. Formerly, under the National Assistance Act (1948) the welfare state had a duty to produce services which were of material value to its beneficiaries, benefits such as accommodation, and other welfare services. Under the new Act the only entitlement was to an assessment of needs. In effect a benefit possessing greater symbolic value was substituted for the guarantee of material assistance. In contemporary welfare agencies, an assessment of needs now represents the basic form of entitlement. In this sense then the needs of the 'elderly, infirm and differently described' (National Assistance Act 1948) became the new forces of production in a social care market. Therefore the object of social work activity became the mediation of exchange between needs/desires and the provision of services to deliver customer satisfaction (see Regan 1999).

The community care reforms were sold to unsuspecting public service workers and customers alike on the basis that a shift to market-led provision would result in 'quality services,' 'value for money' and 'consumer choice' (Department of Health 1990). Implicated in the delivery of these desired consumer oriented objectives was some kind of transformative capacity unique to the market which, unfortunately, remained taken for granted rather than fully articulated by reformers.

Thus this essentially arbitrary, abstract and decontextualized set of signifiers formed a powerful system of signs, or communicative frame, which structured the value (meaning) of community care and in doing so successfully emptied out alternative forms of interpretation of the new legislation. 'Quality', 'value' and 'choice' continue to be used interchangeably and repeatedly in all reforms and strategy documents.

The state's national programme of child protection is also illustrative of reform organized by a self-referential system of signs. The signifiers 'protection', 'abuse', 'risk' and 'safety' signal government actions to predict and prevent the murders of children, the subject of much media-generated spectacle. In addition, the actions of social workers to 'protect' children from 'abuse' or keep them 'safe' from the 'risk' of 'abuse' rather than from the effects of poverty or social disadvantage, embody the 'prevalent morality of society', another definition of code (see the Pocket Oxford Dictionary).

Most government reforms now have a (brand) sign as their organizing concept, 'Domestic Violence', 'Bullying', 'Best Value', 'Quality Protects',

'Information Age Government', 'Child Protection', 'Name and Shame' to name but a few. These semiotically organized systems of reform also need to be read as texts which operate as technologies of representation, coding, as the data later shows, the interpretative contexts in which information technology and social work practices are reflexively embedded.

In her book *No Logo* Naomi Klein (2000) observes that what made 1990s-style branding different is that corporations sought to take their brands 'out of the representational realm and make them a lived reality' (p.29). (Corporate sponsorships in particular facilitate an exchange of values when a brand is associated with desirable experiences or worthy causes. Microsoft's sponsorship of the NSPCC's campaigns against 'child abuse' is one such example.)

Turning the benefits of reform into a 'live reality' in the public sector involves the imposition of models of organization which could usefully be described as simulacra, that is to say (fantasy) models and operational simulations. These models tightly prescribe how the perceived benefits of reform will be rendered visible for calculation and measurement on progress. The Community Care simulacra and its operational simulation of purchaser/provider arrangements, and the Child Protection simulacra and its simulation of the investigation of 'child abuse' exist as evidence of how contemporaneous reforms derive from fantasy worlds rather than from lifeworld reality.

In the new millennium, 'the public sector will transform itself by implementing business models which exploit the possibility of new technology' (www.e-envoy.gov.uk/ukonline/progress/estrategy/context. htm, p.1). The named benefits of 'lower transaction costs', 'reducing the regulatory burden for business', 'better inventory management', flexible working', 'more personal service and democratic participation' strangely echo those elucidated by Price Waterhouse (now known as Price Waterhouse Coopers) as the perceived benefits of the separation of the workforce into commissioners, purchasers and providers (Department of Health and Price Waterhouse 1991).

The operational simulations designed to derive the benefits of the 'information age' revolution include all the same components of the standard reform package: a national framework of standards, infrastructure, partnerships and support structures. Their implementation will involve purchases of new technology, growth in customer services and call centres, the recruitment of staff to devise action plans, performance targets and so on.

All of which will bring added profits to the private sector computer industry. Baudrillard argues that codes, simulations and models have less and less relationship to an outside external 'reality' and that the image or signifier of an event has replaced direct experience and knowledge of what an event signifies (Sarup 1993, p.164). These thoughts are useful to consider in the light of the analysis of the data.

The background to the research

The analysis of social work referral-taking systems was commissioned as part of wider research into the outcomes of local child protection systems in 15 local authorities (Thorpe 1994–2002). The impetus for agencies to commission this research arose in response to a range of Department of Health sponsored child protection studies which drew attention to the negative impact of heavy-handed child protection investigations on families wrongly reported as having harmed, injured or neglected their children (Department of Health 1995). Thorpe's research identified a fundamental problem in that many referrals were shown to have been wrongly categorized as child protection rather than as cases where either families were in need of support or referrers were expressing concerns over the care of children.

Of the 15 agencies commissioning child protection outcome studies, 13 also commissioned focused ethnographic studies of their existing referral-taking systems with a view to making the changes necessary to improve the categorization process (Regan 1998–2002). The material from these studies informs the discussion in this chapter.

In carrying out the organization research, a total of 59 local authority referral-taking settings were visited over a period of four years. In the tradition of ethnomethodologically informed ethnography (Hughes *et al.* 2002), the researchers were particularly interested in capturing the interactions between workers, their computers, telephones and action baskets. On most sites, workers generally included social workers on duty as well as other intake workers of various designations such as customer services officers, access workers, customer liaison officers or information and advice workers, team managers, receptionists and clerical workers. The video recordings of workers engaged in their usual, everyday activity significantly enhanced the capacity for observing the extent to which activity was oriented by the technology in use.

In the six local authorities retaining traditional models of referral taking, social workers in twenty-nine settings were usually placed on a duty rota to receive referrals directly from other professionals and the general public. Interactions with referrers occurred either by telephone, home visits or in the office. In these settings computers, wire baskets, filing cabinets, appointment diaries etc. were viewed as technologies which supported social work responses rather than organized them.

The other seven local authorities had established non-traditional modes of referral taking in favouring centralized models of referral taking. Thirty separate settings were included in the research. Four of the seven authorities employed a combination of social workers and non-social work staff while the remaining three were staffed by non-social work staff only. The analysis will mainly focus on the 25 settings where customer services were not located in the same building as the fieldwork teams. Fewer problems were reported from authorities where the social work teams were located in the same building as the customer services workers. In these situations the opportunity for conversations to occur improved the quality of referral taking (although this tended to be less so in situations where the initial referral had been received by non-social work staff). The purpose of making this distinction is to sharpen the analysis of sites where the assumptions about the efficacy of technology in improving services for customers can be fully explored. The discussion begins with some general observations of customer services before moving on to a more critical analysis.

The particular claims made about the capacities of technology described earlier find their realization in the establishment of dedicated customer services sites (variably called central duty teams, access points, customer liaison or customer services). Government performance reviews, strategies for e-government, and grants for service modernization favour local authorities planning to centralize their systems of referral taking. The targets set for on-line access to public services have also led to the fast growth of call centres in the public sector (IDS 2000). The particular benefits of these arrangements (hereafter referred to as customer services) were usually given in local authority documents as the following:

1. The model produces a transparent interface between the public and otherwise complex local authority systems and processes.

2. Intake processes are streamlined and paperwork, in the early stages (at least), is kept to a minimum.

3. Best use is made of the possibilities of available technology to create and support standardized county or borough-wide systems of referral taking.

4. Customer services workers can be used more flexibly in large authorities with more than one customer services site to support. Replacing workers on sick leave, holiday or study leave is easier when workers who are not fixed in any one location can be called upon at short notice to take up duty in other locations.

5. The initial screening of referrals diverts inappropriate referrals away from hard-pressed social workers and other professionals.

6. Customer services workers are more readily available and cost less than professionally trained social workers.

7. The arrangement provides readily identifiable locations for the future development of e-government and other modes of technologically integrated on-line and web-based service delivery.

In an organizational sense these benefits of technology-led customer-orientated services can be summarized as increased accessibility, efficiency, uniformity, rationalization of technological and human resources, standardization and flexibility. The benefits can also be said to be symbolic in that the very existence of a customer services site signals both the competence of the agency in utilizing information technology and its compliance with a crucial aspect of the government's most recent reform agenda.

The analysis of the research data revealed that the benefits of this way of organizing had very little to do with the technology in use. Rather the benefits to customers were directly attributable to other features of this way of organizing. Customer services workers were generally fixed in one location and so a degree of continuity and consistency was generated for customers and for professionals from other agencies.

Workers in customer services settings did not carry caseloads and only dealt with initial enquiries from the public either by telephone or in person; their sole activity was to address demands for information or advice. The customer services workers we observed offered prompt assistance when they could and they contacted other agencies on behalf of their callers and returned calls promptly, thus demonstrating an essential but often underestimated element of reciprocity embedded in customer services work.

It was interesting to note that many of the sites had become 'beacons' for people, including other professionals, wanting all kinds of information, a growing proportion of which did not fall within the remit of social services. On one site visit, a worker was seen co-ordinating assistance for an elderly man whose neighbour had reported that the man's milk bottles had not been collected for some days. On another occasion, a court officer had telephoned to report problems concerning a person who had been apprehended by railway police. The man was penniless and had a mild disability. The officer wanted to know what social services were going to do for him. One central site had become the focus of an inter-agency emergency plan to cover the cross-over period to the new millennium. In general customer services workers had extended their knowledge about the workings of other government departments and voluntary agencies.

Another salient organizational feature of the customer services model was the insulation of workers from the operations of their own agencies and from the outcomes of their decision making. Referrals which were already open for service or those which were considered to need longer-term intervention or home visits were transferred either by fax or computer terminal to the relevant local area team. Being able to effect satisfactory closures on referrals brought its own rewards; social workers in these settings rarely had time to worry about the difficult cases which they transferred to their colleagues in the local team. The consumer satisfaction surveys routinely distributed by one authority with a call centre arrangement indicated that most of their customers were very satisfied with the service they received. Despite the unremitting flow of telephone calls, customer services workers, particularly in sites where the technology had been 'bedded down', also expressed satisfaction with customer services work which they described as non-routine, unpredictable and challenging.

To borrow a term from Lingus (1994), a new 'surface of production' had emerged from the coupling of the ideologies of information technology and customer services. New skills, new forms of knowledge and a broadening but flattening out of relations could be said to have emerged across a wider surface of production than was previously the case in localized duty social work (a characteristic of service also known as net-widening).

In one long-term ethnographic study of telephone work in a large retail bank, Hughes *et al.* (2002) identified the particular skills required by workers in 'customer-facing' settings as 'demeanour work'. The skills involved in demeanour work included responding to customers who ask questions which did not conform to the institutions' 'order of things' while simultaneously navigating through screens which did not match the flow of enquiries. Hughes *et al.* observed that customer confidence came from this 'seamless, apparently unproblematic way in which bank workers are *manifestly* [their emphasis], demonstrably, able to do the work necessitated by customer demands and thereby produce an orderly flow of transactions' (p.2).

In the contexts of referral taking in social services very few of the workers, apart perhaps from experienced social workers in the call centre, were observed responding to their customers in this seamless kind of way. Very few workers wore headsets which would enable them to manipulate a computer keyboard while speaking on the telephone. More often workers were observed placing receivers on their desk or cradling them in the crook of their shoulders while they either wrote down details on a notepad as they spoke or accessed a computer screen. The production of an orderly flow of transactions presented problems for customer services workers in social services. The reasons for this are best illustrated by data selected from the video-taped material.

In the first example, Gail (not her real name), an experienced social worker and the manager of three customer services sites, was observed answering a call from a person wanting to know the whereabouts of an agency employee. She was seen reaching for and consulting a small tatty booklet to trace this information:

> Gail: Yes I think that he's in the Westwood Team…do you have the fax number?… OK? Thanks.
>
> Researcher: Gail, what is the little book you have there?
>
> Gail: Oh, this is an old-fashioned little book…it was provided in August 1997…I think that we all find this quite useful because it's a local [area] book. The alternative one is a county one. All you have to do is look up the name of someone. I suppose because quite a lot of us here have local knowledge…for example if I wanted to speak to Susan Bailey, I know that she took over Margaret Goodman's job and I know which team she was in. It's convoluted [*laughing*] but it works. The problem is that in the days

> before LGR [local government review] we had a lot more secretaries who produced these every year and they were excellent because they were regularly updated. Unfortunately that doesn't happen any more... you can't substitute for the knowledge in your head.

Gail observed that it was her local knowledge acquired over a lengthy period of employment in this department which enabled her to respond by going through 'detours and side roads' to answer the most basic of questions: 'where is this person working?' (Geertz 1983). The new customer services officer also present in the office would not have known about the usefulness of the 'old-fashioned little book'. The glossy county-wide directory he had been presented with during his training would have listed an out-of-date location for the person. It was simply chance that Gail answered the call. The episode shows the notion of uniformity and standardization to be somewhat illusory and unstable.

Workers in fieldwork offices, particularly clerical workers, were more consistently recorded voicing their familiarity with the local area and case details. For example, in one busy inner-London borough, a person turned up at the reception desk to let social workers know of his concerns about a neighbour. The reception workers rang through to the duty room on the second floor. The social worker responded immediately: 'Look, I know Cyril, he wouldn't have come in unless something was wrong. Tell him to wait. I'll be down'.

Since the establishment of customer services sites, the task of logging on data about all new referrals in some authorities has been transferred to customer services. Referrals from hospital wards to social workers on the same site were also included in the transfer arrangement. Previously, requests for social work interventions would be discussed directly between the ward sisters and the hospital social workers. The referral details would be logged on to the server at the hospital. Under the new regime, ward sisters from hospitals in one authority were requested to fax the details of a new referral to the customer services site for logging on to the central database. The customer services workers would then post a hard copy of the referral back to the hospital ward and alert the hospital social workers by telephone that a new referral had been logged onto the system:

Researcher: Does this mean that no action can be taken on a discharge until the referral is logged on here then?

Kate: Yes, but it also means that the [hospital] wards phone us [for information] rather than phone the hospital [social work] team direct and we would have less knowledge about the person. Sometimes [when] the wards phone us we have to phone the social workers [in the same hospital] to tell them what is going on.

On another occasion a customer services worker was observed taking referral details from a ward sister about a patient requiring a home care service after her discharge from hospital. After first asking for a name and date of birth, the worker then turned to her computer screen to do a 'trace' (i.e. a search for a corresponding name or address on the database). After finding no match with the name, the worker told the ward sister that there was no social worker involved. At a later point in the conversation, the ward sister mentioned that the patient was already receiving home care. Very quickly it became obvious to the worker that the referral was a request for a resumption of services and not a new referral. The conversation then finished with the customer services worker suggesting that the ward nurse ring the hospital social worker for more information. Shortly afterwards, the hospital's occupational therapist also telephoned for discharge information. She too was told to contact the hospital social work team.

These two episodes demonstrate how the illusion of consistency and standardization is the product of certain kinds of processes. In these examples inefficiency was deliberately embedded into the ordering of work routines in order for standardization and consistency to be rendered as a visible effect of the new arrangement. The customer services workers were aware that their interventions were unnecessary and could result in delays in the organization of discharge arrangements. Despite their protests at this obvious example of unreason in their working practices the procedure remained.

The next episode highlighted the shortcomings of computer technology in simultaneously ordering and *dis*ordering the work of three workers in three different contexts of activity:

Researcher:	Can you tell me what you're working on at the moment?
Frances:	I took this referral about ten minutes ago. It's from Ward 26, a patient admitted to Ward 26 yesterday…an elderly lady who it is felt needs some support at home. So I asked the ward workers [*looking at the computer screen*] for the reason for admission, what support she is having already…if there is any family support, does she live on her own and so on.
Researcher:	So you take all this information from the ward and load it on to the computer?
Frances:	In fact with this one when I came to load it I found that she [the patient] was already open to a social worker.
Researcher:	So you weren't able to check that while you were on the phone to the ward sister?
Frances:	I could have done but I was in the middle of loading up another referral on the screen and I would have lost what I was working on…anyway I will phone the social worker and ask her to phone the ward.

In this example, the absence of a multi-screen tasking facility on the computer coupled with the customer services worker's lack of knowledge about the case succeeded in generating more telephone contacts and time wasting for all concerned. The on-screen referral form had been designed as if each referral transaction would flow in a linear fashion and without interruption. Many workers (in both central and local sites) had developed idiosyncratic adaptations to technology which were the cause of much frustration and inefficiency.

The following example reveals the limitations of the customer services model in producing flexible working arrangements. Service users who presented to their local social services office for a service caused problems for local workers who were not authorized to take referrals. When this happened the service user was taken to an interview room to telephone customer services in order for their referral to be logged on the central database and their request dealt with by a worker at the 'central' site. In most agencies, customer services workers are first recruited to larger sites and then placed on a duty rota to provide a service to a smaller site in an outlying locality. Often these workers' knowledge of local service situations was limited, necessitating further conversations with a social worker already on duty at the smaller site.

So far the examples from the research have raised questions over the perceived benefits of centralizing referral taking. In each of the situations described, the most effective and efficient responses would have come from the social work teams responsible for the actual provision of a service. In addition, two-tier systems of duty were in evidence as fieldwork teams already have duty systems in place to cover emergencies on open cases. Thus duplication is embedded into the customer services arrangement.

Transferring referrals from customer services to the local team

In turning to referrals concerning the care of children, the impact of customer services models of referral taking on practice were thrown into sharp relief. Essentially, the model of centralization is predicated on the belief that up-to-date technology will facilitate a timely response from the fieldwork office when one is required. As part of the research into how referral taking was ordered in each setting, the pathway of a referral beginning in the customer services office would be tracked through various workers, baskets, in-trays, computers, fax machines and finally to an allocated social worker in the local team. Sometimes, as many as 12 points of contact were identified.

At each point of contact a referral would be read through by a different worker and often a referrer will be re-contacted by that worker. In one large authority one referrer had to retell his story, which concerned an allegation of a criminal assault on a child, to four different workers over a period of two days: first to the customer services worker, second to the duty worker at the local team, third to the team manager on 'duty back-up' at a different office from the one where the first social worker was on duty and finally to the team manager from whose area the allegation originated. The referrer was not impressed as each worker to whom he spoke asked him a different set of questions with the effect that the workers and not the system were deemed by him to be incompetent.

With the introduction of centralized customer services sites and new procedures for assessment, many authorities have reorganized into customer services, referral and assessment (short term) teams and family support/looked after/permanency (longer term) teams. The fragmentation of formerly integrated social work teams into prescriptive, task-focused units of activity began with the introduction of purchaser/provider arrangements in adult services in the early 1990s and has since become the standard mode of organization across local authority social services (Regan 2000a).

Many authorities have adopted this model to demonstrate compliance with government performance measures. One such measure is the time taken for either a Section 47 (child protection investigation) or Section 17 (initial assessment) to be carried out (Department of Health 2000). In order to comply with the time-frame of one day/seven day turnaround for new referrals, customer services workers were observed alerting fieldwork teams to referrals where allegations of 'abuse' or serious neglect had been made. In most local authorities these referrals are coded according to the Department of Health guidelines as (1) urgent same-day response (2) seven days or (3) 35 days core assessment.

Many social workers and team managers complained to the researcher that the referrals they received from customer services were either wrongly coded or did not contain sufficient information to enable the social workers to determine an appropriate response. In the words of one referral and assessment team manager:

> When I first came over here to this office [from another authority] customer services were screening out a percentage [*said with emphasis*] of the referrals but they were sending most of them through to me on my [computer] system. I would be screening twenty to thirty referrals a day… It only needed to have two CP [child protection] enquiries on two consecutive days for the back-up social workers to become extremely busy and for you to have a system which would be totally clogged with referrals that hadn't been screened.

The following example was typical of many 'CP' referrals documented in Thorpe's case-file studies or captured on video tape during the period of the research:

Stephen: This referral came in at 9.51 this morning.

Researcher: You can tell that from your computer?

Stephen: I can tell that… well, actually the first thing I did was check to see if the family was known to the department. And the child wasn't. So I took the child's details, his name, date of birth, who the GP was, the next of kin, the siblings and so on. Then I took the referral [*pointing to his screen*]. This was a referral from an assistant manager at a day care centre. He had concerns about a child who came into the nursery this morning and who had some bruises on him. One of the workers noticed it and therefore they thought that it was a child protection referral and so they referred it on to us.

Researcher: What made the manager suspect that this child had been deliberately injured?

Stephen: First of all he said that a worker had noticed the bruising and had taken the child into the manager's office to show him. There was some bruising around certain areas of the face and ears. They were red and about a day old. They did stress that they had spoken to Mum and told her that they had concerns that they would be reporting to social services…it's classed as an NAI [non-accidental injury].

This information was then logged onto the computer and coded as 'abuse' and given an urgent priority. A hard copy was delivered to the childcare team manager and another sent via the computer system to the duty computer.

The team manager assigned two social workers to meet the mother at the nursery at 12.00 p.m. It was decided that the police would not be called until after the visit. (Joint visits with the police on matters like this constitute standard 'working together' practices in childcare.) The referrer was contacted again so that aspects of the referral could be clarified. The social worker also telephoned the mother to inform her that she and a colleague would be meeting her at the nursery. 'Register checks' were also carried out to see if the child had been registered as a child protection case.

On their return to the office the workers reported that they were satisfied with the mother's explanation that the child had fallen out of the cot on two recent occasions. One social worker commented that the injuries were consistent with her story. The mother, a single parent, was described as open and forthcoming. The social workers acknowledged that life was difficult for her as a single parent with three children under school age. She was working part-time and had recently moved house to be nearer to her mother and sister. The children were already receiving a subsidized nursery service (a service which she would have been offered had she not already been receiving it).

The mother was informed that no further action would be taken and the matter would be drawn to a close. (Thorpe's studies (1988–2002) show that

65 per cent of all child protection investigations concern similar matters and end in much the same way.)

However, the triumph of the 'situated moral reasoning' exercised by the social workers was short-lived (Parton, Thorpe and Wattam 1997) . Once the referral was entered into the computer (as a 'child abuse'code) the narrative account became incidental to the 'real' work of the agency. Two parallel modes of activity, both concerned with the demonstration of compliance with the model of child protection vied for the social worker's attention.

The social worker was first seen completing an initial assessment form for every child in the woman's family despite enquiries being carried out under Section 47 of the Children Act (1989). Even though the nursery manager had wrongly suspected 'child abuse' and the matter dealt with, the completion of an initial assessment on every child (and on every referral) constituted standard practice in this authority.[1] The woman's health visitor was contacted as were the previous nurseries attended by her children. There were spaces in the initial assessment form for judgement to be exercised by the social worker as to the health and general well-being of the children, their attachment to the parents and significant others, their progress at school and so on. The social worker then completed her written assessment summarizing her reasons for closure. Details of the referral were then entered into five different screens on the agency's computer database. This process could have taken up to two or three hours, but as there was only one computer between two workers, the inputting might not have taken place immediately. Both the paperwork and the computer-based accounts have to be checked and signed off by the team manager. The initial coding of 'abuse' was likely to remain in the systems as the representation of activity.

In the following interview the team manager explains the routine involved in closing this case:

> When I want to allocate a case or close a case, I have to go though five screens on my system...I have to first go into the referrals tab and complete the details there of the close date and close reasons...I would have to go into involvements and complete the details there...take the person's name off that so that next time when someone goes into the system that person is not identified as the key worker...so then it would be back into referrals tab and into further details. I go into the actions tab and again it's a process you go through of ensuring that it's fully closed

down. You need to complete the front tabs as to the date it was closed down and the reasons why it was closed down.

Then really as a team manager part of my responsibility is obviously auditing and checking that all the appropriate work that has to be inputted onto the system has been done. Now given the referrals you can see there, the two piles [*pointing to two piles of thick files on her desk*]...those two have been put there over the past two weeks so it is a considerable amount of closures for me to audit. Obviously I have to read through those and sign them off. I then have to close them down...but I should [*said with emphasis*] then move across the screen and go into what they call the assessments tab. What you then do is ensure that the assessment field has been completed by the worker... that is the date that the assessment was completed...you then have to go into the attachments tab because on every referral now you can attach the assessments that were completed for that child. It's really quite time-consuming... And of course when you're dealing with computers you can have mechanical failures or the fact that it's working quite slowly that day can just make the process take that bit longer...

So I would then come out of the assessment tab and go into the further details tab because there has to be a final outcome put in...so you can see that she's forgotten to do that. One of the irritating things for me is that we have all adults and children [outcomes] as one. I think that they should really make it quite specific... But again I think that there's so many [options] to go through they [the social workers] think 'I'm just closing this down. I just want to get rid of it'. Sometimes I think that we end up watering down the system because there are so many options to choose from.

So for me this is a very lengthy process. I have to say I do not go through those checks on every case. I just keep reminding people that that's what they're supposed to do. My main concern is that I do read all the paperwork that's coming through...I would read the assessment summary because that indicates to me the decision making and outcomes. There's a brief closure summary on file... There's two systems here really.

This manager's description of her work showed how the technology in use, far from supporting her work, was duplicating and elaborating on the routines already embedded in the paperwork system. However, it was the manager's reading of the case closure summary on the file which gave her the information she thought was important to making sense of what had happened.

The following transcript of a conversation with another highly experienced local childcare team manager was similarly revealing. This manager is describing what she does when receiving a referral from customer services.

> Well, I would look at the information on the referral. I would take in the narrative of the referral. I would actually look at what outcome code the central duty had put on that and whether it has been assessed as urgent, immediate or routine. I would actually look whether this was a child who was known before and whether there were papers. If it was a referral from the P area then papers would be attached [by the team administrator] because we store the papers for this particular area here. But if the address was either the area covering the N team or the area covering the M team or L team then those papers would be at those offices and I wouldn't be able to quickly look at the previous involvement.

Essentially, both managers in different ways were connecting with the form of ordering common to local knowledge in which experience, context and 'common sense' knowledge are intertwined (Geertz 1983). The sequencing of questions: 'Do we know this family? If so where are the papers? What was the outcome of our previous involvement?' reasserts the primacy of processes characteristic of proximal contexts of action (Cooper and Law 1995). In traditional forms of social work narratives are constructed from the 'running records' on a file which connect up events and stories. They embody temporal and spatial dimensions in an agency's relationship with a family which contextualize events. In some agencies case-files and local knowledge were viewed as powerful technologies in effecting positive outcomes for vulnerable families (Regan 1998). Unwittingly, these managers' comments drew attention to the displacement of these proximal technologies by the fragmentation of social work activity.

The following transcript from a video recording highlighted how a form of 'moral invisibility' (Bauman 1989) emerged in a situation where this social worker in a customer services setting was distanced from the 'lifeworld' of the service user:

> *Iris:*   This referral is from a neighbour who wanted to remain anonymous. She phoned up because she was concerned about the conditions at a particular home. She had heard that the [family's] previous address had to be fumigated when they'd left. The referrer had visited the house that

particular day following an argument between children. She said that there was a horrendous smell coming from the house and that the mother was aggressive…shaking… and she knew about this – but the referrer knew about this [*repeated for emphasis, smiling and looking up at me*] because her sister-in-law had lived next door to this family previously …we often get similar types of things and what we do is welfare, what we call welfare checks…checks with the schools, health visitors, GPs, anybody who might have some knowledge of the family…

Researcher: So you routinely check, you call them welfare checks, on everything even from anonymous referrers?

Iris: Yes absolutely…we do check up on every one. We have our suspicions as we have plenty of experience where ex-partners…or there's been a row and people use us to get back…but we do notify families…we don't work in secrecy.

The worker had found a previous child protection referral on her database. Three years ago the family had been reported following a kitchen fire. The woman, a single parent, was then described as being 'emotional and not coping after the birth of a premature baby'. Checks [2] had been carried out but the woman had not received any family support. On the strength of the account given by an anonymous referrer, the action of the customer services worker was to send a letter to the woman's home. The letter read:

This department has received information regarding the welfare of your daughter. We've also received information about the poor condition of your home. I have notified your health visitor of these concerns and asked for her opinion. Depending on the outcome of this and other enquiries we make regarding this matter we will contact you to discuss any issues that arise.

In reporting back to the customer services worker, the health visitor informed her that 'Mum had been very upset' at receiving the letter, but that she had tidied the house. The worker considered that this was a good outcome for the children and closed the case. When asked if she thought that the mother would come to social services for help in the future, she simply shrugged.

Many people telephoning social services to report their concerns are not disinterested bystanders simply reporting on self-evident, factual phenomena. They usually have a particular stake in how a social service agency responds to a situation which they consider contravenes normal child-rearing practices. As a result many of the referrals coming to the attention of an agency are characterized by varying degrees of uncertainty and complexity. Many referrals occur in the context of custody access disputes, neighbourhood disputes and problems over adolescent behaviour (Thorpe 1994).

The video-recorded data revealed that decisions over referral categorization occur, not in any formal or sequential way, but in response to partial fragments of information emerging in settings where a number of interlinked factors come into play. For example, the time of day when the referral arrives, who is on duty, whether or not a senior is available, the local interpretation of procedures in place to guide action and the proximity of workers to case-files and computer databases. All of these factors could be seen to play a part in how referral information is interpreted and ultimately what outcome is produced.

Conclusions

From the distal perspective of Department of Health policy makers, politicians, social services inspectors, auditors and agency managers, centralized systems of referral taking create an overarching illusion of order, control and efficiency. The arrangement also offers visibility to those performance measures which link information technology to services which provide 'citizen focus, accessibility, inclusiveness and accountability' (Department of Health 2001).

The focused ethnographic studies of the organizing of referral-taking settings across 13 local authorities drew attention to the paradoxes at the heart of the government's modernization agenda. Embedded in the everyday practices of workers routinely using computers to order the referral-taking process were examples of inefficiency, duplication of effort, variability, fragmentation and ultimately new forms of disorder and unreason. Instead of producing order, efficiency and uniformity, technologically driven customer services sites were observed embedding their opposites.

The benefits to be derived from referral taking by customer services workers were attributable, not to technology, but to the possibilities generated for focused conversations between callers and customer services workers. Freed from the baggage of casework, paper-trails and difficult cases and isolated from the day-to-day operations of their agencies, workers in these settings were paid to listen and respond, provide advice, follow up on behalf of callers and pass on information. More importantly, they were able to exercise discretion over the boundaries of their engagement with callers.

The limitations of the model were observed in situations where more complex referrals were transferred to workers in operational areas. At that point the simple assumption that referral taking is a straightforward task which can occur independently of detailed knowledge of day-to-day operations or casework experience was subjected to doubt.

With the best of plans and technology it was extraordinarily difficult for isolated workers in large organizations to keep track of the minutiae of changes in staffing arrangements, policy and details of service delivery in their own and other agencies. Yet that fantasy lies at the heart of the 'information age' agenda. Customer services, 'e-government' business, local e-government and system interoperability all rely upon the allegedly tranformative capacities of technology to bridge the lacuna between fantasy and the heterogeneity of the lifeworld and public sector organizations.

Following on from Woolgar and Grint (1997) this chapter adopted an 'anti-essentialist' stance in its exploration of these transformative capacities. This stance proved to be particularly fruitful in the analysis of referrals concerning the care and protection of children. In tracking responses to typical child protection referrals from customer services via technology to the local fieldwork teams, a number of distinctive features in the contemporaneous organization of social work were observed.

Social work in referral and assessment teams was characterized by time-consuming repertoires of activity which were oriented towards compliance with prescribed models of practice reform. These models, unlike all previous reforms, were seen to be organized by a system of signs that coded the meaning and interpretation of events as symptomatic variants of 'abuse' in one form or another.

The 'child abuse' sign (with its litany of well-known names of murdered children as its signifiers) could be seen regulating institutional, technical and social boundaries of everyday practice in childcare social work. The most direct route to social work attention and supportive services could be seen to emerge through this route. In this, the 'abuse' sign has been as globally successful as the McDonald's 'M' sign in generating a boundless field of consumption. Concerned members of the public, malicious neighbours, disgruntled ex-spouses, worried teachers, education welfare officers, police officers and health visitors have all become experts in recognizing the signs of 'abuse' and in commissioning prompt investigation/assessment services.

The discussion in this chapter has, it is hoped, highlighted the epistemological poverty and moral ambivalence embedded in codes and models of reform which empty out the value of situated interpretations of narratives and events, reducing the knowledge which emerges from these contexts to the status of mere spectra. In this view, codes were seen to control the production of knowledge and representations in everyday practice and were reflexively embedded in the technologies in use.

References

Abercrombie, N., Hill, S. and Turner, B. (1988) *Dictionary of Sociology*. London: Penguin Books (second edition).

Adam, A., Beck, U. and Van Loon, J. (2000) *The Risk Society and Beyond*. London: Sage.

Baudrillard, J. (1970) 'Consumer society.' In *Jean Baudrillard: Selected Writings*. (1988) (trans M. Poster) Oxford: Polity Press.

Baudrillard, J. (1976) 'Symbolic exchange and death.' In *Jean Baudrillard: Selected Writings*. (1988) (trans M. Poster) Oxford: Polity Press.

Baudrillard, J. (1981) 'Simulacra and Simulations' in *Jean Baudrillard: Selected Writings*. (1988) (trans M. Poster) Oxford: Polity Press.

Baudrillard, J. (1988) *Jean Baudrillard: Selected Writings*. (trans M. Poster) Oxford: Polity Press.

Bauman, Z. (1989) *Modernity and the Holocaust*. Cambridge: Polity Press.

Beck, U. (1992) *Risk Society: Towards a New Modernity*. (trans M. Ritter) London: Sage.

Castells, M. (2000) *The Information Age: Economy, Society and Culture. Volume 1. The Rise of the Network Society*. Oxford: Blackwell (second edition).

Collins English Dictionary (1986) Glasgow: Collins (second edition).

Cooper, R. and Law, J. (1995) 'Organisation: distal and proximal views.' *Sociology of Organisation 13*, 237–274.

Cubbitt, S. (2001) *Simulation and Social Theory*. London: Sage.

db@socialworkalliance.net (October 2001) Reference to the launch of the Cabinet Office's e-government strategic framework for public services in the information age.

www.e-envoy.gov.uk/ukonline/progress/estrategy/context.htm

db@socialworkalliance.net (April 2002) Reference to the launch of the draft national strategy for local e-government. www.local-regions.dtlr/egov

Denzin, N. (1992) *Symbolic Interactionism and Cultural Studies*. Oxford: Blackwell.

Department of Health (1990) *Community Care in the Next Decade and Beyond: Policy Guidance*. London: HMSO.

Department of Health (1995) *Messages from Research.* London: HMSO

Department of Health (1999) *Working Together to Safeguard Children.* London: HMSO.

Department of Health (2000) *Framework for the Assessment of Children in Need and their Families.* London: The Stationery Office.

Department of Health (2001) *Information for Social Care.* London: HMSO. http://www.doh.gov.uk/scg/infsoc/qualserv/index.htm.

Department of Health and Price Waterhouse (1991) *Purchaser, Commissioner and Provider Roles.* London: HMSO.

Douglas, M. and Isherwood, B. (1979) *The World of Goods.* London: Allen Lane.

Flynn, N. (2002) *Public Sector Management.* London: Harvester Wheatsheaf (third edition).

Geertz, C. (1983) *Local Knowledge.* New York: Basic Books.

Hughes, J., O'Brien, J., Rouncefield, M. and Tolmie, P. (2002) *Virtual Organizations and the Customer: How Virtual Organizations Deal with Real Customers.* www.comp.lancs.ac.uk/sociology/VSOC/Yorkpaper.

IDS (2000) *Pay and Conditions in Call Centres.* London: Income Data Services Ltd.

Jackson, N. and Carter, P. (2000) *Rethinking Organizational Behaviour.* Harlow: Pearson Education.

Klein, N. (2000) *No Logo.* London: Flamingo.

Kling, R. (1992) 'Audiences, narratives and human values in social studies of technology.' *Science Technology and Human Values 17,* 3, 349–365.

Lingus, A. (1994) 'The society of dismembered body parts.' In C. Boundis and D. Olkowsi (eds) *Gilles Delueze.* London: Routledge.

Parton, N., Thorpe, D. and Wattam, C. (1997) *Child Protection, Risk and the Moral Order.* London: Macmillan Press.

Pocket Oxford Dictionary (1960) Oxford: Clarendon Press.

Regan, S. (1998) *Evaluating the Organizational Dimensions of the Action Research Pilot Project in the Wellingborough Office.* Research report for Northamptonshire Social Services.

Regan, S. (1998–2002) *The Organization and Analysis of Referral Taking in Children and Families Services.* Research reports for thirteen local authorities.

Regan, S. (1999) *Transformation in the Organization of Social Work in the Public Sector.* Unpublished PhD thesis, University of Lancaster.

Regan, S. (2001) 'When forms fail the reality test.' *Community Care,* 25–31October.

Sarup, M. (1993) *Post-structuralism and Postmodernism.* London: Harvester Wheatsheaf.

Simpson, L. C. (1995) *Technology, Time and the Conversations of Modernity.* London: Routledge.

Smith, G. (2001) 'Three ideas for e-government.' *Management Issues in Social Care 8,* 2, 17–19.

Thorpe, D. (1994) *Evaluating Child Protection.* Milton Keynes: Open University Press.

Thorpe, D. (1988–2002) *Reports on the Outcomes of Child Protection Referrals.* Research reports of fifteen local authorities.

Woolgar, S. and Grint, K. (1997) *The Machine at Work.* Oxford: Polity Press.

Endnotes

1.   The incident highlighted a fundamental confusion introduced by the framework for the Assessment of Children in Need and their Families (Department of Health 2000). Children about whom enquiries are made under Section 47 of the Children Act 1989 are at the same time treated as 'children in need/no significant harm'. In this case, as with many others a child who is reported to the authorities is often not 'in need' of either safeguarding or local authority services. Often such referrals simply reflect the 'concerns' of well-intentioned individuals. The new framework wrongly assumes that Section 17 and Section 47 are 'two sides of the same coin' (see Regan 2000b).

2.   The carrying out of 'welfare' checks on families who have been reported to social services is routine practice under *Working Together* policies (Department of Health 1999). It is now called 'information sharing'. Undertaking these checks without the consent of the families now contravenes the Human Rights Act (1998). However, under Section 47 of the Children Act (1989), social workers can continue to carry out checks without consent if they have reason to believe that there is a likelihood of significant harm or injury to a child. The definition of what constitutes significant harm varies from office to office. In some agencies checks are made following a routine notification from the police about a domestic incident where a child happens to be present in the household when the police arrive. These notifications are treated as child protection cases.

CHAPTER 5

Internet Child Abuse

Brian Relph and Stephen A. Webb

In September 2001 the UK government published the *National Plan for Safeguarding Children from Commercial Sexual Exploitation* (Department of Health 2001). A steering group comprising professional and voluntary organizations with a responsibility for children's safety and protection put the plan together. It included sections dealing with 'Child Pornography and the Internet' and 'Other Risks to Children posed by the Internet'. The plan was produced in preparation for the second World Congress Against Commercial Sexual Exploitation of Children that was held in Yokohama in Japan in December 2001. The plan represents the first attempt to produce a systematic response to these types of crime by child protection agencies in the UK. Prior to this, in November 2000, the Home Secretary, Jack Straw, announced that £25 million would be allocated to establish a 'hi-tech' crime unit to help British police combat computer-related crime. The Internet squad will liaise with local UK forces and overseas police in the cross-border battle against computer-based criminals. Straw said 'The crimes concerned cover a wide spectrum from hacking and financial fraud to obscenity and the unlawful activities of paedophiles'. The unit Project Manager Mark Castell explained 'Tactics to trap paedophiles will include undercover police lying in "virtual" wait in Internet chat rooms and attempting to make contact with criminals' (Society Guardian 2000). These 'sting operations' have been used for some time in the US where police officers pretend to be young children in Internet chat forums as a means of identifying paedophiles. The reality is, of course, as a recent television documentary 'Paedophiles: Assessing the Risk' showed, many predatory paedophiles are not monitored at all. Their court cases are not dealt with speedily and many fall through the crime prosecution net (Channel 4, November 14, 2001). Most convicted paedophiles are left to their own devices because of the lack of police and social services resources.

In a landmark legal case on 24 September 2000, the paedophile Patrick Green was sentenced to five years in prison at Aylesbury Crown Court, following charges of unlawful sexual assault of a 13-year-old girl. Green, pretending to be a 15-year-old boy, had lured the girl to his house after using chat forums, email and telephone calls. A spokesperson for Thames Valley police hailed the decision as a landmark in English criminal justice. The Internet Watch Foundation commented on how the sentencing of Patrick Green to five years in jail for sexually abusing a 13-year-old girl he first met through a chat room underlined the importance of safety consciousness on the Internet. Celebrity stars such as Carol Vorderman, the television presenter and journalist, are supporting Chatdanger.com, a website that was established in response to the Green case. These developments demonstrate varying responses to Internet sex crimes.

New technology enhances performance and leisure, but as we have seen in medicine, the environment and the workplace, what might begin as an improvement can often end up shifting a problem or magnifying it. Technology introduces new risks into social life. This chapter considers the likely impact of the use of new communication technologies by paedophiles, for child protection policy and intervention. It critically locates new risks associated with the Internet and computers in the field of child sexual abuse. The chapter begins by considering the two main challenges related to new communication technologies: (a) the proliferation of child pornography and (b) the increased opportunities for contact provided by the Internet. We then consider the issues arising from a series of representative case studies and we will conclude by considering the practice and theoretical implications.

It is our contention that the Internet poses a difficult challenge to child protection agencies, both nationally and internationally. There are two primary loci of this challenge, one related to the proliferation of child pornography, and the other related to the new opportunities the Internet provides for communication and contact, both between offenders and between sex offenders and children. These two loci give rise to a series of practice issues for agencies relating to:

- national and international law
- the assessment and investigation of child sexual abuse

- the treatment and monitoring arrangements for sex offenders
- the treatment of victims
- the raising of public awareness and risk management strategies
- the development of technological responses.

This chapter also asks whether new technology magnifies, shifts or reframes the problem of child sexual abuse. By examining a number of case studies we draw out the implications of the effects of new computer technologies on the remit of child protection work. The contention here is that Internet-derived sex crimes constitute less visible risks than physical or material ones and are potentially persistent. We suggest that sexual abusers may flourish by taking advantage of technological change in a way that can harm vulnerable children. Moreover, it is contended that new communication technologies facilitate alternative strategies by which sex abusers can target, cultivate and groom potential victims. The alternative opportunities modify the offending habitat, the level of absorption and cycle of criminal involvement. Whilst physical involvement with children is a more definite and material mode of sexual engagement for offenders it is likely that virtual imagery, text and morphing permit a different mode of sexual appropriation. By imposing a virtual form on an imaginary person it gradually comes to acquire an independent reality or 'life world' which offers alternative sexual stimulation. The material reality of sexually fetishized phenomena ceases to be restricted to the necessity of the presence of a here-and-now embodied being. This can result in an alternative form of sexual possession that might be best described as 'control at a distance'. This type of possession represents a pathway whereby sex offenders accomplish their desire to mark the potential victim by imposing their will upon her or him. Research has shown the significance that sexualized images of children have for child sex abusers (see Durkin and Bryant 1999). New communication technologies facilitate this mode of predatory sexual crime. Internet technology thus becomes a means by which offenders successfully use virtual territory for imagining, planning and executing their crime.

The challenges of the Internet to child protection agencies
The proliferation of child pornography
Researchers in this field indicate that, due to the abhorrent and in most countries illegal nature of the material involved, precise estimates are not

possible (Carr 2001; Taylor, Quayle and Holland 2001). However as John Carr has said: 'In 1995 Inspector Terry Jones of the Greater Manchester Police Obscene Publication Squad was involved in seizing a total of 12 child pornographic images and all of them were either in the form of photographs or videos'. In 1999 he seized 41,000 child pornographic images and all except for three were computer based (Carr 2001). The prosecution of the members of the 'Wonderland Club' in 2001 revealed a collection of more than 750,000 computer images of 1263 different children (Davies and Vascar 2001). The COPINE Project (Combating Paedophile Information Networks in Europe) based at University College Cork has estimated that currently photographs 'are appearing in the newsgroups monitored by the project at the rate of two new children a month' (Taylor *et al.* 2001, p.4). Under the 1978 Protection of Children Act, the UK has seen a steady increase in the number of successful prosecutions for the possession or distribution of child pornography. From 215 in 1997 numbers have risen to 303 in 1999. This is in marked contrast to the average of 40 cases per annum between 1985 and 1995 (Hansard 2001). If we contrast this with the research carried out by Christopher Bagley in the 1980s (Bagley 1997) which indicated a considerably more restricted trade in images, we can see there has been a considerable increase in both the production and distribution of child pornography.

The rise of new communication technologies can be linked to this increase in child pornography. The new technology has allowed for a deregulated global space where images can be traded both commercially and non-commercially. The increasing availability of cheap computers with more sophisticated software packages, including digital cameras and video, has made the production of home-made child pornography much easier. The perceived anonymity of the Internet has removed one of the powerful inhibitors against the acquisition of this material. An important question has yet to be answered: does this rise in the number of images produced reflect a pre-existing demand that has now become more visible, or is the Internet propagating an increased demand? The effects, however, are the same, and there has been a renewed victimization of children in the production of this material which has led some researchers to indicate a growth in the commercial exploitation of children (Carr 2001).

The role that pornography plays in causing sex offending is highly contested (see Itzin 1996; Marshall 2000; Wyre 1992). What can be said is that it does have an influence, and it does play a part at the fantasy stage of the offending cycle (Wyre 1992). Child pornography is the record of abuse itself, and its distribution has been seen by some as a continuation of the abuse (Taylor *et al.* 2001). It has also been noted that pornography and child pornography are used by offenders as part of the grooming process (Carr 2001). The new challenge for child protection agencies is the instantaneous and global nature of these developments, which call for policy initiatives at both the national and international level.

The increased opportunities for contact provided by the Internet

This part of the discussion relates to two areas: (a) opportunities for contact between offenders and (b) opportunities for offenders to contact children.

OPPORTUNITIES FOR CONTACT BETWEEN OFFENDERS

In 2001 members of the Wonderland Club were brought to trial as a result of Operation Cathedra. One hundred people were arrested across three continents for the possession and production of child pornography; this included seven Britons (Davies and Vascar 2001). The most striking feature of the membership was the diversity of their social backgrounds. There were commonalities in that they were all men, predominantly white, and most had a link to the computer industry in some way. However, their backgrounds suggest that they would not normally have associated. The Internet allowed them to form a virtual community around their shared interest in sexual abuse. Their technical proficiency allowed them to safeguard that community through encryption software and thus build up a network of security. This added to the salience of the group and allowed for the legitimization of distorted thinking in terms of shared values and solidarity.

David Hines, a convicted member of the Wonderland club, said in interview:

> The Internet is great. It is a whole world that sucks you in. Within 24 hours of going on-line I'd found the child porn...I found people I could talk to. People who felt like me...I had friends. (quoted in Carr 2001)

From research on treatment programmes with sex offenders (Marshall 1990) and work on sexual abuse generally (Finkelhor 1984), we are aware of the role of disinhibitors and positive reinforcement in building up patterns of offending behaviour. The Internet, through accessibility and anonymity, can offer a ready source of positive reinforcement to potential offenders and build a sense of shared solidarity.

Researchers have noted the 'addictive' behaviour of some offenders who use the Internet to build up a 'collection' of images (Taylor *et al.* 2001). Some offenders use pay-per-view access to Internet child pornography and engage in trading images with other offenders through chat rooms or password-controlled websites. Ethel Quayle has noted that this 'trading' can play a large role in legitimizing and normalizing the offender's distorted thinking in respect of child sexual abuse (Quayle 2002). At its most extreme the Internet has been used to carry out real-time organized abuse. In the case of the Orchid Club, one offender procured a child and received instructions about what to do from other members of the 'club' who were watching via a web camera (Carr 2001). In this example, new technologies facilitated criminality by permitting more experienced sex abusers to effectively train novices and voyeuristically initiate them into different types of offence.

OPPORTUNITIES FOR OFFENDERS TO CONTACT CHILDREN

The case of Patrick Green, cited earlier, brought about a national debate concerning the risk to children using forms of 'Internet chat' (Williams 2000). For the government, 'where adults were abusing chat rooms to try and establish contact with children...in order to groom them for inappropriate or abusive relationships', there were 'particular problems because they occur in real time and there is no record of the material held' (Department of Health 2001, p.12). Research carried out by the FBI had raised the issue of 'traveller children', meaning children who had been reported as missing after arranging to meet someone through the Internet (Carr 2001). Of note is the extreme distance some paedophiles have been prepared to travel in order to contact children they initially meet through the Internet (Williams 2000).

Given what is known of offending behaviour, this form of contact has many positives for the potential abuser: identity can be disguised, communication can be planned and vulnerable children targeted. It also allows the offender to maintain multiple contacts with minimal effort in comparison to real-world grooming (Salter 1991). However, it has disadvantages in connection with the later stages of grooming and the maintenance of children in the abusive situation (Berliner and Conte 1990), as it does not allow for the building of dependency. Nevertheless, offenders seem to be able to adapt to this new medium and there are examples of offenders asking children to swap images which may be a way of attempting to gain control at a distance (Quayle 2002). Although the number of recorded offences resulting from this kind of contact remains relatively small, the prevalence of this sort of behaviour has still to be fully researched.

Case studies on Internet sex crimes

To illustrate some of the issues concerning child pornography and new communication technologies, the following case studies are considered. They help shed light on the changing context of child protection work as it is influenced by Internet-derived computer technology. The cases have been anonymized and some the details have been altered to prevent identification. The cases are drawn from practice-based examples occurring between 1995 and 2000 in Britain.

Case A

Mr White was a software systems support manager for a large company. He was described as reclusive by work colleagues and had few outside interests apart from a passion for science fiction. Mr White used the most sophisticated and advanced Internet technology in his criminal activities. He lived alone in a house opposite a school. During an external audit his computer was found to have thousands of pornographic images, a number of which were of pre-pubescent girls. He had no previous criminal convictions, or contact with social services. He was sentenced to three months imprisonment and placed on the register of sex offenders. This example raises a new question: should offences committed primarily in cyberspace be treated in the same way as offences in the 'real world'? Put another way, are the treatment and assessment structures used for 'real world' offenders still appropriate? Although the number of individuals arrested for offences similar to the above has increased, it should be noted that the majority of possession offences have been discovered by the police during enquiries concerning 'real world' abuse. For example, police in Hertfordshire investigating a sports coach for alleged sexual abuse seized his computer and found downloaded images of young boys of similar age and likeness to his victims (personal communication with DI Tilley, Hertfordshire Constabulary). Typically, the discovery of Internet use is secondary to an investigation into 'real world' activity.

The case of Mr White demonstrates the ease with which new technologies such as the Internet permit users rapidly to become producers of sexually explicit images of children (see Taylor *et al.* 2001). Individuals are enabled to engage actively in the production of pornographic material to suit their own personal preferences and interests. Such images can then be circulated via the Internet. In general, Internet activity leaves an electronic 'trace' that can lead to the detection of such practices. However, there are now means by which this trace can be avoided, making the task of detection and prosecution even more difficult.

Case B

Mr Blue is a 14-year-old male. Schoolteachers described him as a high achiever academically. He had a computer in his bedroom and came from a comfortable middle-class background. He was reported to police and social services following an incident where he was charged with indecent assault. The youth justice worker in the course of pre-sentencing work with him found that he had gathered a large collection of hard-core child pornography from the Internet.

This case touches on the frequently debated issue of the role of pornography in motivating or inciting sexually aggressive behaviour (see Cowburn and Pringle 2000). It also highlights the need for a growing awareness among professionals of the impact of the Internet on young people's access to sexually explicit material, the ease with which it can be obtained, and the value system which may be imparted with it. There has been a steady increase in public awareness of the issue of sexual abuse committed by children and young people. Erooga and Mason (1999) referring to Home Office figures for 1997 state that, of the 6400 persons cautioned or found guilty of sexual offences, 47 per cent were under 21 years of age, with 10.5 per cent being under 13 years of age. However, the authors make no reference to the role the Internet may have played in the promotion of this behaviour. There is a clear need for qualitative research on the effect of the Internet on the development of opinions and attitudes on sexual behaviour. There is also a need to consider current treatment programmes for young people who have committed sexual offences. How far is their Internet use questioned or challenged? A brief telephone survey of treatment programmes found that the majority had an awareness of potential Internet use, but none made it a significant area of questioning. It was treated as pornography through other media.

Case C

Mr Green was a married father of two. He had been married to his current partner for ten years at the point he was referred to police and social services. He was arrested and charged with indecently assaulting an 11-year-old boy who was a friend of the family. During post-sentencing work with the probation service on a programme for sex offenders he began to discuss his Internet use. He had begun using the Internet two years prior to his arrest; initially he had collected images of adult pornography. He then described using chat rooms to explore issues concerning his own sexuality. Following this, he decided to experiment with bisexuality and used the Internet to make contacts. From this early experimentation he then described the 'discovery' of his romantic feelings towards younger boys.

This case may illustrate the pattern of behaviour found during research carried out as part of the COPINE (Combating Paedophile Information Networks in Europe) project (see Taylor et al. 2001). Individuals initially acquire computer skill, then download adult pornography. Advanced computing skills are developed and there is a further engagement with the virtual community. This community reinforces the pattern of behaviour. A progression to the collection of child pornographic material is followed by a further period where the material is used within the subject's fantasy world. In some cases this will be followed by progression to real-world contact and abuse. It is interesting to note the standard avoidance techniques in Mr Green's account, and the classic defence of placing the abuse within the context of a 'loving' relationship (see Salter 1991). It is also interesting to note that in this case the offender has shifted the locus of responsibility for his offending behaviour onto the Internet itself, which is portrayed as acting as a seducer.

Research into the role the Internet plays in developing offending behaviour is at an early stage. Previously, the Internet was seen as another tool used by those with a predisposition to offend against children. Further research needs to be conducted into the role of the Internet as a trigger for offending behaviour. This can be especially relevant given the interactive nature of the medium and its ability to reinforce modes of conduct through membership in an alternative virtual community. Mr Green's case shows how Internet technology accommodates crime displacement opportunities for sex offenders. Here displacement refers to the possibility that, in response to reduced opportunities to commit a particular crime, sex offenders will adapt by either: (1) choosing other targets; (2) offending at a different time or place or (3) changing their methods for committing the crime based on available opportunities.

The opportunity structure for crime places a limit on the ability to act. Internet chat forums, for example, extend the opportunity for sex offenders to engage in criminality. They are able to operate in a search or proactive mode, actively scanning the range of potential targets within a chat forum before considering which vulnerable child to focus on. As part of the displacement process, they can move around different chat forums unnoticed and change identities to suit particular strategies of involvement. In this sense they resemble shoplifters, in that there is little chance of being observed until the actual act of crime takes place. The use of 'untraceable pseudonymity' in Internet chat forums poses a particular set of problems for child protection agencies. They allow for multiple identities or the continuity of a false identity to be maintained over a period of time. A person posting under a 'nym' can develop an image and a reputation just like any other on-line personality. Most people we interact with on-line are just a name and an email address, plus whatever impression we have formed of them by what they write.

Case D

Mr Grey was reported to the local police and social services department following the discovery of emails he was sending to a chat room. Another police authority was monitoring the chat room and it detected his potential paedophilic activity. A police search was conducted at his home and computer equipment seized. It was discovered that his stepdaughter's bedroom had been set up with a hidden digital video camera. Mr Grey was found to have been abusing his daughter and producing pornography that he then traded on the Internet.

This case highlights the sophisticated nature of some modes of offending behaviour, and the necessity of monitoring and surveillance. It also highlights the need for close co-operation between police forces at national and local level, and with local child protection agencies. It is representative of an increase in the 'domestic production' of pornography, a trend noticed by COPINE, Internet Watch and the Movement Against Paedophilia on the Internet (MAPI) (see Taylor *et al.* 2001). As can be seen, this is linked to advances in technology, specifically the video camera, digital camera and video capture software. These have enabled the production of images without the need for outside laboratories to develop the films. This removes a significant deterrent and has led to a rapid rise in the number of new images being produced. According to Taylor *et al.*, approximately two new children appear each month on the Internet pages monitored by COPINE. Recently there has been a growth in the number of photographs of Eastern European children. The victim in this case was white. This is consistent with research findings that show a relative absence of pictures of black children. Taylor and his colleagues emphasize that the link between the market, domestic and commercial production of child pornography should not be overlooked by child protection agencies.

The case of Mr Grey also demonstrates the importance of Internet chat forums in the construction of sex crimes against children. As mentioned above, offender's strategies are often dependent on disguise (e.g. false age and gender) and the multiple identities that can be used in Internet chat (see Herring 1999). Failure to lure and cultivate a child using one virtual identity can lead to its replacement with another. This gives a paedophile a new approach and set of cultivating tactics. Whilst this case illustrates some success, in general, crime control in relation to Internet chat is weak. With reference to sexual offences against children, Felson (1986) describes informal control (where no formal legal sanctions or rules are in place) as most secure when the four elements of handled offender (whose behaviour is informally regulated by another person), suitable target, intimate handler (who is close to the offender and informally regulates their behaviour) and capable guardian (of the suitable target) are in direct physical contact and when relevant people know one another very well. There are few potential 'informants' in Internet chat. The dispersion of individuals in chat forums makes it much more difficult to develop the kind of informal control discussed by Felson. Sex offenders who use Internet technology have no intimate handler near (e.g. the parents, the neighbours, social worker or probation officer) and can get to a target with the guardian away. When using the Internet children are dispersed away from family and neighbourhood situations. Sex offenders can find targets with guardians absent. In addition, they are able to get away from their handlers, and can be fairly certain that it will be difficult for Internet handlers (e.g. Internet chat hosts) to recognize them, or compare notes with the guardians (e.g. parents, social workers) (see Walsh 1986). Here we see how handlers and guardians are segregated from suitable targets in Internet chat and informants are less likely to link the handler to the evidence. Even if other on-line participants have suspicions, they will not be able to know the (potential) offender's real name or location. Internet chat lacks the conditions of a tight community where handlers and guardians can have greater presence and ability to control sex crimes.

Practice issues arising from the challenges and case studies

Child pornography is a global problem in terms of its production, dissemination and the involvement of offenders. The challenge for governments has been to produce an international consensus about the nature of the problem, to increase international co-operation in terms of the prosecution of offenders (e.g. harmonizing the rules on extradition), and to develop internationally consistent internal legal frameworks for dealing with offenders. This latter development is vital given the ability of the Internet to transcend national boundaries. 'Sites' are now being hosted in countries without a legal framework. The UNESCO Conference in Paris (1999), for example, highlighted Venezuela and Japan as countries which failed to prosecute hosted websites that involved sexually explicit material of children.

The difficulties in achieving a consensus have been recognized for some time. The United Nations Convention on the Rights of the Child uses a qualified definition of what constitutes a child. (A child is 'Every human being below the age of 18 years unless under the law applicable to the child majority is attained earlier'.) A joint internationally agreed definition of child pornography has still to be formally ratified. According to the INTERPOL working group 'child pornography is the consequence of the exploitation or sexual abuse perpetrated against a child. It can be defined as any means of depicting or promoting sexual abuse of a child, including print and audio, centred on sex acts or the genital organs of children'. Notice that this definition does not include digital imagery or computer graphics. This definition has, however, gained wide acceptance and was used at the World Congress against the Commercial Sexual Exploitation of Children in Stockholm in 1996. This definition, although useful, does not take into account the recent phenomena of 'pseudo images'. Pseudo images are pornographic images produced by using computer graphics software to alter existing photographs. In this case an actual child may not have been abused directly. The definition also does not cover the 'morphed' images (in which disparate images are grafted onto each other to create a new image) of children paedophiles acquire, which may not contain obscene images, but may play a key part in the offender cycle.

There has been a degree of success in producing broadly similar legal frameworks in a range of countries. For example: the Protection of Children Act (1978) in the UK; the Omnibus Bill currently being debated in Canada; the Child Trafficking and Pornography Act (1998) in the Republic of Ireland; and the Child Pornography Prevention Act (1996) in the US. All these acts have similar terms of reference concerning the production, possession and trafficking of pornographic materials.

In the UK, the issue of child pornography has been primarily dealt with via the Protection of Children Act (1978) with amendments, and the Obscene Publications Act (1959) and its various amendments. How these laws have been modified provides useful illustrations of some emerging themes in relation to new communication technologies. The 1978 Act arose out of public concerns about the growing availability of child pornography in print and film. This had resulted from a liberalization in certain countries on laws on pornography that led to an increase in the commercial availability of such material. Section 1 of the Act made it an offence 'to take, or permit to be taken or to make, any indecent photographs...of a child.' The Act was strengthened by Section 160 of the Criminal Justice Act (1988) which made it an offence 'for a person to have any indecent photograph...in his possession'; this initially carried a maximum sentence of six months which has now been increased to five years. The amendments made by the Criminal Justice and Public Order Act (1994), Section 84, extended the definition of photograph given in Section 7(4) of the 1978 Act to include images stored as data on computers. It also created a new section in the 1978 Child Protection Act at 7(7) which defined pseudo-photographs as 'an image, whether made by computer graphics or otherwise howsoever which appears to be a photograph'. For the first time the amendment allowed for the prosecution of persons for the production, trading and possession of 'pseudo-photographs'.

The issue of pseudo-photographs has raised many complex questions about the use of new technologies in relation to child sex offences. Civil liberties groups have raised the question of whether there is an offence if a child has not been directly involved in the production of the material, and the material has only been produced for private consumption by the individual concerned. This was seen in the case of R. v. Sharpe in the Supreme Court of Canada (2001) (for details of this case see Yaman Akdeniz, Regulation of child pornography on the Internet: cases and materials, at http://www.cyber-right.org/reports/chil.htm) where Sharpe appealed that Section 163.1(4) of the Criminal Code dealing with possession of child pornography infringed his constitutional rights under the Canadian Charter of Rights and Freedoms. The UK position, as described by Akdeniz, is one where the 'police believe that the creators or possessors of pseudo-photographs will end up abusing children, so the purpose of the new legislation may be seen as a preparatory act being criminalized'. He also notes that the criminalization of pseudo-photographs is regarded as a preventative measure concerning future prosecution problems regarding pornographic images, the origins of which might be increasingly difficult to prove.

There have been a series of successful prosecutions in the UK using the legislation and the number of possession offences has increased rapidly over the past five years. As a result of Operation Starburst, which was led by the West Midland Police, the first prosecutions took place in 1995 with Christopher Sharp receiving a £9000 fine for possession of child pornography, and with Martin Crumpton being the first person to be imprisoned in early 1996. The case of Allan Fellows and Stephen Arnold held in Manchester in 1996 set various legal precedents in the UK. Arnold and Fellows (who had been based at the University of Birmingham) were charged with a number of offences under the Obscene Publications Act (1959), the Protection of Children Act (1978), and Section 160 of the Criminal Justice Act (1988), including the transmission and possession of child pornography. Fellows set up an Internet website and had been supplied with photographs by Arnold.

This case widened the definition of publication to include computer-transmitted digital imagery and set the precedent that images retained on computer hard drives as data could still be considered as 'photographs' for the purpose of prosecution. The sentencing of Fellows to three years imprisonment also underlined the seriousness with which the offence was taken. The trial judge in his summing up added that 'the pictures could fuel the fantasies of those with perverted attitudes towards the young and they might incite sexual abuse on innocent children'. This is a good example of the commonly held opinion of the corrupting nature of the visual material and its potential role in 'inciting acts of abuse' via the use of new technologies. It also implies that there is a causal relationship between virtual forms of the digital imagery production and actual physical sexual abuse that is characterized by a continuum of criminal stages of involvement.

The proposed criminal continuum of paedophile crime can be helpfully understood in terms of what Cornish and Clarke (1986) refer to as a distinction between *involvement* and *event* stages in criminal activity. Put another way, it is likely that sex offenders move through involvement and event stages in their offending behaviour. This distinction might be particularly useful in shedding light on Internet chat forums as environments for cultivating potential victims and linking on-line to off-line activities. It has affinities to models of reflexively organized crime, whereby criminals weigh up the pros and cons involved in particular opportunities for crime. For Cornish and Clarke the 'involvement zone' refers to the processes through which offenders choose to become involved in particular forms of sexual abuse, and then to continue or to desist. The 'event zone', on the other hand, refers to the commission of specific sex crimes which utilizes specialized knowledge of criminal opportunities (also see Finkelhor 1989). Involvement decisions are characteristically multi-stage, extended over substantial periods of time. A depository of information will be drawn upon, only some of which will be related to the sex crimes themselves. Event decisions on the other hand are frequently shorter processes, utilizing more circumscribed information relating to immediate abusive circumstances and situations. The use of new communication technologies by paedophiles can have the following effects: (1) it enables them take a more casual approach across time, and (2) browsing activity can occur at the involvement stage. This might suggest that more time elapses between the involvement and event stage when sex offenders use new technologies. Brantingham (1984) refers to the involvement stage as 'awareness space' in which a criminal familiarizes himself with the opportunities for crime. As a planning stage it allows for free-range opportunism whereby offenders catalogue any obstacles and potential problems involved in sex crimes.

The case of Father Adrian McLeish is another good example of a highly sophisticated paedophile making effective use of new communication technologies to execute sexual abuse. Father McLeish was discovered as part of Operation Starburst and was successfully prosecuted and sentenced to six years in prison in Newcastle in 1996. He was found to have a vast store of images held on four computers and to be in possession of a range of other material including magazines and videos. At trial he was charged with a series of specimen charges in relation to indecent assaults carried out on boys aged between 10 and 18 years. Police checks on McLeish's email found him to be in contact with a number of individuals across the world, including the

US, Sweden, Germany and France. The prosecution claimed he was part of an international paedophile ring that used Internet technology to discuss 'grooming', and other cultivation issues, as well as to exchange pornographic images. Prior to his arrest, McLeish erased his digital records, and borrowed a colleague's computer to alert the wider network using anonymous email software. In McLeish's case the images collected formed part of the backdrop of an already established pattern of offending behaviour, which adapted to incorporate the new opportunities presented by the Internet medium. The central concern here is the powerful way in which the Internet was used to form and develop wider paedophile networks. McLeish was a cautious and careful character who used information technology not only to deepen his involvement in sex crimes, but also as a security device against criminal detection. Typically, he was involved in 'flaw hunting' whereby sex offenders search for chinks in any safety system (e.g. parents, influential authoritative adults or the police) that protects vulnerable children.

In producing legal frameworks to deal with child pornography there is a need for common definitions. There is also a need, however, for the legislation to be regularly reviewed to keep up with the rate of technological innovation and change. It has been seen in the field of intellectual property law that legal instruments have to be continuously adapted to reflect changed circumstances. This rate of change poses significant problems for governments and investigating agencies alike. Clearly, the question of individual liberties needs to be taken into account, but this should be balanced with the risks to children as well as their rights to safety and protection. The complex role of pornography in the offending cycle needs to be considered in respect of sentencing policy and legislation.

Detection, assessment and investigation of Internet child abuse

Child protection agencies in the developed world need to develop a greater awareness of the role information technology plays in perpetrating and staging sexual abuse. Clearer lines of communication between national agencies and centres of excellence also need to be developed in relation to investigating this type of abuse. A series of recommendations were made at the Yokohama Conference in Japan in December 2001 to improve international co-operation and tighter agency-based networking.

The government's policy outlined in the publication *Working Together to Safeguard Children* (Department of Health *et al.* 1999) requires local authorities in England and Wales to consider the protection of children in relation to the Internet. The *National Plan for Safeguarding Children from Commercial Sexual Exploitation* published in 2001 unified this with guidance for Northern Ireland and Scotland. The plan requires Area Child Protection Committees to ensure that effective services are in place to support children who may be exploited. This is primarily in relation to children involved in prostitution, however, there are clear links between this form of exploitation, the Internet and the production of child pornography (Carr 2001). The national plan also indicates that the Association of Chief Police Officers (ACPO) are 'developing a strategy to combat abuse on-line [which] will provide cohesive direction, co-ordinating operations across forces to ensure maximum impact'. The Regulation of Investigatory Powers Act (2000) is designed to assist the investigation of child pornography on the Internet by providing 'a statutory basis for the acquisition of communications data from communications service providers'. It also allows the police to require an individual 'to deliver up the plain text of lawfully obtained electronic material which has been protected in some way'. The civil liberties aspect of this legislation has caused a great deal of concern and debate in the UK.

Increasingly, child protection agencies will be compelled to use information technology to monitor and detect the activities of paedophiles using new media and the Internet. A recent development, for instance, in the detection methods of the police has included the use of 'trace programmes'. These programmes have been used to identify the ISP addresses of computers that have contacted specific 'flagged' sites. This has then been used as the basis of applications for search and the confiscation of computer equipment. Whilst this is a resource-intensive method, it significantly widens the level of surveillance and detection. The view here is that the focus should be on the offenders' decision-making and context of the offenders' activities. The hi-tech crime unit recently set up to combat computer-related crime will uncover covert or illegal networks. Malcolm Sparrow (1991) examines the application of social network analysis to criminal activity. Sparrow describes three problems of criminal network analysis that are relevant to Internet child abuse:

1. Incompleteness – the inevitability of missing nodes and links in the network that the investigators will not uncover.

2. Fuzzy boundaries – the difficulty in deciding who to include and who not to include.

3.   Dynamic networks – these networks are not static; they are always changing.

Instead of looking at the presence or absence of a tie between two individuals using the Internet, Sparrow suggests looking at the waxing and waning strength of a tie, depending upon the time and the task at hand. Covert networks of paedophiles, for example, are unlikely to behave like normal social networks (see Baker and Faulkner 1993). Child abusers using the Internet seem to have a preference for networking with other offenders, perhaps for economic and time resource reasons. This means they do not form many ties outside of their immediate cluster and regulate co-option and recruitment to existing ties inside the network. Strong ties between prior contacts, which are likely to have been formed over time, and therefore established on trust, will tend to keep the cells linked. Yet, unlike normal social networks, these strong ties will remain mostly dormant and therefore hidden to outsiders, until the time for organized crime arrives. In a covert network, such as an Internet paedophile ring, because of their low frequency of activation, strong ties may appear to be weak ties. The less active the network, the more difficult it is to discover. Krebs (2002) summarizes some of the key network responses necessary to detect and prosecute networked crimes such as Internet child abuse. This summary is shown in Table 5.1.

Table 5.1

Relationships and/or network	Data sources
Trust relation	Prior contacts in family, neighbourhood, school, military, club or organization. Public and court records. Data may only be available in suspect's native country.
Surveillance Task	Logs and records of phone calls, electronic mail, chat rooms, instant messages, website visits. Travel records. Observation of meetings and attendance at common events.
Operational Strategy	Websites. Videos, DVDs and encrypted disks delivered by courier. Travel records. Observation of meetings and attendance at crime-related events.

The treatment and monitoring arrangements for sex offenders

As we have seen, much of the research in this area is only at an early stage in respect of evaluating the impact of Internet use on sex-offending behaviour (Quayle 2002; Taylor *et al.* 2001). Current sex offender treatment programmes tend to view the Internet as just another source of pornography for offenders, tending to disregard the way that it can reinforce different types of sex offence and shape behaviour. The Internet can reinforce addictive qualities and offer a source of legitimization and shared knowledge (Quayle 2002). It can also enable sex abusers to develop offence specialization and avoid police contact because much information technology is knowledge based (see Kempf 1986). There needs to be more systematic collection of data concerning offenders' use of the Internet in treatment programmes. The role of the probation service in respect of offenders' access to computer equipment also needs to be considered.

The treatment of victims

Computer technology and the Internet are too new to establish whether the long-term impact of this type of abuse may differ from other forms of sexual abuse. However, according to Taylor *et al.* (2001), the impact on children abused through Internet pornography, and the fact that their images will continue to be replicated by other sex offenders, is an issue for consideration.

The raising of public awareness

The second World Congress Against Commercial Sexual Exploitation of Children, held in December 2001 at Yokohama, made clear the responsibility of Internet services to play their part in 'policing' the Internet. The industry has responded globally with the production of sites to which child pornography can be reported. Co-operation with international law enforcement agencies has also been improved. Nigel Williams of Child Net International has raised the need for further monitoring and guidance to be provided in chat rooms. In 1996 the UK funded the Internet Watch Foundation which takes referrals and monitors concern about child pornography.

There have been some good examples of public awareness campaigns in relation to children and the use of new technologies. Nationally the UK government, through the Internet crime forum, produced 'Chat Wise, Street Wise' which made recommendations to the industry, and through the

Department for Education and Skills (DfES) (2002) produced the 'Super-highway Safety Guidance' for parents and teachers. As noted above, the policy *Working Together to Safeguard Children* (Department of Health *et al.* 1999) and the *National Plan for Safeguarding Children from Commercial Sexual Exploitation* (Department of Health 2001) require Area Child Protection Committees (ACPCs) to develop services to prevent the sexual exploitation of children. In consequence, ACPCs should be developing communication strategies. Anecdotal evidence indicates that, unfortunately, this work has been slow to start due to the low priority it has been given.

The development of technological responses

With the accelerated pace of technological change within the computing industry, child protection agencies need help in understanding the implications of the latest developments. This could be offered in centres of forensic excellence. Nationally, child protection agencies require training on the implications of computer use for child safety, and also for dealing with sex offenders.

Through government objectives children are being increasingly familiarized with computers and the Internet. Studies have found that children are spending more time communicating via the new technologies. The risk is that children are ahead of the child protection agencies in their computer literacy and knowledge. They are increasingly entering a virtual world of their own with child protection agencies lagging behind in their understanding. Child protection agencies need to engage with this new technology as it offers a new medium for communicating with children. A good example of this happening is the NSPCC's Virtual Children Centre. Here children are enabled to communicate directly with workers on-line.

Conclusion

In this chapter it has been suggested that research and policy should focus on the decision-making processes (e.g. pattern-planning) of the sex offenders who use new communication technologies such as the Internet. It has also been indicated that these offenders are reasoning decision makers and that new technologies can facilitate the process involved. Rather than concentrating on factors disposing sex offenders to criminal behaviour, there is a need to emphasize subsequent networked decisions (such as the initial use of Internet chat rooms) in the offender's career. This means conceptualizing the various contingent factors that are involved. The case studies also suggest that a crime-specific focus is necessary. This is because the situational context of the decision making, and the information being handled, varies according to the offences committed. A crime-specific focus for sexual abuse is likely to involve rather finer distinctions than those commonly made in the child protection literature. This might mean that the explanatory focus is on the crimes themselves rather than on offender characteristics. Through the use of case examples from child pornography and Internet sex chat we have identified that new communication technologies are likely to:

- increase accessibility to vulnerable children as a medium which can extend or enhance criminal activity for sex offenders (this boils down to a simple model of crime production via new technologies)

- provide a virtual alternative to real-time sexual abuse whilst retaining key elements of its criminality

- reduce the risk of detection and prosecution

- permit a more rigorous targeting and cultivation of potential victims by sex offenders

- weaken social regulation of sex offenders who cannot be effectively 'handled' by a capable guardian, authority or regulator

- modify expert perceptions about the nature of the sexual offence and might thereby alter investigation and assessment procedures.

It is often suggested that new forms of communication involve a constellation of knowledge, processes, skills and products which aim to control and transform. This view tends to rely on the autonomy of new technologies as an independent force. There is, however, an alternative perspective that challenges this kind of technological determinism. This alternative perspective emphasizes the intentional use made of technology in terms of extending the range of social action and networks for individuals. This chapter shows how technology is used to control and transform the behaviour of others. New communication technologies, such as the Internet, can be used to magnify and reframe the potential for child sexual abuse. It might be correct to say that examples such as those discussed here demonstrate how the use of new technology by sex offenders is nevertheless 'technological': the examples refer to various dimensions of criminal practice that are characterized in specific ways. The particular manner in which new communications have been appropriated is 'technological' in that they are end-oriented. Simply put, they are used as devices to obtain sexual possession and abuse. Sex offenders look at the world technologically when they see it as either a resource to be used or as a constraint to be overcome. New communication technologies are therefore a part of a problem-solving process in that they are used to satisfy various wants and desires.

References

Bagley, C. (1997) *Children, Sex and Social Policy.* Suffolk: Avebury.

Baker, W. E. and Faulkner, R. R. (1993) 'The social organization of conspiracy and illegal networks in the heavy electrical equipment industry.' *American Sociological Review 58*, 6, 837–860.

Berliner, L. and Conte, J. R. (1990) 'The process of victimization: the victim's perspective.' *Child Abuse and Neglect 14*, 29–40.

Brantingham, M. (1984) *Patterns in Crime.* New York: Macmillan.

Carr, J. (2001) 'Child pornography.' Paper presented in preparation for the Yokohama Conference by John Carr on behalf of EPCAT. Available through the conference website: www.focalpointngo.org/yokohama/themepapers

Cornish, D. B. and Clarke, R. V. (eds) (1986) *The Reasoning Criminal: Rational Choice Perspectives on Offending.* New York: Springer-Verlag.

Cowburn, M. and Pringle, K. (2000) 'Pornography and men's practices.' *Journal of Sexual Aggression 6*, 1, 52–66.

Davies, N. and Vascar, J. (2001) 'Global child porn ring broken.' *The Guardian*, 1 November.

Department for Education and Skills (2002) *Superhighway Safety: Safe use of the Internet at home and at school.* http://safety.ngfl.gov.uk/schools.

Department of Health (2001) *National Plan for Safeguarding Children from Commercial Sexual Exploitation.* London: TSO.

Department of Health, Home Office and Department for Education and Employment (1999) *Working Together to Safeguard Children.* London: TSO.

Durkin, K. and Bryant, C. (1999) 'Propagandising pederasty: a thematic analysis of the on-line exculpatory accounts of unrepentant paedophiles.' *Deviant Behaviour: An Interdisciplinary Journal 20*, 103–127.

Erooga, M. and Mason, H. (1999) *Children and Young People who Sexually Abuse Others.* London: Routledge.

Felson, D. (1986) 'Linking criminal choices, routine activities, informal control, and criminal outcomes.' In D. Cornish and R. Clarke (eds) *The Reasoning Criminal: Rational Choice Perspectives on Offending.* New York: Springer-Verlag.

Finkelhor, D. (1984) *Child Sexual Abuse: New Theory and Research.* New York: Free Press.

Finkelhor, D. (1989) *Nursery Crime: Sexual Abuse in Day Care.* London: Sage.

Finkelhor, D. (1993) 'Epidemiological factors in the clinical identification of child sexual abuse.' *Child Abuse and Neglect 17,* 67–70.

Hansard (2001) Lords Hansard text for 15 Jan 2001 (210115w03).

Herring, S. (1999) 'The rhetorical dynamics of gender harassment on-line.' *The Information Society 15,* 3, 151–168.

Itzin, C. (2001) 'Incest, paedophilia, pornography and prostitution: making familial males more visible as abusers.' *Child Abuse Review 10,* 35–48.

Itzin, C. (1996) 'Pornography and the organization of child sexual abuse.' In P. Bibby (ed) *Organized Abuse: The Current Debate.* Aldershot: Ashgate.

Kempf, K. (1986) 'Offense specialization: does it exist?' In D. Cornish and R. Clarke (eds) *The Reasoning Criminal: Rational Choice Perspectives on Offending.* New York: Springer-Verlag.

Krebs, V. E. (2002) 'Uncloaking terrorist networks.' *First Monday 7,* 4, 1 April.

Marshall, W. L. (2000) 'Revisiting the use of pornography by sexual offenders: implications for theory and practice.' *Journal of Sexual Aggression 6,* 1/2, 67–77.

Marshall, W.L., Laws, D.R., Barbaree, H.E. (1990) *Handbook of Sexual Assault: Issues, Theories and Treatment of the Offender.* New York: Plenum Press.

Quayle, E. (2002) 'Modus operandi of internet sex offenders'. Lecture given at Sexual Abuse and the Internet Conference, London, 30th October.

Salter, A. C. (1991) *Treating Child Sex Offenders and Victims.* Sage: London.

Society Guardian (2000) http://society.guardian.co.uk/ 16 November.

Sparrow, M. K. (1991) 'The application of network analysis to criminal intelligence: an assessment of the prospects.' *Social Networks 13,* 251–274.

Taylor, M., Quayle, E. and Holland, G. (2001) 'Child pornography, the Internet and Offending.' *Ete,* Summer, 94–100.

Walsh, D. (1986) 'Victim selection procedures among economic criminals: the rational choice perspective.' In D. Cornish and R. Clarke (eds) *The Reasoning Criminal: Rational Choice Perspectives on Offending.* New York: Springer-Verlag.

Williams, N. (2000) 'Using hard cases for good purposes – the example of Chatdanger.com.' Paper presented at International Forum of Researchers, Young People and the Media, Sydney, Australia, November. Available via the ChildNet.com website.

Wyre, R. (1992) 'Pornography and sexual violence; working with sex offenders.' In C. Itzin (ed) *Pornography: Women, Violence and Civil Liberties: A Radical New View.* Buckingham: Open University Press.

Further Reading

Beck, U. (1992) *Risk Society.* London: Sage.

Bilson, A. (1999) *Child Safety, Child Rights and the Net.* Birmingham: BASW.

Jenkins, P. (2001) *Pedophiles and Priests – Anatomy of a Contemporary Crisis.* Oxford: Oxford University Press.

Marshall, W. L. and Marshall, L. E. (2000) *Origins of Sexual Offending.* London: Routledge.

Quayle, E., Holland, G., Lineham, C. and Taylor, M. (2000) 'The Internet and offending behaviour: case study.' *The Journal of Sexual Aggression 6,* 1/2, 78–96.

Note

The issue of Internet child abuse is constantly changing – since going to press, the preferred reference for child pornography has become 'abusive images of children'. The authors support this term as it emphasises the abusive nature of this medium.

Part Two
Health and Welfare

CHAPTER 6

Information Technology and the Organization of Patient Care

Walter Sermeus

In 1999, the US Institute of Medicine (IOM) published the report *To Err Is Human: Building a Safer Health System* (Kohn, Corrigan and Donaldson 1999) estimating that in the US as many as 44,000 to 98,000 people die yearly from medical errors that occur in hospitals. The report breaks the silence that has surrounded medical errors and their consequences, not by pointing fingers at caring professionals who make these mistakes – after all, to err is human – but by aiming to design a safer health system.

Two remarks can be made on the report. Until data show the opposite, we can assume that this particular US situation is prevalent in all health care systems across the western world. Second, the findings in the report amounted to only the tip of the iceberg. A health system is a tangled, highly fragmented web that often wastes resources by providing unnecessary services and duplicating efforts, leaving unaccountable gaps in care and failing to build on the strengths of all health professionals.

The new IOM 2001 report *Crossing the Quality Chasm: A New Health System for the 21st Century* (Institute of Medicine 2001) offers a comprehensive strategy to improve care. The report envisions a system that not only is centered on the needs, preferences, and values of patients, but also encourages teamwork among health care workers and makes much greater use of information technology. Health care organizations are only beginning to apply technological advances. For example, patient information typically is dispersed in a collection of paper records, which often are poorly organized, illegible, and not easy to retrieve, making it nearly impossible to manage various chronic illnesses that require frequent monitoring and ongoing patient support. In addition, many patients could have their needs met more quickly and at a lower cost if they had the option of communicating with health care professionals through email. The use of automated medication order entry systems can reduce errors in prescribing and dosing drugs, and computerized reminders can help both patients and clinicians identify needed services. The commission said that a nationwide effort is needed to build a technology-based information infrastructure that would lead to the elimination of most hand-written clinical data within the next ten years. Without a national pledge to create and fund such a technological framework, progress to enhance quality of care will be painfully slow.

The IOM Commission proposed six areas: safety, effectiveness, patient-centredness, timeliness, efficiency and equity. The first section of this chapter will describe the transition from the actual health care system to a patient-focused health care system. The second section will provide a conceptual framework in which the patient-centred dimension is translated into organizational systems. In the third and last section, the focus is on the information systems that are required to fulfil these goals.

From functional departments to patient-focused care

Health care organizations are very complex. According to Mintzberg (1997) running even a highly complicated corporation must be simple compared to managing any hospital. But, according to Mintzberg, if we can succeed in giving hospitals a more appropriate organizational structure, they become 'more manageable than anyone thought'.

Many authors (for example, Fetter and Freeman 1986; Herzlinger 1999; Lathrop 1993; Mintzberg 1997) agree that the main problem in managing health care is the dual organizational structure. Two distinct processes are functioning in an almost independent way: the clinical process and the organizational process. The medical doctor drives the clinical process. When a patient has a health problem, he/she sees a medical doctor. The doctor examines the patient. A wide variety of diagnostic tests can be ordered. In terms of treatment, drugs can be prescribed and a number of therapeutic options are available. The hospital managers drive the organizational processes. They ensure that resources are available to the clinicians. Although this way of providing clinical care is still in evidence, for the following reasons it is outdated and no longer appropriate.

Historically, this two-tier model of health care was relevant 50 years ago, when the medical doctor was an independent professional treating patients in a one-to-one relationship. Only when a patient's family was unable to provide care was the patient transferred to the hospital. The evolution in capital-intensive diagnostics (e.g. x-ray) and therapeutics (e.g. operating theatres) started a trend towards doctors spending more time in hospitals. Their practice, however, remained independent. Clinicians value and wish to protect their independence and this one-to-one relationship with patients. However, the reality is that once a patient is admitted to hospital, care is provided by a complex network of highly educated professionals. Abersnagel and van Vliet (1998) suggest that a patient undergoing open heart surgery in the Utrecht Academic Centre may meet on average 100 people from 18 different disciplines.

Also, the link between the clinical and the organizational processes is very weak. This link consists of prescriptions, orders and medical procedures. In most hospitals the link is not automated; therefore, communication is slow and time-consuming. About a century ago, this order-link was satisfactory. On average, patients stayed in hospitals for 20 days. Medical doctors visited their patients from once a day to three times a week. Following this visit, orders were made. Nowadays, the number of orders has exponentially increased. Lesar, Briceland and Stein (1997) found that almost 300,000 medication orders were written during one year in a tertiary-care teaching hospital. The Mayo Foundation (http://www.mayo.edu/facts/factsheetfoundv2.html), taking care of about half a million patients yearly on an inpatient or outpatient basis, performs about 4500 diagnostic X-ray procedures, more than 40,000 lab tests and more than 300 admissions and surgical operations a day. An average hospital of 500 beds is probably processing 10,000 to 20,000 orders a day.

There are several problems with this order-link system. Turnaround times are extensive: it takes about four hours to process and deliver a routine service such as an initial drug order, a lab test or an X-ray examination. For an X-ray examination more than 40 work steps are routinely involved (Lathrop 1993). In addition, the overall error rate is high. Lesar *et al.* (1997) found 313 errors per 1000 medication orders. Moreover, because a patient's day consists of a complicated series of transactions, professionals are competing for time with him or her. Lathrop (1993) shows that respiratory therapists, on first attempt, managed to provide a service for only about half of the patients referred to them. It requires an average of three visits to deliver two respiratory therapy treatments. This means that 33 per cent of their time is used inefficiently. This paper-based order system leads to high costs as well as poor service. Only 24 per cent of the time of hospital personnel is devoted to patient care (medical-technical as well as hotel services). Seventy-six per cent of the time is spent on: documentation (30 per cent); scheduling and co-ordination (14 per cent); transportation (6 per cent); management and supervision (7 per cent); and finally 19 per cent is idle time being ready for action (Lathrop 1993). This ready-for-action time is important. By way of the order-link, the clinical process is driving the organization. Because of the fact that the clinical process is individually designed, together with a high emphasis on the therapeutic freedom of the clinician, clinical processes are treated as highly unpredictable, leading to this need for such a high proportion of structured idle time:

> Hospitals seem to have designed their operations around the following baseline parameters: describe the busiest time on the busiest day of the year; then add to that demand the sickest possible patient with the most complex set of needs; then design operations to meet that standard at all times. (Lathrop 1993, p.68)

Cost cutting in hospitals has led to a reduction in the level of resources and beds which, in turn, has impacted on the clinical process. This has led to increased waiting lists and waiting times. This indicates that it is very difficult to balance input (organization) and output (clinical processes) if these two processes are functioning almost independently with a slow order-link.

Defining the hospital as an organizational duality, with the medical doctor deciding on the clinical process and the manager deciding on the organization, is oversimplifying the current system. The role of the nurse complexifies matters. He/she was seen as part of the clinical process, but also regarded as part of the organizational aspect by the medical doctor and the manager. By seeing the nurse as part of the organizational system, the medical doctor could be sure that the unique patient–doctor relationship stayed intact, knowing at the same time that the nurse constituted a link between the medical and organizational dimensions of the hospital. It is often said that medical doctors would be helpless in hospitals if it were not for nurses. Nurses not only take care of patients, they take care of doctors also. For managers, negotiations with medical doctors are already tough enough without adding nurses to the clinical side of the equation. New nursing roles such as nurse specialists, nurse practitioners and case managers emphasize both the professional and clinical dimension of their role. Nowadays, it is seen that steering the clinical process is no longer the single-handed right of the medical doctor. Increasingly, decisions are made in teams consisting of various specialists such as nurses, physiotherapists and social workers. Decisions are more likely to be made across organizational borders taking into account the general practitioner and the community nurse, as well as the family network. Even more important is the role of the patient. Gone are the days of the patient as a passive recipient of care. The patient is now taking a more active role, looking for evidence on the Internet, seeking second opinions and requesting information and treatment options.

Due to the changing interaction between the clinical processes and the organizational management, hospital structures are changing. Traditionally hospitals were structured in a functional way according to professional groupings: for example, the medical department, the nursing department and the technical department. The medical department is not even a 'real' department. In most organograms the medical department is linked to the health care organization with a dotted line, indicating a relationship, but uncertainty as to its 'fit'. Most other departments are structured hierarchically. The nursing department is led by a chief nursing officer. Below the chief nursing officer will be nurse directors, nurse managers, head nurses and lead nurses. In many hospitals, it is the head nurse who is the lynchpin between the medical doctor and the organization's management. He/she is involved in co-ordination, negotiation and the resolution of conflicts between the clinical and organizational processes. In practice, this can mean undertaking such tasks as admitting patients, scheduling X-ray examinations, and retrieving patients' records.

A first step towards making organizational improvement involves the creation of a divisional structure. One of the first occurances of this took place in Johns Hopkins Hospital at the beginning of the 1980s (Heyssel *et al.* 1984). The outcome of this experiment has inspired the clinical directorate structure in the UK today. The divisions have an interdisciplinary composition (including, for example, medical doctors, nurses, paramedics and clerical staff). Divisions are led by a management team: a medical doctor, a nurse, and an administrator. The number and different roles can vary from organization to organization (de Vries and Beijers 1999; Wulff 1996). The medical doctor, called clinical director, has the final responsibility of the division and takes care of all relations with the medical staff. The co-ordinating principle is management by results. The divisions get a budget according to volume and quality indicators. They are independent in their decision making as long as they get the final results within budget constraints. The main advantages of this model are that decision making is decentralized and that medical doctors are more integrated into the hospital. One of the main disadvantages is that the organizational structure becomes more complex. The existing functional professional structure does not disappear but is given a new role. For example, all operational responsibilities within the nursing department are decentralized to the divisions. The nursing department, an 'umbrella' department for professional nurses, acquires an increasingly professional role in terms of quality control, accreditation and the drawing up of guidelines.

The number of divisions and the way they are organized can vary. They are mainly ordered in terms of: specialized patient units (for example, according to medical specialities, length of stay, level of intensity, age groups and patient problems); centralized ancillary units (for example, radiology, laboratory and pharmacy); and centralized hospital services (such as maintenance, housekeeping and laundry). This means that every patient will have contacts beyond the level of division. This requires co-ordination and problems can occur. Every division will try to optimize its output according to annual targets or performance indicators. However, patient processes cut across divisions and these are seldom optimized. Thus patients experience poor service and high levels of inefficiency. From the perspective of the medical doctor a divisional structure of low quality is experienced. This leads to reduced motivation for engaging with this kind of arrangement.

In consequence, this has led to a third type of organizational structure known as service-line. In service-line organizations the leading principle is the patient's journey through the system. A division, frequently renamed as a patient care centre, takes the lead for a group of patients with similar needs. Results are not solely defined at the divisional level but are dependent on the ability of each division to facilitate the patient care process. Therefore, results and incentives are mainly set from the patient's perspective. These are often to do with safety, effectiveness, and timeliness of service. Hospitals become yet more complex with the introduction of this third patient-focused dimension. The first layer of organization, which revolves around professional groups, is tangible by means of diplomas and credentials. The second layer of divisional organization is visible due to geographical location. The third layer is relatively virtual, being embedded in the connections and the information systems.

A health care model

In the mid 1980s, James Heskett set forth a set of relationships for service organizations. It was called the strategic service vision and consisted of four important principles: markets should be targeted; service concepts should be formulated in terms of results produced for customers and should be related to the needs of the customers and the offerings of competitors; organizational operations should value customers over costs to the offering organization; and service delivery systems, which include buildings, equipment, and information systems, should complement the associated operating strategies and operations. These four principles can be applied to any service organization, including a hospital.

One example of these principles in practice is the Shouldice Hospital, near Toronto, Canada (Heskett, Sasser and Schesinger 1997). This hospital specializes in one type of surgery: fixing external inguinal hernias. Being extremely good in that particular procedure, as showed by very low complication rates, they admit more than 6000 patients a year. These patients come from Canada, the US and even Europe. The success of the hospital lies mainly in its clear concept of care. Because of a special operating technique, which involves not only fixing the hernia but also inforcing the muscular wall of the abdomen, patients can gain mobility more quickly. The concept of care is built around self-care and patient involvement, with a focus on health rather than on sickness. This concept is translated into all aspects of practice. On arriving at the hospital the patient is examined by the surgeon. Patients are kept informed by nurses and other patients. The other patients, who had their own operation just a few hours before, can offer reassurance and advice. For patients, the most memorable aspect of their treatment is being invited to get up from the operating table after the operation, and walking to the door of the operating room on the arms of their surgeons. It is the start of a remarkable recovery process. For two or three days following the operation, they exercise slowly but relentlessly, swapping stories with other patients. This approach allows them to return to work twice as fast as other approaches. Because of the high emphasis on self-care, the cost of care is lower than in every other hospital dealing with similar patient populations. Shouldice does not look like a hospital. It is set on a country-club-like estate that encourages outdoor exercises. The strong market and operating focus make this hospital almost unbeatable for hernia procedures. In the following sub-sections the different aspects of this service orientation will be discussed.

The focus of the hospital

Many studies show a strong relationship between the volume and the outcome of care. Two volume parameters are taken into account: the number of procedures per physician and the size of the hospital. Brennan *et al.'s* (1991) classic study described the relationship between surgeon volume and risk-adjusted mortality for Coronary Artery Bypass Grafting (CABG) in New York in 1989. High-volume surgeons at high-volume hospitals experienced a risk-adjusted mortality of 2.2 per cent compared with low-volume surgeons at low-volume hospitals, who demonstrated a risk-adjusted mortality of 14.1 per cent.

A systematic review of the research undertaken since 1980 (Halm, Lee and Chassin 2000) shows that for a wide variety of medical conditions and surgical procedures, patients treated at higher-volume hospitals or by higher-volume physicians experience on average lower mortality rates than those treated by low-volume hospitals and physicians. Seventy-seven per cent of all the assessments in the studies in the review found statistically significant associations between either hospital or physician volume and health outcomes. In all cases the association was in the direction of higher volume being associated with better outcomes. No study documented a statistically significant association between higher volume and poorer outcomes. The volume itself cannot directly produce good (or bad) outcomes. Other features of patient care, correlated with volume, are the most likely explanatory factors. One of the hypotheses, besides skills and experience of the physicians or surgeons involved in the procedure, is related to the skills and experience of the health care team and the whole organization. High-volume hospitals are adopting specific organizational strategies that are particularly effective in enhancing outcomes, for high-volume procedures. They employ standardized protocols to reduce errors. Large hospitals have an advantage because house staff and fellows provide 24-hour physician coverage. The more complex the treatment process, the more likely it is that physician or surgeon skill will be only one of many important components of the full complement of effective care.

Concepts of care

Concepts of care are essentially built and evaluated on their level of evidence and patient involvement. Although these characteristics are almost opposites, they are interrelated in practice. Prahalad and Ramaswamy (2000) suggest that the changing role of the patient from passive to active is leading to their involvement as co-creator of value. Three changes will be discussed: first the change whereby patient preferences are taken into account in clinical decision making. The second change involves the patient's self-care. The third change involves the patient co-operating in the whole health care plan.

First, patients vary in their ability to acquire, process and understand relevant medical information as well as in their need for involvement in medical decision making (Taylor 2000). Some patients value involvement in decision making whilst others find it intolerable and want physicians to decide on what should happen. Research shows, however, that the will to be involved in decision making has an effect on the outcome of care and therefore should be taken into account when the care plan is drawn up. Two key elements in any decision are (1) what is likely to happen, and (2) the value of the outcome. The first element is mainly the focus of evidence-based clinical practice. Evidence-based medicine should help to clarify the various probable outcomes of each treatment alternative. This is clearly the professional side of the decision-making process. The second element is related to the value invested by the patient and/or his family in each of these adverse or positive outcomes. This is clearly the client side of the decision-making process. The clinicians should help the client to come to the most reasoned decision. This does not mean the same decision in all cases. For example, a woman with breast carcinoma can face two main choices for her treatment: a simple mastectomy or a lumpectomy with radiation. Some patients will give greatest value to the quality of life, whilst others will prefer survival or the quantity of life. Also, preferences regarding risk influence decision making (Morris *et al.* 1997). Valuing the different outcomes and their probabilities helps to obtain balanced decision making.

Nursing care should assist the anyone, whether sick or well, in performing activities contributing to health, its recovery, or to peaceful death, that would be performed unaided if the individual had the necessary strength, will or knowledge (Henderson and Nite 1960). From this definition it is clear that a nurse assists a patient in the activities of daily living only when he or she is unable to perform them independently. It is important that patients, when able, undertake these activities themselves. In consequence, in-depth assessments of self-care abilities are crucial (Evers 1998). If a patient is unable to care for him/herself in some way, a nurse must search for the cause. Insufficient knowledge, skills and motivation are usually the core reasons for self-neglect. A nurse must then assess whether the individual's state will allow self-care, either at present or at some time in the future. This assessment provides the necessary information regarding appropriate nursing intervention. It is of utmost importance that patients or their family members are taught how to handle these problems effectively. Only when patients or family members are not able to provide this care, will professional care be appropriate. In short, nurses should put every effort into improving the self-care abilities of the patient and the family rather than taking over the care in a ritualistic way.

Instead of patients being viewed as passive recipients of information or care, patients should be viewed as active participants in the caring process. This means that they must actively participate in constructing the options. This requires medical personnel to value patients' knowledge of their illness. In certain instances a patient can be even more informed about his illness than his or her GP or medical specialist. Also, practitioners should learn more from patients' experiences. Many self-help organizations help patients gain control over their lives. They do this by means of psychological support and practical advice. The involvement of medical doctors or nurses in these organizations has traditionally been very low, and in most working relationships the direction of information has been one-way – from professional to 'layman'. It has become obvious that, due to their experience, networks and living knowledge, these 'laymen' are in fact real experts. The working relationship has increasingly become more of a dialogue, in which self-care organizations are supporting professional organizations in improving priorities and patient care.

The provision of care and organizational processes

This concept of care, with its foundations in evidence-based practice and patients' experiences, preferences and expectations, has to be translated into organizational practice. Because of the complexity of health care, most patients require their care to be explicitly managed. In general, two methods for care management exist: (1) clinical pathways, and (2) case management. In the latter option, a person has responsibility for leading the patient through the organization. Eighty per cent of patients can be managed through clinical pathways whilst twenty per cent need case management. The main principle in deciding on the above options is the predictability of care. Predictable care can be managed in clinical pathways. Less predictable care needs day-to-day or even minute-to-minute case management. In practice, both methods can be combined. They can vary in time. There is no clear-cut line dividing clinical pathways and case management. There is a wide variety of methods varying from generic standardized pathways to customized pathways.

Clinical pathways are defined as 'schedules of medical and nursing procedures, including diagnostic tests, medications, and consultations designed to effect an efficient, co-ordinated program of treatment' (National Library of Medicine 2002). Most importantly, they aim to be patient-centred and multidisciplinary. Developing and implementing clinical pathways is always difficult. The difficulties revolve around the co-ordination of the professional team, gaining agreement on aims and goals of a programme, defining the various roles, and setting up procedures.

The best analogy for understanding the setting up of a clinical pathway is that of an airline deciding to fly to a new destination. First they have to find out about the market. How many customers might be interested? How frequently has this flight to be offered? What are the expectations? Should the focus be on service (as in business class) or on cost control (as in economy class)? This is still the easiest aspect of the task. Transforming the plan into operations is the hardest part. It takes about 18 months from making the decision to fly to a new destination to reach the first take-off. Landing rights and slots have to be booked. The crew has to be recruited and trained. The new destination has to be scheduled. The ground crew, such as caterers, cleaners and baggage handlers, have to be organized. Prices have to be set and so on.

From a patient's point of view, clinical pathways are similar tools to control processes. If a hospital decides to carry out cardiac surgery, the number of yearly operations is estimated through strategic analysis. The team of cardiac surgeons, nurses and technicians has to be recruited and trained. The hospital has to plan operating, bed and policlinic capacity. All arrangements for rehabilitation, blood supplies, X-rays, patient information brochures and advertising have to be made. In addition, accreditation and financing has to be secured. Clinical pathways involve the full scenario of a programme: aims and goals; the key players and their various roles; structure and procedures; how evaluation should be conducted. It takes about nine months to one year to build such a programme. From the perspective of a service industry, this approach is the most logical. In health care, however, dominated by the dual organizational structure described above, this hardly occurs. Indeed, the reverse is often the case. The surgeon, based on his/her personal skill and reputation, may decide to start a new programme without being sure whether the organization is prepared. One of the most common critiques on the actual provision of health care, as formulated by the Institute of Medicine in the US or by the Bristol Royal Infirmary Inquiry in the UK (2001), is not in the personal commitment of the care givers, but in the lack of appropriate systems.

Organizational support systems

The fourth part in the model is the support systems. To organize requires an explicit level of awareness. Systems often function on an implicit level. This next section focuses on information systems, the information system being just one of the systems that supports health care management and delivery.

Information systems

Information systems can support clinical decision making, the design of clinical pathways, the delivery of care and the evaluation of outcomes. Each of these aspects will be discussed in the following sub-sections.

Information systems and clinical decision making

The first generation of systems aimed at supporting the clinician in making medical decisions appeared in the late 1950s. The degree to which clinicians are assisted varies from the provision of information to systematic decision support by means of decision trees, probabilities and expert systems. Recently, these systems have also been used to help patients make decisions. Their benefit lies in their ability to couple medical evidence with patient-specific data. In consequence, an evaluation of treatment options can be made. Most commonly, systems are used to provide guidelines, evidence reports, and access to systematic reviews and meta-analysis. Examples are: the Cochrane library; the National Institute of Clinical Effectiveness; the Agency for Health Quality and Research; the Institute for Clinical Improvement; the Scottish Intercollegiate Guidelines Network; and PubMed. It is most important that this information is easily accessed by the clinicians, for example, from their office desk, the policlinic or the hospital wards. An example is the Columbia Presbytarian Medical Centre (CPMC) medical entities dictionary used in the New York Presbyterian Hospital (Cimino 2000) to link data in the clinical record to medical literature. Formats such as Guideline Interchange Format (GLIF) or Arden Syntax have been developed to link up guidelines with clinical information systems.

Patients also have access to health information by means of webservices that guide a patient through the systems, for example, Medlineplus, NHS Direct, Cancerfacts.com, Healthfinder, and Healthwise. A recent study confirmed that more than 100 million Americans went on-line in search of health-related information (Berland 2001). In fact, more than 70 per cent of users say on-line health information has influenced a decision about their treatment. At the same time, it has become obvious that accessing health information using search engines and simple search terms is not efficient. Coverage of key information on English and Spanish-language websites is poor and inconsistent, although the accuracy of the information provided is generally good. High reading levels are required to comprehend web-based health information.

Also, health care outcomes for individual hospitals and/or physicians should be made available for the public and should help patients in deciding which doctor to see or which hospital to go to. One example is Quality Check, a service delivered by the Joint Commission for the Accreditation of Healthcare Organisations. Quality Check enables the general public to have access to the accreditation reports of specific health care organizations. Other examples include hospital performance reports published by the Pennsylvania Health Care Cost Containment Council. Volume, risk-adjusted mortality rates, risk-adjusted length-of-stay and average charges are available for each hospital for 73 treatment categories (http:// www.phc4.org/idb/hpr/).

Information systems in the design of patient care programmes
The quality of decision making should be complemented by the quality of care. A recent study by the American Hospital Association (2001) revealed that, for a typical surgical patient, physicians, nurses and other hospital staff spend on average 30 minutes on paperwork for every hour of direct patient care. Partly due to the vast array of federal, state and local health regulations, in the emergency department, every hour of patient care generates an hour of paperwork. Health care systems are renowned for delays and lengthy cycle times. For example, delays occur in getting appointments with specialists or

in starting therapy. These delays adversely affect clinical outcomes, patient satisfaction, and cost. People often assume that reducing delays and increasing access will increase cost. In fact the opposite is true: delays and restricted access are properties of poorly designed, costly systems. Re-engineering and redesigning the system using clinical pathways and workflow information systems can reduce delays and improve the quality of the process.

The success of a clinical pathway is determined by the ways in which change is achieved. The systematic approach through the Plan–Do–Check–Act (PDCA) cycle, is highly recommended (Vanhaecht *et al.* 2001). In a first phase (plan phase), the patient population is determined and the interdisciplinary team is compiled. A temporary task force is assigned. The task force will determine aims and goals of the programme. These aims and goals are translated into concrete measurable indicators, for further follow-up and evaluation. The clinical pathway is outlined in its first draft. A time–task matrix is used. The focus is on key interventions. Based on this first outline, the resources and infrastructure are determined. The procedures for running the programme are set.

In the second phase (do phase), all data are gathered to test and document actual care and the intentions set in the first phase. It is a time-consuming phase (one to two months) and consists of the following:

1. Patient record analyses: the actual care process is evaluated and visualized by analysing 15 to 20 patient records focusing on the length of stay, key interventions, major delays, major overlaps and gaps.

2. Pre-test: a few outcome indicators (such as patient satisfaction or clinical indicators) are prospectively assessed for 10 to 15 patients. The main goal is to evaluate the performance of the actual programme and to gather baseline data for evaluating the effect of the clinical pathway after implementation.

3. Literature review: to compare actual practice with the 'Best Practice' guidelines (by means of the Center for Disease Control or Cochrane, for example, which provide an overview of guidelines). The evaluation is multidisciplinary.

4. Patient surveys: the expectations of patients and their families are assessed by patient surveys (about ten patients). The Picker

Institute, which works in the UK, the USA and Europe, focuses on: respecting a patient's values, preferences and expressed needs; access to care; emotional support; information, communication and education; co-ordination of care; physical comfort; involvement of family and friends; continuity and transition. An alternative for patient surveys in ambulatory care settings is a 'walkthrough'; this means walking anonymously with the patient through the system.

5.   'Peer' review: a clinical pathway is usually designed by the inner circle of the interdisciplinary team. The outer circle, which might consist of radiologists, pharmacists or pathologists for example, are only indirectly involved. The clinical pathway can be improved by discussing the effectiveness of each test among clinicians and ancillary services departments. The discussion focuses on the appropriateness of the test, the alternatives, the practical organization and very often a review of each role in the process.

6.   Process mapping: for a few patients, the complete process is analysed, with exact time intervals, length and frequencies of the different contacts. Specific software is available to visualize these processes (http://www.ashhouse.co.uk/process.htm). Process mapping helps to simplify the process and visualize 'bottlenecks'.

7.   Documentary analysis: a complete inventory is made of all order and prescription forms, patient information, written protocols, procedures and so on. Very often, data is collected two, three or even more times during a hospital stay.

In the third phase (check of study phase) the task force studies all the information. The first version of the clinical pathway is revised and will end in a few additional tasks:

1.   The definitive version of the clinical pathway is written in a time–task matrix. It is important that not only interventions but also aims and goals (intermediate and final goals) are specified in the time–task matrix. Specific software is available to support this process: for example Pathlinks (www.achievehealthcare.com), Excelcare (www.excelcare.com), HBOC (www.hboc.com), Curapath (www.curapath.com), Q.works (www.qworks.com),

PathCare (www.ecyber.com/pathcare.htm), Clinical Pathway ConstructorTM (www.zynx.com).

2. The time–task matrix is only the start of a complete design process, which takes into account the capacity and resources for running the programme: policlinic, X-ray capacity, lab-capacity, inpatient capacity, time of nurses, physicians, physiotherapists and so on.

3. Service level agreements (SLAs) link the inner interdisciplinary team (those who are committed) to the outer interdisciplinary team (all those who are involved in the programme). An SLA describes how the department will contribute to the specific programme. All elements, such as activity, service level, quality, time, frequency, and resources, are taken into account.

Information systems in the delivery of care

The 1990s were characterized by a major shift from administrative hospital information systems to clinical information systems. A clinical information system is used by nurses, physicians and others for the purpose of delivering health care. Although these systems already focus on patients, they still have a departmental remit (medical system, nursing system, pharmacy system, lab systems, and intensive care system). The challenge today is to enable these systems to communicate with each other. It can be done by setting up client–server systems, middle-ware systems (software which connects two separate applications), and communication standards such as HL-7, a Standards Developing Organization specializing in providing standards for the management of data in healthcare. Web-based technology will facilitate the integration of hospital information systems. When this occurs it will be the patient and not the department that will play the central role.

Information systems and the evaluation of care

Continuous follow-up and evaluation of the outcomes is necessary. The most appropriate instrument is the 'Value Compass' (Hill and Zander 2001; Nelson 1996; Zander and Bower 2000). It is equivalent to 'Balanced Scorecards' (Kaplan and Norton 1996), but more suited for evaluating clinical practice. Four domains are assessed:

1. THE PROCESS

The quality of the care process is evaluated by tracking the level of deviation from the clinical pathway. These deviations or variances are classified according to cause (patient, professional or system), directions of the variance (positive or negative), and the actions taken to resolve the variance. Reports are made every three to six months, analysed, discussed with the team and then used as the basis for continuous quality improvement. An automated patient record helps to track the variances (Spath 1994).

2. THE CLINICAL OUTCOME

Indicators of clinical outcome can be general (such as mortality, complication rates, or readmission rates) or specific to each patient group (the whole range of quality of life measures for a series of patient groups would be used). Most important is the use of standardized valid and reliable scales.

3. THE FINANCIAL OUTCOME

Because a patient's length of stay in hospital is closely related to cost, it is probably one of the most frequently used indicators. A more sensitive measure is a patient's 'Bill Of Service' (BOS). This lists all interventions provided for a particular patient. For each of the interventions, a standard cost is added and so the total cost of a patient's care can be derived. This indicator can be used to measure the impact of cost-reducing efforts.

4. THE SERVICE OUTCOME

Service indicators measure the quality of the care as perceived by patients and their families. To arrive at a valid Value Compass, a few steps are needed:

(a)   The election of a standardized, valid and reliable set of indicators (De Paepe *et al.* 2000; Sermeus *et al.* 2000).

(b)   Benchmarks need to be established in order to compare the outcomes with those of other health care organizations. Networking facilitates the gathering of data necessary for meaningful comparisons to be made.

(c)   Timely, systematic and readable feedback reports should be provided to the clinical teams.

(d)   In order to be able to set up such an information system, a data warehouse (DW) has to be built. The DW is designed to input, store, and search a large amount of related data. These data are derived from multiple sources; therefore, the DW provides a single, consistent interface to data derived from various sources. It is a specialized and powerful tool that can support managerial decision making. It can also be used for making responses to service users and for the purpose of enabling users to make reports.

Conclusion

The Institute of Medicine (2001) recognizes the enormous potential of information technology in improving the quality and organization of health care. Automated order entry systems can reduce errors in drug prescribing and dosing. There is considerable evidence that computer-assisted diagnosis and automated reminder systems improve quality of decision making. Access to reliable websites and on-line support groups help patients to become more involved in their care. Telemedicine, e-visits and scheduling systems lead to improvements in time management. IT systems in general have the potential to transform the traditional health care system into a highly flexible, patient-centred, demand-led service. For this to happen, however, professionals and managers need to integrate this new technology into their day-to-day practice.

References

Abersnagel, E. and van Vliet, J. (1998) 'De invulling van kwalificatieniveau 5.' ('Implementing nursing qualification Level 5.') *Tijdschrift voor Ziekenverpleging 17,* 506–507.

American Hospital Association (2001) *Patients or Paperwork: The Regulatory Burden Facing America's Hospitals.* New York: Price Waterhouse Coopers.

Berland, G. (2001) '"With just one click": online health information is abundant, but can it be trusted?' *Western Journal of Medicine 175,* 6, 391.

Brennan, T., Troyen, A., Leape, L. and Laird, N. (1991) 'Incidence of adverse events and negligence in hospitalized patients. Results of the Harvard Medical Practice Study.' *New England Journal of Medicine 324,* 6, 370–376.

Bristol Royal Infirmary Inquiry (2001) *Learning from Bristol: The Report of the Public Inquiry into Children's Heart Surgery at the Bristol Royal Infirmary, 1984–1995.* Norwich: The Stationery Office.

Cimino, J. (2000) 'Harnessing world wide web technology and standardised terminology to improve decision making for patients.' In V. Saba, R. Carr, W. Sermeus and P. Rocha (eds) *One Step Beyond: The Evolution of Technology and Nursing, 7th International Congress Nursing Informatics 28/4–3/5/2000.* Auckland: Auckland Healthcare Services Ltd.

de Vries, P. and Beijers, R. P. (1999) *Management van het Patiëntenproces (Management of the Patient Process.)* Houten: Bohn Stafleu Van Loghum.

De Paepe, L., Quaethoven, P., Sermeus, W. and Vleugels, A. (2000) 'Klinische indicatoren voor het meten van klinische performantie toepassing: het quality indicator project.' ('Clinical indicators for measuring clinical performance: the quality indicator project.') *Acta Hospitalia 40,* 1, 55–67.

Evers, G. (1998) *Meten van Zelfzorg, verpleegkundige instrumenten voor onderzoek en klinische praktijk.* (Measuring patient selfcare: nursing instruments for research and clinical practice.) Leuven: Universitaire Pers.

Fetter, R. and Freeman, J. (1986) 'Diagnosis related groups: product line management within hospitals.' *Academic Management Review 11,* 1, 41–54.

Halm, E., Lee, C. and Chassin, M. (2000) 'How is volume related to the quality of health care: a systematic review of research literature.' In M. Hewitt (ed) *Interpreting the Volume–Outcome Relationship in the Context of Health Care Quality.* Washington DC: Institute of Medicine. (http://books.nap.edu/catalog/10005 .html)

Henderson, V. and Nite, G. (1960) *Principles and Practice of Nursing.* New York: MacMillan (fifth edition).

Herzlinger, R. (1999) *Market-Driven Healthcare: Who Wins, Who Loses in the Transformation of America's Largest Service Industry.* Cambridge: Perseus Books Group.

Heskett, J., Sasser, W. and Schesinger, L. (1997) *The Service Profit Chain: How Leading Companies Link Profit and Growth to Loyalty, Satisfaction and Value.* New York: Free Press.

Heyssel, R., Gaintner, J., Kues, I., Jones, A. and Lipstein, S. (1984) 'Decentralised management in a teaching hospital.' *New England Journal of Medicine 310,* 22, 1477–1480.

Hill, M. and Zander, K. (2001) 'DataMap: a dashboard to guide the executive team.' *New Definition 16,* 1.

Institute of Medicine (2001) *Crossing the Quality Chasm: A New Health System for the 21st Century.* Washington DC: National Academy Press.

Kaplan, R. and Norton, D. (1996) *The Balanced Scorecard: Translating Strategy into Action.* Boston: Harvard Business School Press.

Kohn, L., Corrigan, J. and Donaldson, M. (1999) *To Err is Human: Building a Safer Health System.* Washington DC: National Academy Press.

Lathrop, J. (1993) *Restructuring Health Care: The Patient Focused Paradigm. The Healthcare Forum.* San Francisco: Jossey-Bass.

Lesar, T., Briceland, L. and Stein, D. (1997) 'Factors related to errors in medication prescribing.' *Journal of the American Medical Association 277,* 4, 312–317.

Mintzberg, H. (1997) 'Toward healthier hospitals.' *Health Care Management Review 22,* 4, 9–18.

Morris, A. D., Morris, R., Wilson, J., White, J., Steinberg, S., Okunieff, P., Arriagada, R., Le, M., Blichert-Toft, M. and Van Dongen, J. (1997) 'Breast-conserving therapy vs mastectomy in early-stage breast cancer: a meta-analysis of 10-year survival.' *Cancer Journal from Scientific American 3*, 1, 6–12.

National Library of Medicine (2001) *Medical Subject Headings (MeSH)* (http://www.hlm.kih.gov)

Nelson, E. C. (1996) 'Improving health care, Part I: the Clinical Value Compass.' *Journal of Community and Quality Improvement 22*, 4, 155–166.

Prahalad, C. K. and Ramaswamy, V. (2000) 'Co-opting customer competence.' *Harvard Business Review*, January–February, 79–87.

Sermeus, W., Kearney, N., Kinnunen, J., Goossens, L. and Miller, M. (eds) (2000) *Wisecare, Workflow Information Systems for European Nursing Care.* Amsterdam: IOS-Press.

Spath, P. (ed) (1994) *Clinical Paths, Tools for Outcomes Management.* Chicago: American Hospital Publication.

Taylor, T. (2000) 'Understanding the choices that patients make.' In J. Geyman, R. A. Day and S. D. Ramsay (eds) *Evidence-based Clinical Practice: Concepts and Approaches.* London: Butterworth Heinemann.

Vanhaecht, K., Sermeus, W., Vleugels, A. and Peeters, G. (2002) 'Ontwikkeling en gebruik van klinische paden in de gezondheidszorg.' ('Development and use of clinical pathways in health care.') *Tijdschrift voor Geneeskunde.*

Wulff, R. (1996) *Het ontwerpen van ziekenhuisorganisaties, een onderzoek naar de organisatiestructuur van het algemene ziekenhuis.* Eindhoven: Technische Universiteit.

Zander, K. and Bower, K. (2000) *Implementing Systems for Managing Care.* Boston: Center for Case Management.

CHAPTER 7

Health, Collaborative Learning and the Collapse of Professionalism?

The Information Brothel

Joe Cullen

Salman Rushdie once referred to the Internet as 'that brothel of information' (*Guardian* 1999). Rushdie's observation is a revealing signifier for the ambivalence and anxiety members of the establishment (be it political, social or literary) often exhibit towards new technologies. The history of technological revolution is a history of a dialectical struggle between the application of technology by ruling élites to maintain their hegemony, and the application of technology to emancipate those who are controlled.

Medicine has not been immune from this 'power struggle'. Over the last three centuries, health technology, or more precisely the technologization of health, has been a powerful force for social control. As Foucault put it:

> Medicine, as a general technique of health even more than as a service to the sick or an art of cures, assumes an increasingly important place in the administrative system and the machinery of power. (Foucault 1984, p.283)

Foucault equates the sudden importance assumed by medicine in the eighteenth century with the state's increasing control over economic regulation, public order and rules of hygiene, and with the emergence of a general 'police of health' (p.278). This made it possible for the state to exercise control over demographic processes, by annexing the family from communal life, and to harness 'population' to the political economy of the state. At the same time, the state professionalized medical practice, and in turn medical practice formalized and classified the body, its functions and its social life world. Medical terminology and lexicon reinforced the separation of medicine from the everyday life of humans. The clinician began to assume a major function in the subjectification of individuals through medical practice, by mediating between the processes of domination and the processes through which individuals relinquish their autonomy and control over the body (Cullen 1998).

In the post-millennium information society, however, increasing credibility is being given to the argument that the present generation of medical technologies – 'health informatics' – is beginning to erode the power base of the 'police of health' by making it more and more possible for laymen to regain control of their bodies and of the process of 'subjectification'. In this sense, the self-management of health by individuals comes much closer to Foucault's interpretation of the Greek concept of *epimeleia heautou* – taking care of oneself (Foucault 1984).

This argument also reflects ideas drawn from concepts such as 'dialogic reflexivity'. With the advent of the information society, the tensions generated by the interplay between the state and the market are compounded, according to a number of writers, by complexities associated with what Habermas (1992), along similar lines to those espoused by Foucault, refers to as the 'rationalisation of the communicative practice of everyday life' (p.138). As a consequence of increasing professionalization, the distance between 'expert cultures' and the broader public is growing fast, precipitating a corresponding cultural impoverishment of social relations, and the cutting off of cultural tradition in the face of the expanding formalization of 'organised domains of action'. The role played by new communication technologies in this rationalization process is complex. Instantaneous global communication, as Giddens (1994) puts it, tends to marginalize cultural diversity, and so reinforces the tendency for globalization to limit the capacity of local communities to develop and implement their own forms of social action. As a result, personal identity becomes highly reflexive, and everyday 'experiments with the self' become an intrinsic part of daily activities, utilizing information coming from a variety of sources.

Giddens therefore argues that the proliferation of social movements and self-help groups in recent years is directly related to the growth of the information society and reflects both this heightened self-reflexivity and the effects of instantaneous global communication. Such movements have played a major role in retrieving power from experts and in the lay retrieval of expertise, almost as an antidote to the dividing practices portrayed by Foucault.

Supporters of this prevailing view point to the raft of policy initiatives aimed at empowering citizens and patients in decisions about health and health care that have been implemented in recent years in the UK (and more widely within the EU) as evidence of the increasing involvement of ordinary people in the social construction of health. These policies have been aimed primarily at 'putting information to work' in order to improve the effectiveness and efficiency of the NHS and ultimately the health of the nation. The 1998 policy document *Information for Health* (Department of Health 1998), for example, proposes a number of initiatives – lifelong Electronic Patient Records (EPR) for every citizen; instant access to patient data and evidence-based practice; and on-line public access to health information, through NHS On-line and Digital Interactive Television – each intended to promote the 'information society for all' with regard to health care. This can be set against the broader policy background of 'joined up government' – for example the integration of patient-centred health within an overarching framework of e-government, and its place within the Government's vision of communications integration (in, for example, the Department of Trade and Industry 2000 White Paper). As the centrepiece of modern, joined-up government, the e-Government Interoperability Framework (GIF) envisages that all key government services should be available electronically by the year 2005, and available over a wide variety of channels.

Against this background, this chapter attempts to shed some light on two fundamental questions associated with health informatics. First, do the new technologies of health really empower individuals in the process of 'taking care of oneself'? Second, are they contributing towards a convergence of knowledge and power in terms of the relationship between clinicians, other health professionals and non-professionals?

To make a contribution, at least in part, towards answering these questions, the following discussion draws on a range of research and research and technology development (RTD) work in which the author has been involved in recent years in the field of health informatics.[1] The first part of the discussion below focuses in more detail on the policy background. This analysis is followed by a brief summary of the types of health informatics systems currently being developed and used in the UK and further afield. A number of typical examples of these applications are then analysed as forms of social and organizational practices. These are presented below in the form of vignettes or mini-ethnographies showing how these new technologies are applied in their social and organizational settings. Finally, the concluding section attempts to draw some conclusions with regard to these two key questions on the basis of the vignettes.

The discussion therefore applies a hermeneutic approach to assessing health informatics (Habermas 1984; Strydom 1987). It considers health informatics as historically unique socio-technical and 'techno-economic paradigms' (Dosi 1988). Health informatics innovations (applications) as socio-technical artefacts can be considered as spaces which contain internalized representations of the external environment, reflecting a particular cultural logic. This cultural logic is a complex configuration of symbolic and concrete features that are derived from the particular socio-cultural and historical context in which health care is evolving. The cultural logic will reflect a particular vision of society, and what society should be like. For example, a European RTD programme such as AIM (Telematics Systems for Health Care Programme – a medical informatics RTD programme supported by the EC in the early 1990s) reflects (at least in principle) notions of using health technologies to combat social exclusion. This vision may be very different from that embraced by the International Telecommunication Union, which in turn may vary dramatically from conceptions of user needs identified by groups of clinicians. Typically, the cultural logic of the innovation – its internalized representation of the external environment – takes the form of four main aspects of innovation: technological, economic, institutional and organizational arrangements. These might involve, for example, the implementation of new forms of cost reimbursement for health care delivery, involving new partnership arrangements between health providers and purchasers, and utilizing hospital information systems to re-engineer the nature of work inside the hospital. The vignettes below represent typical exemplars of these cultural logics.

The policy background to health informatics

The policy dynamic of health informatics is being driven by escalating pressures on welfare budgets as well as changing patterns of diseases. These pressures are mainly caused by: demographic changes resulting in an increasingly ageing population; an intensification of competition in international markets; changes in labour and employment markets; and political restructuring of health care systems. Another factor is the increasing prevalence of 'expensive to treat' (and to some extent preventable) conditions such as certain forms of coronary illnesses and cancers, and HIV/AIDS.

In response to these pressures, health care providers are seeking to do three main things: cut the costs of provision; improve productivity and efficiency; and increase the quality of health care services. One way of doing this is to provide more and better information for citizens and patients, first to promote more effective health behaviours and disease prevention, and second to enable people to take more informed responsibility and control of their health care decisions.

Cost-effectiveness gains are seen as being mainly determined by reduced labour costs arising from efficiencies in the exchange of information and the diffusion of tasks from more highly paid personnel to less highly paid personnel such as nurses and paramedics; reducing length of stays in hospitals through more efficient medical and administrative practices; improving the effectiveness of primary, community-based and self-managed health care; and in preventative health measures.

For example, evaluations of on-line HIV information and support systems suggest that the regular use of such services can reduce the average cost of treatment by around one third (Gustafson 1993). Primarily, this is because patients become better informed about their condition, are less likely to panic when new symptoms occur, make less frequent trips to health professionals and acute care points, and manage their condition generally more efficiently.

In turn, savings on the opportunity costs of chronic illnesses (those costs that are incurred as a result of missed opportunities that could have been taken if a situation had not occurred), realized as a result of better health information provision, can be substantial. For example, in a UNESCO study on the impact of AIDS on the industrial economy of Abidjan, it was estimated that loss of production through AIDS contributed to 25 per cent of all industrial costs and that AIDS contributed to 31 per cent of sick leave and 23 per cent of all medical costs.

Efficiency gains are seen as being derived mainly from improvements in the management of information flows; reduced duplication and the elimination of repetitive keying-in of data; facilitating easier and faster collaboration between different professionals; and 'just in time' diagnosis leading to lower waiting times for patients and easing workload pressures on clinicians.

Quality of care gains are shaped by improvement in the skills, competencies and knowledge of professionals delivered through distance learning; improving evidence-based clinician practices; wider availability of remote expert support for clinical decision making; more accurate diagnosis, care management and care administration; and reducing the effect of unequal access to health resources.

Harnessing health technologies to the pursuit of improvements in cost-effectiveness, efficiency and quality of care implies fundamental changes in social relations between providers and consumers of health information and services. It implies the participation of patients and citizens not just in information sharing, but also more profoundly in actively collaborating with health professionals in the production of knowledge about health – for example by converting their tacit knowledge gained from experience to the explicit knowledge of evidence-based practice.

This reflects a broader objective: the decentralization of health care from acute to primary and self-managed service delivery. It assumes a shift from a medical care and crisis-response emphasis to an emphasis on health care and disease prevention. As a result, it is thought, there will be an increasing involvement of the primary sector in both disease prevention and in a range of practices currently carried out by secondary care providers, such as hospitals. Policies therefore aim to promote a reduction in resources for episodic care and an increase in resources for acute, long-term care. This means less inpatient hospital stays and more outpatient and self-managed care; a movement away from individualized to community-based provision, a breaking down of institutional and organizational structures based on the traditional authority of clinicians and a move towards more collaborative patient-managed partnerships. It is also meant to promote better and more evenly distributed access to health resources and life chances. However, some commentators argue that the health care system is becoming much more supply-led, and that it is more likely that there will be differentiation and unevenness in access to services (Gott 1995).

A typology of health informatics systems

As discussed above, health informatics embodies particular 'visions' for health care. These visions are made concrete in the form of systems applications – specific socio-technical configurations or scenarios of delivery platforms, tools and services. These scenarios can be broadly divided into two main groups: communications infrastructure, and products and services (Cullen 1998). These will be addressed in turn below.

Communications infrastructure scenarios reflect assumptions about the development of 'information highways' and their impact on the spatial and organizational clustering of health care services. Three such generic scenarios are commonly cited by experts:

- Intrahospital communication based on local area networks (LANs) and intranets. These are primarily associated with the widespread use of hospital information systems (HISs) and electronic patient records (EPRs) to manage both the clinical and organizational administration of health care sites.

- Networking between health care actors in a regional context, based on LANs, wide area networks (WANs) and metropolitan area networks (MANs) – and also involving client–server applications using the Internet. This scenario envisages the regionalization of health care telematics to provide a range of services based on common services running on integration platforms, in order to promote co-operative working between primary and secondary care providers, community health monitoring and information services and home telecare.

- Supra-regional communication based on WANs, including Euro-ISDN.[2] This scenario is being driven by the need for more effective dissemination of new diagnostic and therapeutic approaches, and envisages networking between 'centres of excellence' such as medical schools, rather than between 'on the ground' clinicians.

Products and services scenarios reflect clusterings of socio-technical systems centred around a common 'innovation image'. They comprise configurations of particular technological platforms, institutional arrangements and interactions and collaboration between user groups: suppliers and purchasers of health care; providers of telematics services; local, regional and national authorities; and clinicians and health care managers. From the review of the literature and from consultations with experts, six broad clusters of scenarios can be identified:

- Information storage and retrieval systems, such as electronic patient records (or, increasingly, lifelong health records) to facilitate the integration of patient data held by different service providers; 'smart cards' to hold individual patient data on medical history; and insurance and social security data.

- Resource management systems: these facilitate the co-ordination and management of information flows and actions in the management of health care sites. Such systems are typically referred to generically as hospital management systems (HISs).

- Decision support and collaborative working systems for health care professionals: applications areas include knowledge-based systems to assist in the application of medical procedures and protocols; multimedia telematics networks for diagnosis and treatment of medical conditions such as epilepsy; and systems to promote the dissemination of research findings and new techniques in fields such as oncology.

- Regional networks and service integration systems: these typically focus on the development of common telematic systems and services, utilizing open systems architecture in order to promote both technical and organizational integration. A common feature of such scenarios is the adoption of EDI (electronic data interchange) messaging and multimedia services.

- Telecare scenarios embody notions of delivering health care through real-time remote diagnostics; surgical, medical and therapeutic consultancy and emergency telemedicine. They address particularly the problems of delivering health care to remote and transient client groups.

- Telehealth scenarios follow the logic of an expanding and accessible knowledge base for citizens as a result of universal access to information highways. They include automated community health monitoring and evaluation, and health promotion and disease prevention using public access multimedia systems.

The current state of the art in Europe and North America of these health informatics applications and services shows a picture of unevenness of development and diffusion, dictated primarily by cost and availability.

Similarly, community-wide and national networks using digital interactive television (DiTV) are also still at the pilot stage. In relation to delivery mechanisms (network systems interfacing to communications infrastructure, software systems etc.) the main concentration of effort has been in the development and diffusion of PACS (picture archiving and communication systems), electronic patient records and hospital information systems.

Essentially, the diffusion path of health informatics reflects the emerging maturity and dominance of 'top-down' systems that are primarily intended to convert paper-based patient records and administrative information systems into digital format. In other words, they appear to be reinforcing what Foucault would term the 'codification and classification of subjects' (1984, p.280) rather than creating a space for the involvement of patients and citizens in 'practices of the self' (p.362). We explore this theme below with reference to some case study examples.

Telediagnosis and collaborative working

The names in this example have been changed to preserve anonymity.

> Mr H is an avuncular consultant who rules the roost in the accident and emergency department of a large metropolitan teaching hospital. Mr H discovered telemedicine by accident, at a conference in Houston, Texas, and was immediately hooked. Back home, Mr H annexes part of his departmental budget and invests in a high performance teleconferencing system to connect the main hospital campus with a remote minor injuries unit about five kilometres away. I am at the business end of the system – Mr H's expansive office – in which a high resolution video screen gives a bird's eye view of one of the consulting rooms in the minor injuries unit. Or it would if the view were not obscured by a 'modesty screen' behind which a patient is being attended by two nurse practitioners. Faint and unintelligible sounds emanate from the speakers perched on Mr H's desk. He fiddles impatiently with the volume control, taps the intercom and calls into the microphone. There is no answer. Only the scrape of metal and the soothing murmer of the nurses' voices through the hiss of static. We decide to go down to the remote unit to see for ourselves.
>
> There, we are cheerily greeted by the two nurse practitioners, Penny and Angela, who are in the process of performing a routine exploration for a possible nasal polyp. The patient, a middle-aged Asian woman, seems relaxed. I ask Mr H whether his clients find the telemedicine process a little intrusive. 'Not at all,' he replies. 'They find it all very

interesting, don't you my dear?' he says, patting the patient absently on the thigh in his avuncular fashion. He explains later that the patients have really taken to the idea. They are very reassured by the notion that he is watching over them, even if it is from five kilometres away. They now have much less time to wait to be seen – and they get access to top medical know-how. The medical and nursing protocols contained in an on-line database within the unit, and supported by an expert system, are there to ensure that the nurse practitioners know exactly what to do in a difficult or confusing situation. Indeed, he says, patients, particularly those from the Asian community which constitutes the bulk of the unit's clients, are so familiar with using computers at home that they do not consider such equipment in the least unusual.

Later, when Mr H has returned to the main campus, I get to talk with the nurse practitioners. They confess that the modesty screen and the sound problems were not untypical events. It turns out that such things sometimes serve as convenient strategies to prevent Mr H's roving eye from becoming too roving. When the technology was first installed, the consultant's presence, even in virtual form, and the protocols database were essential support mechanisms. As they began to gain more experience, and get more competent, however, they found this virtual presence sometimes got in the way when they were working under pressure. Strategically placed visual impediments are a way of ensuring that the job gets done without unnecessary distractions, and of ensuring that they maintain their learning curve. Sometimes the sound system gets accidentally switched off, so they are unable to respond to the consultant's calls.

So Penny and Angela are able to work remotely, with or without the accident and emergency consultant, and have taken on a range of roles including dispensing drugs, using the protocols database. The nurse practitioners effectively work in their own self-contained nurse-led accident and emergency unit, subconsciously creating two cadres of staff, and a sub-culture that is different from the mainstream nursing culture in the main acute hospital. In addition, the nurses have been promoted to a higher grade pay scale. This has created some resentment from within the 'mainstream' nursing staff. Additional friction derives from the attitudes of some consultants and senior doctors, who feel threatened by the encroachment on their 'territory'. However, as the virtual unit has become more successful, other staff are beginning to see the value of having nurse practitioners perform these roles. Pressure on junior doctors as a result of the build-up of cases in the main emergency room has been reduced by the innovation. Nurses in the acute hospital are beginning to take an interest in acquiring the skills and experience gained from working in the virtual outpost. Undoubtedly, in this case, health informatics is leading to significant changes and re-engineering of professional roles and practices – sometimes in unexpected and unintended ways. But is it collaborative working? As I was leaving, Penny and Angela were putting the finishing touches to a paper they were presenting at a major conference on telemedicine, somewhere in the Far East. They had not told Mr H anything about it.

This example of a virtual minor injuries unit reflects a general steady expansion in health service delivery of nursing, paramedical occupations and other care roles to encompass tasks, such as minor surgical procedures, that were formerly strictly confined to clinicians. Health informatics is clearly accelerating this devolution of professional power, which is accompanied by the re-engineering of organizational procedures, such as regrading and accreditation of nurse practitioner skills.

However, the changes to existing work practices, the new jobs and procedures precipitated by telematics have caused problems. These problems are primarily related to fears about de-skilling and de-professionalization. In the case of consultants and specialists, we found evidence in this and other case studies to support the notion of resistance to the perceived erosion of professional autonomy, and a strong attachment towards holding on to and resisting the sharing of acquired expertise and 'trade secrets':

> Some of the specialists who have been asked to take part in the medical imaging network are scared that it will take their jobs away. But they are wrong because telemedicine is progress, that much is evident. It is not there to annoy them or to take away their patients. They have not understood that the system will lighten their workload, the patients will not have to travel long distances and that is the most important factor. They will have more time to operate, more time to take charge of the patient, to think about the patient pathology and to finally give their opinion. This is a big human problem.

> (Consultant involved in development of teleconsultation system for neurology quoted in Cullen *et al.* 1998, p.43)

In general, we found that the introduction of new technologies invariably creates turbulence within the work culture and within the organization, primarily because the new organizational structures associated with the innovation need to be assimilated within the existing status quo. There are a number of ways in which this assimilation takes place. In the research and R&D examples covered in this discussion, it is possible to identify three key models of organizational re-engineering associated with the introduction of health informatics into the environment of the hospital and the group practice.

In the first model, there is a relaxation of demarcation lines which promotes collaboration between different practitioner disciplines. The second model suggests that health informatics generate initial resistance and hostility which turns to positive organizational change as the organizational structure and the innovation mutually adapt. The third model concludes that the innovation operates as a self-contained organizational sub-system within the wider organizational context.

As an example of the first model, TEAM (Tele-Education and Medicine) is a Welsh project running low-cost PC video telephony to provide dermatology services for rural practices and further education services for doctors and nurses in their own surgeries, within the Powys region. In this case, the introduction of teleconsultation and teleteaching in dermatology provided the catalyst for much closer collaboration between a range of health disciplines, including specialists, GPs, health visitors and nurses.

In contrast, teleconsultation can also promote professional resistance that can be exacerbated as a result of regrading procedures implemented in order to recognize the new skills required by practitioners using the new technologies, as the minor injuries unit example illustrates. Conversely, however, such resistance can itself act as a catalyst for change as the value of the innovation becomes more transparent through its continuing use.

In the third model of organizational impact, the innovation occupies its own organizational sub-space within the wider organizational environment. Although the innovation is in practice 'bolted on' to its host setting, in the sense that it provides services for the operational running of the organization, it may operate under its own 'operational and transformation rules'. A good example is the DIOGENE (Digital Imaging Unit, University Hospital of Geneva) hospital information system. Commencing in 1978, at the Geneva Canton University Hospital, the original objective of DIOGENE was to install health informatics systems in about one hundred ward units. In 1985, a decision was made to 'migrate' the system from mainframes to PCs. This migration process, originally scheduled to last three years, was completed in 1995 after seven years of work at a cost of five million dollars. Such is the complexity and scale of the system that it appears to have engendered a 'system dependency' within the hospital. When the technology fails, there is a high level of disruption to hospital functions. At the same time, DIOGENE seems de-coupled, in organizational terms, from the hospital culture. It has been developed and maintained by a pool of operators and technicians, and there are signs that, as the pool gets smaller and the technicians get older, there will be a shrinking knowledge base that could create problems for the future evolution of the system.

In the case of the minor injuries unit, it is possible to have all three models co-existing equally.

Open SESAME – 'smartcards', pharmacists and the Napoleonic code

In France, the government has driven forward its plan to modernize health data collection, prescription pricing and reimbursement procedures through the use of 'smartcards'. SESAME/VITALE is a system of secured electronic transactions between a range of health professionals and insurance companies. It utilizes a 'smartcard system' comprising micro-chip CPS card (Carte Professional Sante), card reader, terminals and barcode reader to enable pharmacists to read electronic drug codes for prescriptions. Participating health care professionals have to sign a contract with their local State Health Insurance Office to acquire authorized equipment and the invoicing/reimbursement applications programme, which is sold to the healthcare provider via outlets approved by the State Health Insurance Office. Thus, capital investment to enable smart card technology to be implemented at a national level (and in the longer term across Europe) is being underpinned by new forms of arrangements between state authorities and health care providers. In turn, reimbursement procedures for service provision are actioned by electronic transactions involving collaboration between providers, state social security and private health insurers. This is a natural progression from the centralized health system begun by the Napoleonic code.

One aspect of the innovation is the adoption of new working arrangements (including reimbursement) between service providers such as GPs and pharmacists, and government agencies. GPs are encouraged by government agencies to purchase the hardware in order to maintain their 'market position' with patients, and at the same time have to take on some of the responsibilities formerly carried out by health agencies. The reality, however, is that 'encouragement' seems dominated by the stick rather than the carrot. In the words of one pharmacist:

> Eighty per cent of the pharmacists paid for their information system. There will a fine for the health professionals if they refuse to be computerized. Not everyone wants to be computerized especially if they have to pay for the system. There is definitely an absence of choice and of freedom. (Cullen *et al.* 1998, p.51)

As indicated by the example of SESAME/VITALE work re-engineering involving modifications to existing roles usually means the taking on of additional responsibilities by health practitioners for technical and administrative functions associated with the introduction of new technologies. In general, only as a secondary effect does it promote increased collaboration between different health professionals.

As SESAME/VITALE shows, in many cases, this assumption of new technical roles and (particularly for GPs) administrative roles in applying health informatics systems such as electronic patient records has developed without any new resources being made available for the additional tasks. For example, the MEDLINK initiative, involving the introduction of teleradiology services in Finland, meant a higher workload for radiologists as they got more and more involved in the technical support and administration of the systems, and for specialists and nurses who had to process the data generated. These increased responsibilities were carried out without additional resources being made available, except for the provision of training. When work re-engineering develops in this way without accompanying compensatory structural changes, for example in terms of remuneration, then the organizational impact of health care telematics may well be perceived as negative, as the SESAME/VITALE case shows.

SESAME/VITALE also reflects significant changes in health care service delivery funding that are associated with the introduction of health informatics. As another pharmacist observed: 'The pharmacist has taken some of the work of the social security and they have not been paid for this extra workload. Nor is there any talk that they will be.' (Cullen *et al.* 1998, p.42)

The pharmacist's view is echoed by general practitioners:

> There has been no talk about ways to pay the participating health professionals for their extra workload created by the computerization of the GP practice and the new work practice created by the application. On the contrary the health professionals have got to pay for their own computerization. Although I have been computerized since 1989, I have refused to join the SESAME/VITALE scheme because the organizers were lacking in consideration for the medical profession and because of the increased workload. (Cullen *et al.* 1998, p.42)

Essentially, with this smartcard system, health care providers are being rewarded through cost-benefit outcomes rather than through revenue accrued directly from consumers of health care services as a result of direct payment. These cost-benefits are derived in two main ways. First, they are derived as an outcome of retaining and expanding consumer 'market share'. Most health care providers using health informatics applications currently benefit from the added value electronic patient records, teleconsultation services and other applications give to their patient services, by providing them with shorter waiting times, better access to consultants, and more choice. Second, cost-benefits are derived from increasing the efficiency of reimbursement for services provided. Electronic patient records, smartcards and hospital information systems dramatically improve the turnaround of billing and reimbursement processes.

The costs and benefits of health informatics will be defined in different ways according to the particular value chain associated with a particular applications environment, and its associated user groups (Kirby 2000; Somer 1994). Large-scale applications of health informatics, typically implemented on a national scale, such as SESAME/VITALE, inevitably mean high levels of investment and development costs in infrastructure, equipment, software and administration and support that are intended to be offset by expected cost-benefits for national health care provision realized as a result of increased efficiencies in administration, and so on. In contrast, generic and customized applications exhibit the most variable cost structures. Large-scale tailoring of generic systems to help manage the running of a large hospital can mean substantial development and running costs, for example 5.2 million euro to install a major single-site hospital information system and an annual operating budget of 7.5 million euro. At the other end of the scale, 'do it yourself' applications that have been adapted from off-the-shelf equipment can cost as little as 70,000 euro to set up and entail minimal running costs, usually involving only the rental of an ISDN line.

An important point about SESAME/VITALE and other similar large-scale health informatics systems is that not only are they generating organizational change within health services, but also they are in tandem creating new institutional partnerships (typically private/public sector partnerships – PPPs) that in turn work on new financial models based on 'telematics value chains'. For example, there has been considerable interest from pharmaceutical companies recently in the use of both Internet and interactive digital television as a mechanism for expanding the huge potential market in 'over the counter' pharmaceutical products. In a recent US House Commerce Committee Report (*USA Today* 2000), US government investigators concluded that pricing practices and 'price fixing' cost health providers and patients over $1 billion a year. US citizens are increasingly using 'offshore Internet pharmacies' to access drugs that are either significantly cheaper or unobtainable on prescription. Both government agencies and pharmaceutical companies themselves therefore have a vested interest in controlling access to non-prescription drugs available through new technology delivery platforms. The pricing mechanism for this involves complex value chain modelling. For example, advertising banners for on-line travel agency websites can link users both to public agency health promotion sites giving information for example on the inoculations necessary when travelling abroad, and to commercial companies providing over-the-counter products such as sun lotions and travel sickness remedies. Digital television (DiTV) is a convergence technology that is tailor made for this type of value chain financing, because it allows for the integration of different forms of content. This can be pictured as in Figure 7.1.

The DiTV user will be provided with content by their content provider. This content may be drawn from TV production companies, the Internet or other media assets. This implies a range of possibilities for financing service provision through different permutations of the 'content value chain'. But does this lead to more consumer choice, and more empowerment for patients and citizens? Only if there is provision for real collaboration between the different stakeholders involved. In the next section, we look at an example of a health informatics system that attempted to create such a collaborative environment.

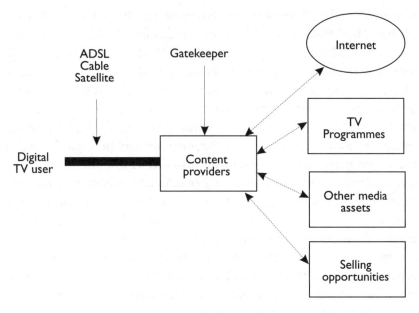

Figure 7.1. Content convergence and the Internet value chain

SEAHORSE – empowerment for people affected by HIV/AIDS

SEAHORSE stands for support, empowerment and awareness for HIV/AIDS: the on-line research and self-help exchange. It aimed to develop a 'European Clearing °House' of information and knowledge about HIV/AIDS in the form of an 'evolving knowledge base' – known as an information repository management system (IRM) – that is accessible via the Internet. SEAHORSE can best be described as a collaborative knowledge production and content management system for health care.

The IRM works by using 'metadata'. Users are provided with a comprehensive database of both existing Internet resources and specially developed 'primary' material (i.e. created from scratch especially for this system). A browser provides navigation around the knowledge base. Registered users can contribute directly to the site by reviewing and commenting on existing websites and articles, suggesting new websites and adding articles of their own. This means that the growing body of material is constantly being evaluated by users working with 'electronic seals of approval' (SOAPs).

In addition, two supporting applications were developed: the Interactive User Monitoring Tool (IUMT) and the Clinician Information Exchange (now called the Health Professional Information Exchange). The IUMT is a web-based tool that captures quantitative and ethnographic data about the users at the SEAHORSE pilot sites. The IUMT allows people with HIV/AIDS to enter their personal, clinical, lifestyle and treatment data, in order to obtain some feedback from the tool, and to support lifestyle change and health decision-making behaviours. The IUMT in SEAHORSE was also linked to the Health Professional Information Exchange, which allows the sharing of information with other support providers through discussion groups, and gives access to on-line databases. Data from the IUMT were made available to doctors, carers and other stakeholders in order to promote collaborative health management for people living with the virus. A key objective of the project was to explore the potential for aggregated data obtained from the interactive functionalities of SEAHORSE to be used in two ways: to enable the pharmaceutical companies providing antiretroviral drugs for people with HIV/AIDS to benefit from a rich evidence base created by users' experiences; and to provide similar data for government agencies monitoring both the prevalence and distribution of HIV/AIDS and the costs of service provision and prevention.

These tools and applications were tested and demonstrated in seven pilot sites, each of which reflects different configurations of user and organizational scenarios, and different models of care. In the UK, for example, SEAHORSE supported the model of 'integrated care' adopted by London Lighthouse – a non-governmental organization (NGO) providing day care, home support and drop-in services for people living with HIV and AIDS by providing a 'virtual drop-in centre' for users. In Bucharest, the health support services concentrated on adding value to the work of NGOs and health professionals working with the families of the 10,000 children affected by the virus – by giving them access, for example, to the latest evidence-based results on antiretroviral therapies. These NGOs and health professionals therefore act as intermediaries who use the information contained in the SEAHORSE repository to develop their own delivery systems – typically using conventional means such as leaflets.

The aim of SEAHORSE was to facilitate real collaborative knowledge production between people living with HIV/AIDS – including people living with the virus, their carers; families and health professionals. SEAHORSE is predicated on developing a 'community of users', individual members of which hold what might be thought of as 'dual nationality'. On the one hand, the users are consumers of information. On the other, they are providers of knowledge – for example they allow peers to share experiences of using particular combinations of drugs. Because the information corpus in SEAHORSE is an evolving knowledge base that is developed by users themselves, in collaboration with both their peers and other stakeholders, the project is aimed at fostering 'community empowerment' in the design, implementation, monitoring and evaluation of health interventions. This dialogic approach to health promotion is in line with current thinking around the wider benefits of health – for example in terms of the relationship between health, social capital and community capacity building, and economic and environmental amenity.

More than this, the collaborative knowledge production and content management concept underlying the SEAHORSE technology is 'collaborative learning'. Collaborative learning is about 'sensemaking' (Weick 1995). It is about learning as a 'participative mode of action-reflection' (Lave and Wenger 1991). It provides the context in which individuals can become 'insiders' and acquire the language, syntax and shared values that will tie them into a 'community' – whether it be an NGO, a 'community of practice' (such as health professionals) or a virtual community of disparate individuals.

This was the theory. In practice, SEAHORSE did not work very well. It functioned perfectly as a standard web-based information service for people wanting to access efficiently an extensive database of material on HIV/AIDS available in several languages. Where it did not perform so well was in terms of all the sophisticated collaborative knowledge production functions designed to facilitate user empowerment.

On the one hand, the project had a significant impact. The SEAHORSE tools and services were used by 500 registered users. In addition, the website attracted increasing numbers of 'casual' users – running at a level of around 60 per day. SEAHORSE established seven local versions of the central information repository in four EU countries: the UK, Greece, Spain and Italy, and also in Romania. These local sites provided culturally relevant support and information in users' own language.

But, as a means of empowering people with HIV/AIDS to make key decisions on self-managing their health, and as an evidence base for adding value to clinical and social practice in the HIV/AIDS field, SEAHORSE was not a success. In a limited way, the use of the interactive collaborative learning features – the content editing and evaluation tools – did lead to the formulation of new knowledge that might otherwise have emerged only after some considerable time had elapsed, if at all. As an example, it was as a result of collaboration between SEAHORSE users that a particular side-effect associated with the use of antiretroviral drugs (ingrowing toe-nails) was identified as a common experience. This had not previously been reported in the medical journals.

But the statistics on the usage of the SEAHORSE interactive tools show that collaborative knowledge production ran at a relatively low level. Many potential SEAHORSE users did not use SEAHORSE. Those who did were reluctant to explore its more interactive features – such as the annotation and content evaluation tools, and the interactive monitoring tool. Furthermore, many users were reluctant to empower themselves as part of their own self-managed health care. Users – especially those who are not computer literate, and those who have to deal with a chronic illness on a day-to-day basis – are not inclined to complete intensive, detailed and technical evaluation instruments. This underlines the need for new forms of evaluation methodologies and tools that can address this problem of user resistance. Ultimately, a paradigm shift for health telematics is required. Despite its integration of stable technologies, SEAHORSE was – for many users including health professionals, and also for investors – ahead of its time. SEAHORSE has to be seen as part of the vanguard of seamless information society technology (IST) services that ultimately need to be embedded within their social context.

Conclusions

It is often cited that in the US the biggest proportion of the searches made of Internet websites are for information on health issues. Indeed, there is already an embryonic and growing business in on-line health-related product advertising in that country, with a total value projected to reach $250 million per annum by the year 2002 (Schoenfeld, Harrison and Kosarajhu 1999). Whilst this suggests that there is an expanding consumer base for health informatics services, it does not necessarily reflect a universal trend towards citizen or patient empowerment. A recent survey carried out in the EU (in Spain, Portugal, Germany and the UK), for example, showed marked divergence in health information and support seeking behaviours (MELIC Consortium 2000). The survey showed that, even for regular Internet users, whilst 29 per cent used the web to obtain information on health, 75 per cent went directly to their physician, and 44 per cent got advice from 'personal conversations', that is, discourse with friends, family and peers. There were also variations from country to country – with proportionately more respondents using the Internet for health information in Germany compared to Spain. In a parallel 'off-line' survey (i.e. carried out on a sample of the general public rather than regular Internet users) only 4 per cent of respondents used Internet or other 'high technology' sources to obtain health information.

As the SEAHORSE experience discussed above indicates, whilst individuals are increasingly comfortable using the Internet as information consumers, they are still resistant to playing the role of knowledge producers or knowledge collaborators. I think this reflects what Foucault refers to as the difference between the *practice* of the self and the *culture* of the self. In the latter case, Foucualt makes a reference to the 'Californian cult of the self', where:

> one is supposed to discover one's true self, to separate it from that which might obscure or alienate it, to decipher its truth thanks to psychological or psychoanalytic science, which is supposed to be able to tell you what your true self is. (Foucault 1984, p.362)

In contrast, the practice of the self developed, according to Foucault, over a long period, linking paganism to Christianity, and had its apex in the rise to prominence of Greco-Roman asceticism. In practices of the self, knowledge plays a very different role than in the 'cult of the self'. Knowledge was a tool that enabled individuals better to understand the necessity of the world, in order that the world could be mastered in the service of the self. For the Stoics, self was defined by the capacity to familiarize oneself with and more importantly apply technologies to 'taking care of the self' – for example via an understanding of cosmology or physics. Following the rise of Christianity, however, 'the self was no longer something to be made but something to be renounced and deciphered' (Foucault 1984, p.280).

Foucault argues that, as a result of the transition from practices of the self to the culture of the self in Christianity, knowledge and the development of 'techniques of the self' became put to work in the exercise of pastoral power. *Epimeleia heautou* gave way to *epimeleia tonallon* – essentially taking care of others. Particularly from the seventeenth century onwards, this pastoral power is reified in the annexation of knowledge about the body, about health, and about techniques of the self – by professionals: surgeons, public health administrators and psychiatrists.

There is no real evidence to suggest that the onset of the information society is bringing about a re-emergence of 'practices of the self'. Indeed, the typical pattern of use of web-based health information and support services by citizens and members of patient interest groups replicates almost precisely the process of 'deciphering of the self' highlighted by Foucault as a characteristic feature of the opposing 'cult of self' – especially it would seem in the case of the US. What is lacking in the current generation of so-called collaborative knowledge-based health information and support systems is something that Foucault maintains is an essential ingredient of 'practices of the self' or techniques of self-mastery. The missing ingredient is what Foucault identifies as 'literature of the self'. In classical times, these took the form of diaries, private notebooks and other examples of *hypomnemata* (personal narratives and individual ethnographies). In the information age, tools and services such as chat rooms, annotations systems, enriched document systems and distributed knowledge bases provide a potentially rich source of *hypomnemata* to enable citizens and patients to become actively engaged in their own 'self-policing' of health.

The most widely developed and disseminated health technologies, however, are those that reinforce established parameters and procedures of control, surveillance and classification. A clear example of this is the significant investment by public health services in health smartcards and electronic patient records. In contrast, there has been comparatively little investment in large-scale community-based health information and support services. Although there are a small number of pilot examples of community-based health telematics initiatives, implemented mainly in Scandinavia, these have focused on connecting spatially dispersed points of service delivery in order to make information flow and management more efficient. An example is MEDCOM – a national project supporting the creation of a national health care communication infrastructure to co-ordinate transactions between hospitals, GPs, laboratories and pharmacies, linking up 10 different regions in Denmark, land networking approximately 500 GPs, 12 hospitals, and 10 pharmacies.

In the final analysis, however, even the handful of examples of community-based health informatics systems, such as MEDCOM, are primarily 'top-down' systems based on conventional models of knowledge production. What is now required is a significant investment in collaborative knowledge systems that actively engage lay people in a knowledge production as well as a knowledge consumption role. As the SEAHORSE example discussed above illustrates, such systems have the potential to produce an evidence base for health that is rooted in individual narrative and experience.

At this point in time, however, systems such as SEAHORSE do not actively engage patients and citizens as co-collaborators, along with health professionals, in the process of 'taking care of the self'. For their part, health professionals are engaged in a re-engineering process that is being driven forward by the increasing introduction of new technologies into the workplace. As the above examples indicate, this is beginning to erode established hierarchies of power and control. A characteristic of the effects of health informatics on professional structure and practice is the devolution of knowledge and authority from consultants to a broader professional base. Yet this process is stopping short of a more pervasive convergence of collaboration involving patient self-management.

More significantly, these changes in organizational structure, function and process within health care are accompanied by new forms of institutional innovation, and these in turn are inextricably linked to new forms of economic structure based on the value chains associated with technology delivery platforms. What therefore seems to be emerging through health informatics is not the liberation of the individual from the domination of the 'police of health' but instead new institutional forms of control. These forms of control involve new alliances between government agencies and commercial organizations in the continuing pursuit, in Foucault's terms, of 'harnessing population to the political economy of the State'. In this sense, one might envisage smartcards and the Internet not as an 'information brothel' but as a 'virtual panopticon'.

My opinion is that the emergence of health informatics presents opportunities for either the consolidation of the domination of 'subjects' through new institutional/economic forms of the 'police of health' or, conversely, a re-emergence of 'practices of the self'. In this context, there are broadly three main scenarios for health informatics: the integration model, the strategic model and the collaborative knowledge model.

The integration model is based on the emergence of an 'intelligent network'. This will provide the basis for the seamless integration of information services, stimulating demand-led markets, new forms of competition and collaboration and a corresponding increase in public access to information and services. Also, it entails the 'top-down' structured co-ordination of development and implementation via a common European welfare system and the standardization of platforms and protocols, for example using Euro-ISDN.

The strategic model envisages a primarily market-driven and expert-driven diffusion trajectory for health informatics. It is shaped primarily by differences in the political and administrative structures of health care systems in Europe. This gives rise to opportunistic niche markets developed by telecommunications providers; greater autonomy for hospital administrators and primary care 'fund holders' in the delivery of health care; and the maintenance of a relative status quo in the current hierarchical organizational structure of health care. This process is driven by new institutional arrangements (PPPs) based on value chain funding models. These new partnerships entail some organizational re-engineering. This focuses mainly on the devolution of responsibilities to primary care providers as referral 'gatekeepers', and the broadening of delivery care roles amongst a wider group of service providers, for example nurse practitioners and paramedics. Health informatics products and services are primarily focused on facilitating networking between specialists and GPs, and an emphasis on the utilization of telematics systems for clinician decision support, practice management and teletraining.

The collaborative knowledge model envisages a 'bottom-up' community-led and collaborative health care structure. It foresees a shift from an emphasis on medical care to one of health care and telehealth, and a movement from episodic, acute care to preventative and long-term care, focusing on outpatient and self-managed delivery rather than inpatient care. It anticipates the erosion of traditional authority structures centred on the clinician and the dominance of collaborative patient-managed institutional and administrative structures. This interpretation reflects a common theme of devolving power and control to both the individual and the community, implying a shift in resources from secondary and specialist care centres to primary care and to self-managed care. This notion of managed self-care reflects an emphasis on the empowerment of the users of health care services; the adoption of home-based, patient-managed health monitoring systems (for example in diabetes); and the utilization of Internet-based information and support services.

In my opinion the second model is the most likely.

References

Cullen, J. C., Michelet, E., Goschenberg, E. and Remotti, L. (1998) *The Impact of Telematics on European Healthcare*. Brussels: CEC.

Cullen, J. (1998) 'The needle and the damage done: research, action research and the organisational and social construction of health in the information society.' *Human Relations 51*, 12, 1543–1564.

Department of Health (1998) *Information for Health – An Information Strategy for the Modern NHS 1998–2005*. London: Department of Health.

Department of Trade and Industry (2000) *A New Future for Communications*. White Paper. London: Department of Trade and Industry and Department of Culture, Media and Sport.

Dosi, G. (ed) (1988) *Technical Change and Economic Theory*. London: Pinter.

Foucault, M. (1984) In P. Rabinow (ed) *The Foucault Reader*. Harmondsworth: Penguin.

Giddens, A. (1994) *The Consequences of Modernity*. Cambridge: Polity Press.

Gott, M. (1995) *Telematics for Health: The Role of Telehealth and Telemedicine in Homes and Communities*. Oxford: Radcliffe Medical Press.

Guardian (1999) 26 December.

Gustafson, D., Bosworth, K., Hawkins, R., Boberg, E. and Bricker, E. (1993) 'CHESS: a computer-based system for providing information, referrals, decision support and social support to people facing medical and other health related crises.' *Proceedings of the First National Conference on Consumer Health Informatics*. Wisconsin: University of Wisconsin.

Habermas, J. (1984) *The Philosophical Discourse of Modernity*. Cambridge: Polity.

Habermas, J. (1992) *Postmetaphysical Thinking*. Cambridge: Polity.

Kirby, S. (2000) *SEAHORSE Deliverable 8.1; Exploitation Plan*. London: Tavistock.

Lave, J. and Wenger, E. (1991) *Situated Learning: Legitimate Peripheral Participation*. Cambridge: University Press.

MELIC Consortium (2000) *Report in Direct User Investigation*. Brussels: MELIC Consortium.

Schoenfeld, A., Harrison, M. and Kosarajhu, S. (1999) *Health Industry and the Internet.*. New York: Jupiter Communications.

Somer, T. (1994) *Economic Aspects of Telemedicine*. Brussels: DGXIII/C4 CEC.

Strydom, P. (1987) 'Collective learning: Habermas' concessions and their theoretical implications.' *Philosophy and Social Criticism 13*, 3, 165–181.

USA Today (2000) 'Drugmakers accused of price scheme. Doctors involved, panel says.' 27 September, p.1.A.

Weick, K. (1995) *Sensemaking in Organisations*. London: Sage.

Further Reading

Gammon, D. (1993) 'Restraining and facilitating factors in the diffusion of telemedicine – an interview study.' *Telektronik 89*, 1, 78–84.

Endnotes

1. This includes the following: TELMED: the impact of telematics on European health care, a study commissioned by the EC; SEAHORSE: support, empowerment and awareness for HIV/AIDS, an RTD project funded by the EC; HERO: health and educational support for the rehabilitation of offenders, an RTD project funded by the EC; Informal Learning, a research study funded by the Department for Education and Skills (DfES).

2. Euro-ISDN is a European Telecommunications Standards Institute standard for Integrated Services Digital Network, phased in during March 1994. It allows full transparent interworking between countries that are members of the European Conference of Post and Telecommunications (CEPT) and is available on a commercial basis in most European countries.

CHAPTER 8

From Self-service Welfare to Virtual Self-help

Nicholas Pleace, Roger Burrows, Brian Loader,
Steven Muncer and Sarah Nettleton

Computerisation in welfare and social policy has, more often than not, been about increasing efficiency and reducing costs. Since the early 1980s, a succession of governments in the UK have commissioned expensive and far reaching computerisation drives aimed at reducing the administrative costs of delivering state welfare services. These projects quite often met with only qualified success and tended to fall (sometimes far) short of their original objectives (Hudson 1999, 2000).

More recently there has been a major movement towards e-government and electronic service delivery. Here the intention is that service users will increasingly be encouraged to use automated systems, available via the Internet, digital television and through other networked devices such as Third Generation (G3) phones, to arrange services for themselves. Five years from now, one might be able to claim benefits or ask for a community care assessment through an interactive website or its equivalent. The recently re-elected Labour government announced in March 2000 that all government services were to be 'deliverable electronically' by 2005, having brought the date forward from an earlier 2008 deadline (Cabinet Office 2000). While e-government and electronic service delivery are described as empowering and as improving accessibility, there is also an intention that quite a considerable amount of the administration of welfare services will be completed through a combination of automation and service users, or their carers, taking the lead in applying for and arranging services for themselves.

One of the authors of this chapter has conceptualised these developments as the emergence of 'welfare direct' (Loader 1998a).

It is intended that these on-line, interactive systems will be complemented by an ever increasing degree of networking within and between welfare delivery organisations. It is envisaged that current duplication of record keeping and lack of co-ordination between housing, health, social services and the Benefits Agency, among others, will be reduced and overcome by ever more powerful data management across networks. New organisations, akin to the networked enterprise of the private sector, will be able to function with radically reduced levels of middle management and front-line staff in the medium term.

In essence, government is looking to use ICTs to shunt some of its current costs in the administration and delivery of welfare services onto the users of those services in order to reduce its costs. It is also intending to reduce its costs through using an increasing degree of networking and information sharing to avoid duplication and enhance communication. These developments involve using the same tools and same systems as business has used to shunt some of its costs onto its customers (Castells 1996).

Yet these same technologies are starting to be employed in a radically different way by some individuals who are employing them to provide on-line self-help and social support to one another. This new development in welfare services is quite separate from developments in the provision and commissioning of services by the state, with these technologies being used voluntarily by people to provide mutual support to one another.

Virtual self-help

Virtual self-help (VSH) is not directly comparable with orthodox self-help, although it shares the central characteristic of being based on advice and support from people with the same needs or shared experiences rather than trained professionals or care workers. Unlike orthodox self-help, participants tend not to meet face to face and what can be an international group membership is often fluid, so much so that while some have regular core participants, others cannot really be regarded as being 'groups' as such. Communication is also largely restricted to sending and receiving text messages, though it is possible to exchange video, photos and sound clips.

Rather than seek advice or support from welfare services, or rather from state-provided (or as is increasingly more likely, state-funded) welfare services, individuals can seek advice and support from their peers, peers with a shared understanding gained through having the same needs and experiences that professionals cannot emulate. Finn (1999, p.229), looking at the US experience, takes the view that the virtual self-help group offers the benefits of attending a self-help group with accessibility from one's own home:

> Online groups may be especially useful in providing additional support and information to people who have physical or mental barriers to obtaining services, high needs for support, lack of access to services because of geographic isolation or transportation difficulties, verbal communication difficulties or limited socialization opportunities.

VSH first arose in the US, in what Denzin (1998) has portrayed as the American love of technology and of self-help naturally meshing together. It seems likely that it began life in the discussion groups, called newsgroups. Newsgroups predate mass access to the Internet and allow participants to share an electronic space to which they send notes (called posts) that everyone in that space can read. The posts are organised into chains of interrelated messages called threads by the software using the title of each message. Newsgroups offer asynchronous communication; the nearest analogy might be a group of people sending telegrams to one another that they can all read simultaneously, rather than actual conversation. Newsgroups started on a network called Usenet, which is technically separate from the Internet but accessible via the Internet and World Wide Web. Virtual self-help can also be found in other types of on-line settings that allow communication between two or more people, including Internet Relay Chat which allows what might be described as typed conversations (Pleace *et al.* 2000) and web-based resources. However, VSH is predominately found in newsgroups.

Research on VSH has been quite limited in some respects, with studies tending to look at the phenomenon on a group by group basis. The work that has been done in the US has included analysis of groups for disabled people (Finn 1999), problem drinkers (King 1994), adult survivors of child abuse (Moursund 1997) and people who have negative experiences through living in a family or being in a relationship with someone who was drug or alcohol dependent (Denzin 1998, 1999).

This chapter reports on an exploratory Economic and Social Research Council (ESRC)-funded study conducted during 1998–2000 which looked in detail at individual VSH groups and interviewed 21 British users of VSH. The research was the first to try to get an overview of VSH. Several groups were analysed and a mixture of telephone and face-to-face interviews were carried out. Details of the methodology employed is detailed in Nettleton *et al.* (2001). The chapter provides a brief summary of some of the results of the study. Readers interested in more detailed analyses may care to consult other published outputs from the project which deal with substantive areas such as parenting, depression, problem drinking and diabetes (Burrows *et al.* 2000; Loader *et al.* 2002; Muncer *et al.* 2000a, 2000b; Nettleton *et al.* 2001; Pleace *et al.* 2000).

The exchanges within VSH environments are often long and complex and there is not room in a chapter of this length to use examples that would be properly illustrative. A single 'conversation' between one or more participants will often take up as much space as is available for this chapter, so the focus here will instead be on the views and experiences of those using VSH and on its meanings for social policy and welfare delivery. There are also important ethical questions around quoting from newsgroups and other self-help fora which are briefly considered at the end of this chapter. Examples of VSH newsgroups include alt.support.depression and uk.people.disability, which are accessible via Usenet and the World Wide Web using sites such as www.deja.com.

The meanings of virtual self-help

Some argued, when Internet access was largely confined to academics and students rather than being the mass access medium which it is now, that the Internet would represent a revolution in communication and personal relationships. Some felt this revolution would be positive, that communities based on shared interest rather than geographical location could develop and that relationships would no longer be confined by time and distance. For the paradigmatic statement of the position see Rheingold (1994). Others saw a still more fundamental change on the horizon, the rise of the 'cyborg', a real and a 'virtual' self, participating in life on two levels, in physical reality and on the network (see various of the contributions in Featherstone and Burrows 1995). For others there was the fear that the Internet would, like television before it, reduce social interaction and encourage individual isolation, with people seeking emotional support through simulacra rather than real interaction with one another (see, for instance, Lockard 1997).

None of these predictions can be dismissed out of hand, but while they were at least partly true, they tended to exaggerate to some degree because the researchers or commentators responsible for them had focused on an aspect rather than trying to wrestle with the complexity, diversity and sheer size of the whole. In reality, the Internet has different effects on different individuals in different contexts; it is too diverse for this not to be the case, as Wellman and Gulia have pointed out (1999). One of the fundamental problems with understanding the Internet is its diversity and scale; those looking for child pornography and instructions on bomb making will find them, just as the research team, looking for evidence of mutual support and self-help, found strong evidence of VSH.

The research reported on in this chapter started from this standpoint, expecting to find mixed and, by extension, sometimes rather limited, effects resulting from VSH. From our understanding of orthodox self-help, it might be expected that VSH would be having an impact on the lives of those using it in two ways. In broad terms, the role of orthodox self-help is twofold.

First, it offers the social support of sharing one's needs and experiences with people with the same needs and experiences as oneself. Second, again through the medium of sharing experiences, it can offer an alternative perspective to that offered by care or health professionals. In other words, it can offer advice on parenting from other parents, as an alternative to the advice from a social worker, and advice on which drugs are most effective from fellow sufferers, as an alternative to the diagnosis or advice from the doctor.

Virtual self-help and the provision of social support

A range of social resources are held to act against stress and in turn both reduce the likelihood of the onset of health problems and aid recovery if health problems develop. Simply put, there is considerable evidence that if other factors are equal, people with a good range of positive relationships are less likely to develop disease and more likely to recover from it than those with poor relationships or those who lack relationships. Social support is usually discussed in terms of either the 'buffer' theory in which social supports are held to have a positive effect when individuals are confronted with illness and stress, or the 'main effect' model, in which social supports are held to have a constant and generally beneficial effect (Cohen and Willis 1985). While there is contention over how one can separate out social support from other factors and measure its effects, there is a consensus that it does have an effect on health status (Callaghan and Morrissey 1993). A number of definitions of types of social support exist, but from their review of a large number of studies Cohen and Willis (1985, p.313) were able to condense these into four main 'types' of support. These included esteem support, information that a person is esteemed and accepted; informational support, help in defining, understanding and coping with problematic events; social companionship, spending time with others in leisure or recreational activities; and instrumental support, the provision of financial aid, material resources and needed services.

Some existing research has argued that VSH can provide social companionship, informational support and esteem support (Finn 1999; King 1994; Moursund 1997). As the authors have pointed out elsewhere (Muncer *et al.* 2000a), it cannot deliver instrumental, or practical, support because participants generally do not meet and may live a great distance from one another. The authors have also reported elsewhere that VSH groups quite often seem to focus, though not exclusively, either on informational support or on what might be characterised as esteem support and social companionship (Muncer *et al.* 2000a, 2000b; Pleace *et al.* 2000).

Importantly, the research conducted by the authors also indicates that some groups have a largely transient membership. As we showed in two papers on VSH groups for depression and diabetes (Muncer *et al.* 2000a, 2000b), a group focused on depression had a core of frequent participants who were responsible for the majority of messages, whereas a very active diabetes newsgroup had only a handful of regular participants. The depression group had an emphasis on esteem support and social companionship, the diabetes group on informational support.

The interviews showed that it was the access to a range of individuals, who were able to talk about shared needs in the way those without their experience could not, that had attracted people to VSH.

> ... if you get a condition and you walk away from the doctor's and think to yourself 'I've got this, what's happening?', and there's nobody where you live or round about you that's got it, you think 'Who can I discuss this with?'... And in my case I thought 'Well, look [it] up on a search engine on the Web'... But having said that...that is just, you know, that is, how can I put it, just like reading a text book...whereas with, with Usenet you

can actually dwell on people's life experiences...there are people that actually have got the condition and will come back and tell you about it.

(Man in his thirties)

Oh, I put messages, oh, I mean I've had to post messages up for help and support during all the time I've had all my problems. I've been in and out of hospital and that's how I've met some of these people in the States, you know, they're all people who've had a similar thing to what I've got and it's been a godsend, an absolute godsend, having the computer.

(Woman in her fifties)

The interview results suggested that VSH rarely functioned as someone's sole source of social support, although in two instances where individuals were housebound, it had taken on a role as the main source of social support. Others had used VSH as a means by which to establish ordinary friendships, establishing one-to-one communication with people whom they had met in a VSH group and eventually meeting them if possible.

For other participants some of whom had experienced traumatic events, such as a catastrophic deterioration in health or the death of a loved one, the anonymity of VSH seemed to be important in that it allowed them to give vent to their feelings in a context over which they could exercise control. One respondent talked of VSH in terms of it being an 'interactive diary' into which they could write down their feelings without having to bring themselves to talk about what they were feeling in front of other people; another talked about the advantages of anonymity in discussing difficult and painful subjects:

I think it is because for a very strange reason you tend to get a lot closer to them. And you can build up some quite strong friendships and you might never have met the person. But I think the anonymity actually helps which may sound a little strange but it's easier to talk to a virtual stranger... I mean certainly with my friend, we've got into a far more deeper level of conversation than you would perhaps with a best mate that you've known for years over a relatively short period of time.

(Woman in her thirties)

Two aspects of VSH groups, the inherently limited nature of text-based communication and the tendency for some groups to have a transient population, might be expected to limit the degree of social support that these environments could provide. If the membership of a group is not constant to some degree, it would tend to undermine the chances that it will be an environment in which relationships between participants can develop. Equally, the limitations of only being able to communicate via text messages might also impact on the level of social support that can be provided, if one cannot see, hear or touch those with whom one is communicating.

However, the interview results did not suggest that those participating in VSH viewed it as offering only limited social support. Most of the interviewees were participants in several VSH groups, using the various environments for different purposes. For example, an interviewee might use one or more groups for emotional support related to their needs, but also participate in groups with an informational focus on the same subject and use a range of other groups for leisure and other interests unrelated to VSH. It seems to have been the case that where any one VSH group was not providing everything an individual required, it was often simply a matter of participating in several to meet one's various social support needs.

If one is seeking informational support from people with the same needs, the other individuals involved have to be people like oneself in terms of their characteristics, but not necessarily one's friends or people that one has to form any real relationship with. Indeed, the constantly changing and ephemeral nature of participation in some VSH groups by many of the people who use them may even be characterised as an advantage, as new sources of information are constantly arriving.

For others seeking the social supports that did require the formation of relationships, VSH presented them with the opportunity to meet other people with whom they could develop relationships, working as a catalyst to allow people to develop friendships. Meeting someone via a newsgroup seemed relatively commonplace. In other instances, in groups with more stable memberships, VSH could offer at least some of the social supports that individuals were seeking, although as already noted, it was rarely the sole source of someone's social support.

Since communication is text based, VSH offers none of the usual visual or verbal clues that are part of normal communication. This creates a situation within which individuals could potentially misrepresent themselves to others and it had led some interviewees to exercise some degree of caution when participating in some of the groups.

We've had a lot of people coming in...you find that over time they keep changing their story. I mean I went through it with a new chap a couple of nights ago and they quiz you to find out if you are a genuine MS person, things only somebody with MS would know and it didn't actually occur to me that that's what he was doing until about ten minutes into the conversation and he kept sort of coming back firing questions...and I was quite annoyed actually, but I also realised why he was doing it, because he was new on the site and he was trying to make sure we were genuine.

(Woman in her thirties)

Other aspects of Internet use that might undermine VSH or prevent it did not seem to have been particularly important to the users that were interviewed. The misogyny, race-hate and generally anti-social behaviour of some of the white teenage males who sometimes invaded VSH groups (Spender 1995), while sometimes a pressure, was not undermining participation in VSH.

An alternative perspective

As two of the present authors have argued elsewhere (Burrows and Nettleton 2001) it is the *context* within which VSH has developed that is of particular interest. The 'risk society' thesis interprets the postmodern industrialised society as one that is increasingly characterised by individual insecurity. This insecurity stems from economic change associated with globalisation. It also flows from social change, the situation in which traditional forms of social organisation such as the nuclear family have been undermined (Hampton and Wellman 2001; Wellman and Gulia 1999) at the same time as the welfare state has been cut back, forcing those individuals with the capacity to do so to become increasingly self-reliant. This need for self-reliance also reflects a loss of control by traditional authority and professionals, whether in reference to the inability of governments to control their economy in a situation of globalisation, or in the inability of professionals to counteract problems such as ecological catastrophes or the rise of new diseases (Beck 1992; Giddens 1999). The shorthand term for this situation is the 'privatisation of risk', in which individuals have to cope with new insecurities without the traditional social structures, professional expertise and the powerful politicians they once relied on.

Burrows and Nettleton view VSH as a further mechanism for the voluntary and involuntary privatisation of risk. Virtual self-help is a privatisation of risk management, individuals drawing on the experience and opinions of those with shared needs, rather than professional discourse, as their main source of information. A user of VSH turns up at the doctor's surgery with printouts from their VSH groups, the views of other people with the same health problem, and an opinion about which treatment should be provided (Hardey 1999). Some in the medical profession are already getting worried about the reliability of some information on health on the Internet (Abbott 2000; Kim *et al.* 1999).

The interviews did suggest changing relationships with professional service providers, suggesting that VSH might influence the way in which some people both perceived and related to the professionals they encountered.

> I do read up on everything beforehand and I'm already pretty sure about what it is before I go. But there again I've got quite a good GP that knows me reasonably well and they can usually sort it out. I'm invariably right, you know...
>
> *(Woman in her thirties)*

> [My GP] said 'It's for rheumatoid arthritis' and I had to correct her and tell her it was not for rheumatoid arthritis it was for osteo arthritis which she wasn't very pleased about.
>
> *(Woman in her fifties)*

However, some of the interviewees still felt that information about illnesses or social care needs required expert interpretation, and were not prepared to question the judgements of professionals.

> It's a rerun of... there used to be a programme on the television *Your Life in Their Hands*... And my brother was training to be a doctor... He was a casualty officer and whenever he watched it, he'd go off and find his textbooks...because he said 'I'm going to get twenty people in A and E [accident and emergency] tomorrow with this.
>
> *(Woman in her fifties)*

The quality of the informational support that was available from VSH groups was mentioned much more often than information from the Web. Most seemed happy to seek advice and information from those with the same health or social care needs, but few used the vast array of professionally endorsed information available on-line.

> I've had a discussion on diabetes because I was recently diagnosed as a diabetic as well. And I threw out questions in the disability.uk group about it because I didn't know a lot about it and the doctor hadn't given me [any] information, 'well, just change your diet', well like, what? 'Don't eat sugar'. But I did get back a lot of good suggestions and a lot of things I didn't know, like sugar content in processed food which I hadn't thought about. And quite a few diabetics came back and suggested different strategies...

> *(Woman in her thirties)*

The largest potential problem with VSH in this respect is in the possibility that dubious and misleading information will be taken on board while professional advice is ignored. However, there was caution among the interviewees about trusting any one source of information on the Internet. These British users had sometimes adopted the American term 'snakeoil' (the 'miracle cures' sold by travelling salesmen in nineteenth-century America) to describe much of what could be found on the Internet. The interviewees reported a large number of quacks and charlatans alongside sincere but deluded people, pushing anything from exotic plants through to membership of cults and sects as cures or solutions, but demonstrated a healthy scepticism about the individuals and websites advocating them.

Discussion

The level and nature of access to the Internet are the caveats that must be constantly borne in mind when thinking about VSH and its implications. Given the current expectation of a huge expansion in the ways in which cheap Internet access will be possible over the next decade, many expect that the Internet will be in most people's homes by the end of the next few years. While the UK is still a country in which not everyone has a telephone, it is difficult to counter these arguments given the constantly falling cost of the required technologies. On this basis, it could be asserted that while VSH is not important for many people as yet, it will start to become more and more important as the Internet becomes truly ubiquitous.

Yet fundamental questions remain about whether or not people will engage with VSH even if they have the access to use it. The Internet is already moving away from its original role as a communications medium and being promoted and seen in terms of e-commerce rather than as a means towards people communicating with one another in new ways, so that individuals may see it as a means to shop, rather than as a means to communicate. These technologies also remain relatively inaccessible to people with a visual impairment or disability, or to anyone whose first language is not English. There are also very real barriers to many people in our society who have no experience of or connection with these kinds of technology, through factors such as being beyond the age of retirement or socioeconomic marginalisation (Loader 1998b). It must also be remembered of course, although this is something that is perhaps lost sight of in some of the work on access to the Internet and related technologies, that people may simply not *want* to use it and it may be the case that most people would simply not view VSH as attractive.

Should the use of VSH become more widespread, it may have important implications for social policy. These may be positive. Community care or mental health services have had to focus increasingly on crisis intervention as resources have constricted. Virtual self-help could contribute to the low level social support that can help individuals with support needs to live successfully in the community, which such services now find it difficult to provide (Quilgars 2000) and in so doing reduce some of the calls made on these services. More importantly, VSH could enhance individual quality of life in the way that Finn (1999) has suggested, giving social support to people who are housebound or who would be unable to attend a local support group. Equally, of course, VSH could present the providers of health and welfare services with new challenges, from a new willingness to question professional discourse, through to the challenging of individual and organisational decisions by drawing on VSH resources.

Naturally, VSH may have potentially negative impacts as well. More detailed study is needed of the quality of social support that it is able to deliver. As well as the possibility that individuals may be exploited and abused, which might be more of an imagined problem than a real one, questions need to be asked as to how far VSH can really act as a source of social support. On the basis of the limited evidence to date and allowing for the fact that VSH can be a home to those spouting dangerous nonsense, it can act as a source of informational support, but whether it can really offer emotional and esteem support when participants cannot see, hear or touch one another is perhaps more questionable. On a fundamental level, questions about the reality of VSH social support and the reality of computer-mediated communication, which some argue is an ersatz substitute for real interaction, might also be raised (Kraut *et al.* 1998).

These same concerns arise when one considers the role of VSH as a source of alternative information and perspectives. Of course, when VSH prevents a patient accepting a misdiagnosis by a doctor or challenges the incorrect interpretation of benefit regulations or the incorrect actions of a social worker, there is no problem. Yet if VSH stops someone accepting the drug that will help them, fuels their paranoia about what the mental health team will do to them, or stops them claiming the benefit they are entitled to, then it is another matter. The results of the admittedly limited research conducted thus far indicated a healthy scepticism about information on the Internet, but these were early adopters of VSH who were middle-class professionals.

In summary, there are potentially interesting developments here, but it is really too early to say what the eventual impact will be. More understanding of VSH will be needed to understand its impact fully, should it start to become something that is used by significant numbers of the population. Further research will also have to consider the ethics of quoting from newsgroups and other on-line discussions as these are now being debated. Most studies to date have taken the approach that these are public fora that cannot be compared to an email or telephone call or have not concerned themselves with ethical questions at all. This view is being increasingly questioned and there are some who believe that exchanges should not be quoted without their authors' permission, even though these exchanges are potentially accessible to tens of millions of Internet users. (See Reid 1996; Paccagnella 1997 and Sharif 1999 for a discussion of these issues.)

References

Abbott. V. P. (2000) 'Web page quality: can we measure it and what do we find? A report of exploratory findings.' *Journal of Public Health Medicine 22*, 2, 191–197.

Beck, U. (1992) *Risk Society*. London: Sage.

Burrows, R. and Nettleton, S. (2001) 'Reflexive modernisation and the emergence of wired self-help.' In K. Renniger and W. Shumar (eds) *Building Virtual Communities: Learning and Change in Cyberspace*. New York: Cambridge University Press.

Burrows, R., Nettleton, S., Pleace, N., Loader, B. and Muncer, S. (2000) 'Virtual community care? Social policy and the emergence of computer mediated social support.' *Information, Communication and Society 3*, 1, 95–121.

Cabinet Office (2000) 'Government to speed up introduction of on-line services.' CAB 140/00; 30/3/2000. London: Cabinet Office.

Callaghan, P. and Morrissey, J. (1993) 'Social support and health: a review.' *Journal of Advanced Nursing 18*, 203–213.

Castells, M. (1996) *The Rise of the Network Society: The Information Age: Economy, Society and Culture*. Cambridge, MA: Blackwell.

Cohen, S. and Willis, T. (1985) 'Stress, social support and the buffering hypothesis.' *Psychological Bulletin, 98*, 310–357.

Denzin, N. (1998) 'In search of the inner child: co-dependency and gender in a Cyberspace community.' In G. Bendelow and S. Williams (eds) *Emotions in Social Life*. Routledge: London.

Denzin, N. (1999) 'Cybertalk and the method of instances.' In S. Jones (ed) *Doing Internet Research: Critical Issues and Methods for Examining the Net*. Sage: London.

Featherstone, M. and Burrows, R. (eds) (1995) *Cyberspace/Cyberbodies/Cyberpunk: Cultures of Technological Embodiment*. London: Sage.

Finn, J. (1999) 'An exploration of helping processes in an online self-help group focusing on the issues of disability.' *Health and Social Work 24*, 3, 220–231.

Giddens, A. (1999) *Runaway World*. Reith Lectures. http://news.bbc.co.uk/hi/english/static/events/reith_99/

Hampton, K. and Wellman, B. (2001) 'Long distance community in the network society: contact and support beyond Netville.' *American Behavioral Scientist 45*, 3, 476–495.

Hardey, M. (1999) 'Doctor in the house: the Internet as a source of lay health knowledge and the challenge to expertise.' *Sociology of Health and Illness 21*, 6, 820–835.

Hudson, J. (1999) 'Informatisation and public administration: a political science perspective.' *Information, Communication and Society 2*, 3, 318–339.

Hudson, J. (2000) 'The prospects for information age government.' In R. Burrows and N. Pleace (eds) *Wired Welfare? Essays on the Rhetoric and Reality of e-Social Policy*. York: Centre for Housing Policy, University of York.

Kim, P., Eng, T. R., Deering, M. J. and Maxfield, A. (1999) 'Published criteria for evaluating health related websites: review.' *British Medical Journal 318*, 647–649.

King, S. (1994) 'Analysis of electronic support groups for recovering addicts.' *Interpersonal Computing and Technology 2*, 3, 47–56.

Kraut, R., Patterson, M., Lundmark, V., Kiesler, S., Mukopadhyay, T. and Scherlis, W. (1998) 'Internet paradox: a social technology that reduces social involvement and psychological well being?' *American Psychologist*, September, 1017–1031.

Loader, B. (1998a) 'Welfare direct.' In J. Carter (ed) *Postmodernity and the Fragmentation of Welfare.* London: Routledge.

Loader, B. (1998b) *The Cyberspace Divide: Equality, Agency and Policy in the Information Society.* London: Routledge.

Loader, B., Muncer, S., Burrows, R., Pleace, N. and Nettleton, S. (2002) 'Medicine on the line? Computer mediated social support for people with diabetes.' *International Journal of Social Welfare 11,* 1, 53–66.

Lockard, J. (1997) 'Progressive politics, electronic individualism and the myth of the virtual community.' In D. Porter (ed) *Internet Culture.* London: Routledge.

Moursund, J. (1997) 'SANCTUARY: social support on the Internet.' In J. E. Behar (ed) *Mapping Cyberspace: Social Research on the Electronic Frontier.* Oakdale, NY: Dowling College Press.

Muncer, S., Burrows, R., Pleace, N., Loader, B. and Nettleton, S. (2000a) 'Births, deaths, sex and marriage…but very few presents? A case study of social support in cyberspace.' *Critical Public Health 10,* 1–18.

Muncer, S., Loader, B., Nettleton, S., Pleace, N. and Burrows, R. (2000b) 'Heterogenity in systems of e-support: a systematic qualitative comparison of two on-line self-help groups.' In R. Burrows and N. Pleace (eds) *Wired Welfare? Essays on the Rhetoric and Reality of e-Social Policy.* York: Centre for Housing Policy, University of York.

Nettleton, S., Burrows, R., Pleace, N., Loader, B. and Muncer, S. (2001) 'The reality of virtual social support.' In S. Woolgar (ed) *Virtual Society? Get Real!* Oxford: University Press.

Paccagnella, L. (1997) 'Getting the seat of your pants dirty: strategies for ethnographic research on virtual communities.' *Journal of Computer Mediated Communication 3,* 1. http://www.ascusc.org/jcmc/

Pleace, N., Burrows, R., Loader, B., Muncer, S. and Nettleton, S. (2000) 'On-line with the friends of Bill W: social support and the net.' *Sociological Research Online 5,* 2. http://www.socresonline.org.uk/5/2/pleace.html

Quilgars, D. (2000) *Low Intensity Support Services: A Systematic Review of Effectiveness.* Bristol: Policy Press.

Reid, E. M. (1996) 'Informed consent in the study of on-line communities: a reflection on the effects of computer mediated social research.' *Information Society 12,* 2, 169–174.

Rheingold, H. (1994) *The Virtual Community.* Reading, MA: Addison Wesley.

Sharif, B. F. (1999) 'Beyond netiquette: the ethics of doing naturalistic discourse research on the Internet.' In S. Jones (ed) *Doing Internet Research: Critical Issues and Methods for Examining the Net.* Sage: London.

Spender, D. (1995) *Nattering on the Net: Women, Power and Cyberspace.* Victoria, Australia: Spinifex Press.

Wellman, B. and Gulia, M. (1999) 'Virtual communities as communities: net surfers don't ride alone.' In M. A. Smith and P. Kollock (eds) *Communities in Cyberspace.* London: Routledge.

CHAPTER 9

Consumers, the Internet and the Reconfiguration of Expertise

Michael Hardey

The beginnings of modern medicine are rooted in the Enlightenment and the growing belief in the application of scientific methods to the mysteries of life. The consequent development of scientific medecine created an increasingly complex knowledge base on which the practice of medicine was based. According to Giddens (1991) it is the preservation of and access to such expert knowledge that is one of the defining characteristics of modernity. Based on the new science of biology, medicine evolved in the laboratory and hospital where the investigation and treatment of disease focused on the patient as a body that deviated from normal functioning (Jewson 1976). As knowledge accumulated it became increasingly differentiated into new specialities around which new professions including social work formed. Consequently more scientific disciplines and sub-disciplines continued to emerge to become characteristic of modern expert systems. The Internet, newspapers, magazines, books, televisions, radio and other media present this vast accumulation of differentiated knowledge to a public hungry for the latest medical therapy, diet regime or lifestyle advice. The tension between the availability of information and the specialization and differentiation of expertise is played out in our everyday struggle to know 'both what one is doing and why one is doing it' (Giddens 1991, p.35). Giddens goes on to note that a high degree of specialization effectively makes everyone a lay person in that the more knowledge is differentiated and concentrated 'the smaller the field in which any given individual can claim expertise; in other areas of life he or she will be in the same situation as everyone else' (p.124).

At one level the Internet can be seen simply as another means to transmit information to the public. NHS Direct OnLine[1] displays pictures, short video sequences and voice recordings and places the user in the role of a reader who identifies and chooses what information to access. The Internet is, however, different from earlier forms of media in that it is inherently local/global and interactive. For users it is a simple step to move from using a computer to find and read information to using the same technology to, for example, send an email to a newsgroup or create a home page that offers information to a global audience. This blurs the distinction between consumers and producers of information that further challenges our conceptualization of expertise (Hardey 2001).

This chapter examines how the Internet has created new opportunities and new dilemmas for consumers and producers of health and social care information and services. A technological deterministic approach will be rejected to enable us to explore the complex interweaving of new technology and the nature of knowledge, information and expertise. These have been profoundly altered through the globalizing tendencies of late modernity and growth of human intervention (i.e. 'manufactured' risks and uncertainties) in all aspects of life and the environment (Giddens 1991, 1994; Beck 1992). We will then turn to an examination of lay expertise, looking at two examples of new forms for generating and consuming knowledge. The first involves exploring the personal home page as a venue for publishing information and the second examines the role of newsgroups in providing lay advice and support. We then briefly look at Internet resources provided by the state, commercial and voluntary sectors. This highlights the problem of the veracity of the content of Internet resources and the dilemmas about trust and risk. Finally, the chapter will explore the ways in which the Internet is challenging how expertise is understood and the relationships between practitioners and users.

Expertise and the consumer culture

Health and social policy since the 1980s in the UK has adopted a language that expresses a neo-liberal approach to citizenship and the individual as opposed to post-war values associated with collective responsibilities and state intervention. This language, constructed around notions of 'empowerment', 'rights' and 'partnership', is expressed in terminology that includes service 'users', 'clients' and 'case management'. Within both health and social care professions there has also been a shift towards a rhetoric about evidence-based practice. This holds that practice must be informed by research evidence that is grounded in rigorous methodologies (see Webb 2001). Such an approach is congruent with technocratic organizations that have to justify and compete for resources from the government. The consequent use of 'performance indicators', 'outcome measures' and other techniques prioritizes quantitative approaches to assessment over qualitative and experiential ones (see Department of Health 1999).

Medicine, nursing and social work professionals have national centres that are linked to the Internet and assess and disseminate research evidence (e.g. Cochrane Data Base, University of York; Centre for Evidence-Based Practice, University of Exeter). This evidence is framed in a more or less explicit methodological pyramid that places randomized controlled trials (RCTs), cohort and case control studies at the pinnacle with ethnographies and case studies at the bottom (see Mulrow 1994). This informs a mass of guidelines and review recommendations that shape how health and social care is delivered. It is possible to imagine that evidence-based practice could, for example, in an operating theatre provide the basis for programming a surgical robot that would undertake routinized procedures efficiently and with the minimum of risk. However, the vision of human experts operating within a systematized, technocratic and regimental framework is less appealing because it restricts interpretations and negotiations of problems to an objectively managed process (see Weber's (1976) concept of an 'iron cage' of bureaucracy). This exaggerated model of a 'scientized' evidence-based practice reflects methodological imperatives that are shaped by the specialization and differentiation of expertise.

Accounts of health and social problems by patients or users have commonly been framed within the context of a consultation with an expert. Parsons' (1978) formulation of the sick role is the classic example where the patient is the subordinate member of the encounter. While Parsons acknowledges that there may be some lay knowledge about medicine he argues that 'the evidence is overwhelming that this knowledge is highly limited and that most laymen think that they know more, and have better bases of judgement than is actually the case' (Parsons 1951, p.441). Thus the patient is in a position of 'technical incompetence' (Parsons 1951, p.440). This shows how patient narratives form part of the raw material (in a way similar to parts of the body) which the doctor (or in other circumstances the social worker) uses to find 'the truth' by recourse to esoteric knowledge that reveals answers and privileges one account over another. Such an approach is amenable to evidence-based practice with its implicit methodological baggage. It also reflects the growing specialization and differentiation characteristic of late modernity that creates the circumstances for a mass of often conflicting sources of authority (Giddens 1991). Under such conditions public perceptions of experts of all kind is a mix of 'reverence and reserve, approval and disquiet, enthusiasm and antipathy' (Giddens, 1991 p.7).

Illness and pain, in Parsons' model, involve the emergence of the body as a problem, which hinders individuals' taken-for-granted activities. This suggests that the body remains latent and largely unacknowledged until it makes its presence known. However, it has been argued that contemporary culture is characterized by the treatment of bodies as 'projects' (Shilling 1993). This involves individuals in the surveillance, maintenance and development of their bodies as a central part of their self-identity. Such self-reflexivity is consistent with the constant construction and revising of 'self-narratives' that is characteristic of consumer culture (Giddens 1991). The media and the Internet, for example, publish a vast amount of information about diet, fitness and fashion. This vision of the body as an unfinished project highlights its symbolic meaning and demands continual investment. The centrality of the body emerged in the second half of the twentieth century together with an unprecedented opening up of scientific and technological tools that could be used to develop and change the body (Featherstone 1990; Featherstone and Burrows 1995). We are therefore confronted with many competing ideas about body maintenance and presentation in a society where image is important to social and economic success. Ehrenreich (1990), for example, argues that exercise and diet is embraced by the middle class in order to achieve a 'hard body' and associated lifestyle. This suggests that a 'new health consciousness' shapes choices that include bodily modification, low-fat foods and counselling (Crawford 1987). Such choices are informed by and may be catered for by different expertise and practitioners. It is not surprising that the new media of the Internet should reflect these broad social and cultural changes and become a central space in which the resulting tensions are played out.

The personal home page: lay knowledge and advice

The text below was taken from the personal home page of a young woman in the US. The content of her home page runs to many thousands of words and includes links to other sites about seronegative spondyloarthropy. Some of these have been written by clinicians or form part of patient information services while patients or members of their families have written others. The extract presented here is only a small part of the description of her experiences and advice to others (original spelling and grammar have been retained). Although the graphics and other features that accompany a home page have not been reproduced the text does capture something of the flavour of illness-related home pages that provide unique insights into the experience of chronic sickness (Hardey 2002a):

> This is the Web Page of Ruth Foster. I live in New York and love all things the city has for a 19 year old. I was diagnosed with anklyosing spondylitis (AS) in June 1993 but the doctors tell me they don't really know what is wrong with me. I have long list of symptoms. Here are some to be going on with – inflammation (redness and swelling) of almost all my joints from my toes to my jaw, nausea, eye problems, muscle stiffness, migraines, speech problems (from medication), mood swings and then there is pain. I could go on with this list but it would be so long...I have been diagnosed with over 16 different chronic illnesses including Fibromyalgia Syndrome but I still keep on going.
>
> School and college has been a bit difficult since I have been ill. I had to quit volleyball and was put into adaptive physical education. This turned out not to be adaptive P.E. but a class for kids who had managed to get notes from their doctors to excuse them from P.E. I felt humiliated when I was put into a study hall where I was watched by a security guard who was two times my weight, a foot taller, and growled at everyone because everyone I was with was in there for detention, fighting, or truancies. To the other kids I appeared to be a 'criminal' because I was in a closed classroom in the back of the school for an hour each day. All the staff knew me because I was always having to leave to school to visit doctors. About half of them didn't like me for that. My guidance counselor despised me because I was always coming into her office to get some paper work sorted out or trying to verify my absence. That was all part of school life by the time I was a senior and it didn't get me down. I couldn't carry all my books around the school so I had to have a second set.

For those who don't believe that I have an 'invisible' illness, I try to educate them. I think this is key to understanding and compassion. I'm not looking for pity just the hope that they will give someone the benefit of the doubt and not discriminate. I want people to know I look normal but that I've had a hard time as well. Others who have disabilities don't think I know about pain because there is nothing to see. They think they are 'more handicapped' which is very hard. I've felt rejected by other patients who think 'she is alright' or 'bit of a faker'. They don't realize how sick I really am, and that hurts.

What would I like others to know? That I may look normal, but I've had it hard too. Other people who have disabilities, or are sick, tend to discount any type of pain that I've been through. That type of attitude is very hard to deal with. I've been rejected by fellow patients, they don't realize how sick I really am, and that hurts. When a person is diagnosed like I am, given many different diagnoses and the doctors not knowing what to do about it, it causes (I think) a mental handicap more than anything else. The body may seem healthy, but it's the attitude that keeps the person from functioning in society. I've been there, severely depressed for eight months, and I still fall into it every once in a while.

So what advice do I have for you? Take advantage of what you have now, because you never know when you may lose it. Live life to the fullest. I never thought I'd lose the ability to run, jump, dance... I want to help kids and teens who have or think they might have my kind of problems. I know it's scary but education is the key. My site has lots of information, my whole story and lots of links to stuff that I have found useful or just fun![*]

In the past accounts like Ruth's may been presented to friends, family members, health care professionals and researchers. Sometimes labelled as 'lay referral' the significance of talk about symptoms and health has long been recognized. Freud saw the elicitation of patient narratives of their experiences as a way of understanding the meanings that symptoms have in their lives within the medical discipline. Lay narratives have had a significant place in research since the 1960s and a range of methodologies have been used to collect such material (Hardey 1998). These accounts are constructed

---

[*] This text has been constructed a to illustrate the content of home pages and draws on the study described in Hardey 2002a

in a particular context even when framed within an 'in-depth' and 'open' methodology to be transposed into 'data' by researchers. Other research is more reflexive and can be autobiographical. Frank (1991), for example, has described his heart attack and later cancer; Mapes (1977) showed how he manipulated the 'system' to treat his pneumothorax and Reiner (2000) has described his experience in an intensive care unit. These authors were able to lay claim to academic expertise and wrote about their experiences within the framework of their specialism. Less privileged individuals have only rarely been able to find a means of publishing their experiences before the development of the Internet.

Ruth's home page is distinct from the various illness narratives we have reviewed because it was designed by her to provide understanding and support for a potentially global audience of strangers. Like other personal home page authors Ruth provides information and advice to users who may need to make choices related to their own social and bodily problems and desires. In common with other health-related home pages she also provides an email address and asks readers to post their questions and evaluations of the content. This interactivity makes these pages a dynamic resource and a platform for support, advice and friendship that has commonly been associated with newsgroups and other forums.

Home pages represent a relatively stable presence on the Internet because, unlike newsgroups and other virtual spaces, the author of a web page has control over the content that is not arbitrarily removed, stored or fleeting (e.g. as in chat rooms). The closest analogy to a home page is the published book or article that similarly reaches an unknown readership. However, print publication is confined to those who have an expertise and can claim a potential market that is recognized by a publisher. Samuel Smiles's book *Self-Help* sold some 20,000 copies in the first year it was published in 1857. Written by a doctor, this was an early popular self-improvement text that linked bodily and mental fitness with success in a way that has been followed by many authors since. This reflects the prominence of the body in consumer culture and the mass market for guides to living and advice about self-improvement (Giddens 1991). It is unlikely that many home page authors would be able to (or desire to) add their material to this growing mass of print material. Not only does the Internet allow anyone with a few technical skills to publish, it also proves a far more versatile medium than the printing press. All users have open to them the same technology that enables them to use features that include sound, video and photographs within a web page design. Furthermore, they share the same potential global mass audience with state and other organizations that have traditionally broadcast large amounts of information.

Home page authors are less likely to be driven by the need to compile a large throughput of readers (or 'hits') for revenue or other purposes. This can make the identification of such pages difficult but those concerned to find information about a specific health or social problem may be able to follow hyperlinks through other pages or recommendations made in newsgroup exchanges. Users are therefore likely to be positively seeking out information about their particular problem rather than casually browsing the Internet. There is a similarity here with the way people traditionally seek out information about health or social issues. Family members may be asked about (or initially notice) symptoms that later form the focus for a medical or other consultation. Instead now people may go directly to Internet sites, whether authored by an organization or an individual, to find information on which to base their choices.

Lay expertise: newsgroups and chat rooms

Bulletin boards where users can post notes were part of the early development of the Internet and have evolved into a popular source of electronic sociability represented by Usenet newsgroups. These are arranged around specific topics and can be originated and accessed by any user. As with email users can view previous exchanges and contribute to them. There are newsgroups dedicated to almost every imaginable health or social problem. In the early part of 2000, it was estimated that approximately 30,000 people posted messages to newsgroups each day and that there were over one million passive readers.[3] Search engines or Usenet resources such as Deja News can identify specific newsgroups. They often have a moderator who may be a practitioner where the group has a distinct therapeutic purpose. Chat rooms, unlike newsgroups, allow the simultaneous typing and reading of text but are arranged in a similar manner around different topics. Recent technological innovations have promoted use of the graphically based avatar (virtual cartoon figures that can be chosen and controlled by users) as well as sound and video (Webb 2000). Chat rooms tend to be less 'problem' based than newsgroups but they also provide a forum for people to exchange ideas and beliefs about their situation. The text below is an edited copy of a longer exchange within a UK newsgroup focused on mental health issues[4]. Spelling, grammar and header information has been reproduced but the exchange has been rendered anonymous.

> From: David D<dd2875@mailco.net>
> Newsgroups: uk.people.support.mental-health
> Subject: Please help – Bad things will happen
> Date: 20 Oct 2000 14:11
>
> I have been suffering from chronic depression for 3 years – I have lost my job and am still signed off as incapable of work. I see a psychiatrist and a psychologist on a fairly regular basis. Over the past few weeks I am getting this really strong feeling that if I do something good something 'bad' will happen. This is so difficult to write but an example would be if I show my partner affection somewhere, in the near future, something will happen to pay me back for being nice or enjoying myself. It has got to the stage where I feel really really trapped. I can't eat 'nice' food – if I enjoy it there will be problems. I am existing off water and crackers. I know there is no logic or sense to how I feel – it is ridiculous and completely senseless yet…I really feel trapped, locked down, pinned to this circle. Is this a common complaint – have others suffered? How do you beat it? Can you beat it (I'm sure you can). I am so worried that my psychiatrist will want to admit me that I cannot tell her.
>
> David

> From: Mat Harris<planet372@hotmail.com>
> Newsgroups: uk.people.support.mental-health
> Subject: Re: Please help – Bad things will happen
> Date: 20 Oct 2000 18:12
>
> If you've been seeing these people for more than a few months then you are wasting your time and possibly money as well. There is no reason, with advances in therapy over the past 20 years, why you should need to see someone more than 8 times. You should notice a difference within a few sessions.
>
> Your therapist will, of course, disagree with this because they are paid by the hour, because of professional pride and also because this is what they're taught. They will come up with various excuses for their incompetence. Popular ones are:
>
> 1.   You aren't ready to change.
>
> 2.   Chemical imbalance.

3.   Genetics.

4.   Need to build up a therapeutic relationship over time.

5.   Your problem takes x amount of time to change.

1, 2 and 3 mean that (according to them) the psychiatrist can't help you anyway. 4 and 5 come from ignorance, or worse still, are lies.

I know some of you are compelled to see psychiatrists for various reasons outside of your control. That is another matter entirely.

> 'Over the past few weeks I am getting this really strong feeling that if I do something good something "bad" will happen.'

This is only over the past few weeks??

If so, the most likely possibility (based on what you wrote) is that you are an excellent hypnotic subject and that someone (probably one of your shrinks) has inadvertently suggested that you feel this way. Sounds crazy, doesn't it, but you wouldn't believe how often I get clients for this kind of thing. If this is the case, then you can get a complete cure from all your psychological problems from any vaguely competent hypnotherapist.

Next most likely is that some time in the past, something awful happened to you after you enjoyed yourself or was nice to someone. And that your mind made a connection between the two.

> 'I am so worried that my psychiatrist will want to admit me that I cannot tell her.'

Like I wrote earlier, if your psychiatrist hasn't been able to help you so far then there's little reason to believe she can help you with this either. So why tell her?

Mat

From: Paul L<base5673@btnet.com>
Newsgroups: uk.people.support.mental-health
Subject : Re: Please help – Bad things will happen
Date: 21 Oct 2000 20:40

You have no understanding of mental health problems at all have you?

Paul

The extract above represents a discussion between David D, Mat Harris and Paul L. These are pseudonyms, which hide the off-line identity of the users. Unlike face-to-face communication there are no visual or auditory cues to help assess strangers and few social inhibitions (see Goffman 1967). The anonymity provided by these spaces is important because it allows users to escape their embodied selves and the expectations and norms of off-line sociability. The embarrassment, awkwardness and risks in disclosing difficult or potentially stigmatizing experiences or behaviours associated with other social venues are much reduced. Such spaces also allow people to create 'second selves' and forge relationships unencumbered by physicality and locality, which may alone be therapeutic. In these virtual spaces people with conditions that may confine them to their home or bed can interact as 'normal' participants in Internet society. However, the lack of conventional social constraints and obligations has implications for the trust users may invest in the advice available in these environments (Turner, Grube and Meyres 2001).

Three categories of newsgroup or chat room participant can be discerned. First, what we can label the 'activist' are those who become engaged in the social life of this virtual space. They make frequent visits and the real or virtual identity that they adopt becomes well known to other participants. It is the behaviour of these activists that is important to the claim that the Internet constitutes a 'virtual community' (Rheingold 1994). Within this social environment activists are significant in shaping the interactions and some may construct their own newsgroup or home page. There are instances of health and social care professionals taking an activist role. However, outside of venues that have been designed with an explicit therapeutic purpose their position is uncertain. As activists in general newsgroups, they may not disclose their status out of concern for professional ethics or potential litigation. However, there is evidence that in newsgroups, such as those dedicated to alcohol problems, users who are identified as practitioners may be discouraged from active involvement (Muncer et al. 2000).

The second category of participants are those we can identify as 'traversers' who visit and may be quite active in the environment for a short period and leave. They are more interested in the content and potential advice offered within a newsgroup or chat room than the sense of community it may offer. When they have satisfied their information needs or found that these cannot be answered they move on to another part of the

Internet. Finally, there are passive users who have been more graphically described as 'lurkers'. A less pejorative label would be that of 'flâneur' which captures the way these users may occasionally join in the exchanges but are essentially happy to remain on the fringes of sociability. This apparent voyeuristic activity may reflect the voyeurism of contemporary culture and point to the potential danger of on-line health and welfare advice becoming another 'real life' media entertainment (like the Big Brother television series). More positively it has been argued that these resources constitute a new 'virtual community of care' (Burrows and Nettleton 2000). This suggests that the Internet may empower users of health and social services by providing alternative sources of information and advice to that offered by conventional sources and practitioners. Moreover, research in the US, for example, has shown that virtual communities are a significant source of support, advice and friendship, especially for more socially isolated older people (Wright 2000). It should be remembered that those who take on the role of, for example, activist in one virtual space may adopt that of traverser or flâneur in another context.

Home pages and newsgroups provide information that is potentially subversive of national regulations and professional practice. As a global medium it is easy for users to, for example, identify and exploit differences in the UK and US adoption of practices and regulations. The Internet also brings information and approaches to social and health problems into the same medium that may have a marginal, minority or controversial status elsewhere. For example, there is a proliferation of newsgroups and sites devoted to a vast range of complementary and alternative therapies. This reflects and reinforces their increased popularity especially in developing 'fit' bodies and 'stress free' lifestyles (Select Committee on Science and Technology 2000). Other newsgroups act as forums for information and advice about, for example, the Child Support Agency which may help some participants to circumvent the system.

Professional expertise: the state, commercial and voluntary sectors

NHS Direct Online is essentially an adjunct to the NHS Direct telephone advice service. It has no space for users to post advice, exchange ideas with other people or to contact specialist or service providers though email. Information may be displayed in a number of different languages and some voice-recorded messages are also available. The conservative nature of NHS

Direct Online reflects the need of state-sponsored resources to provide authoritative information and adhere fully to a variety of government and professional policies and guidelines (Loader 1998a). People seeking information about disease-based problems are assured of the clinical reliability of the information that is written from evidence-based material. At a local level an increasing number of medical practices have established Internet sites that provide information about surgery times and services with links to sites such as NHS Direct Online. Other government agencies such as the Public Health Laboratory Service have websites that disseminate the contents of printed information leaflets to users. Local authorities also provide Internet resources that publicize their services and offer information about social and health services. Again these are generally digital copies of paper-based information and do not allow any significant interactive or on-line service provision.

Like other western governments, the UK government has a variety of policies under the umbrella of 'e-government' that include proposals that health and social services will be available 'electronically' to users by 2005 (Department of Health 2000, Section 2, Paragraphs 2–3). This reflects the expectation that the Internet will become a major resource for public information and will potentially make available on-line application forms, the booking of appointments and the registering of complaints (Glastonbury and Gould 1996). However, the HMSO has a monopoly over Crown copyright, which restricts the free distribution of many state documents and contrasts with the US where there is no copyright over equivalent material. More broadly, this tension concerning free public access to material on the Internet has been played out for some years in academic institutions. Users can often read health and social care journals and other research information through the sites provided by universities. Some Internet journals are freely available to any user (e.g. *British Medical Journal*) while others do not allow full access to non-subscribers. There are also many freely available Internet-based journals that follow the same quality control systems long used in academic print journals (e.g. *Sociology Online*). Like universities, research councils and charities are increasingly using the Internet to communicate with the research community and to disseminate the findings of the work they fund.

The BBC OnLine site provides a considerable amount of clinical, health and social information. Less constrained by government policy than NHS Direct Online and able to draw on television and radio programmes the BBC site ranges across the spectrum of health and social care. It is also highly topical in that there are direct links to news stories and some sections offer users a degree of interactivity. For example, following a specific programme users may be able to ask on-line experts questions about the topic. This provides scope for campaigns such as the 'stop smoking' campaign run in 2000 that included radio, television and Internet advice with newsgroup support for smokers organized through the BBC website. Reflecting the content of broadcast media the boundaries between orthodox medicine and complementary and alternative approaches to health are blurred. As digital media develop there is potential for the divisions between these media to fall, as users are able to move from television programme to digital radio and the Internet without leaving their sofa. Indeed this is already possible across cable networks in some parts of the US and via satellite services (Schoech 1996).

Commercial medical sites continue to grow rapidly in the UK and elsewhere. These may be used as advertising media for health insurance, private medical and social care services and may include photographs of clinics, costs of treatments and details of clinical staff. In some cases appointments can be arranged through email; however, like state-sponsored resources, such sites offer few opportunities for interaction. The market-driven US health care system has generated a higher number of more complex and interactive health-related sites. Indeed, second medical opinions have become increasingly negotiated through the Internet alone. In a similar way pharmaceutical companies and sport and fitness centres have developed web resources that provide information and advertise services and products. Reflecting the diversity and plural nature of the consumption of health and lifestyle advice there are many resources that offer users 'new age' treatments for stress, diet and the management of emotions (Hardey 2002b).

There are a growing number of commercial medical sites in the UK that are attempting to deliver services through the integration of information communication and technologies. For example, the 'Pocket Doctor' has a conventional web page with information, a mechanism for sending material to WAP mobile phones and handheld computers as well as a premium rate phone line to a doctor.[5] This sort of facility represents a converging of technologies which can be chosen by the users to fit a lifestyle which demands instant, mobile and 24-hour access to health information. Some large companies provide health and fitness information to employees through in-house intranets. These allow individuals to build up their own health profiles and in some cases consult doctors and councillors.

The direct advertising of prescription drugs to consumers is prohibited in the UK but there is a rapidly expanding market in the US through which products can be sold to the rest of the world (Jenkins 1998). This means that pharmaceutical products that are not approved in one country can be advertized and purchased by residents through the Internet (although this may violate importation regulations). There is also a growing market for people seeking medical treatments in Eastern Europe and Asia that are far less expensive than within the private sector in the UK. In the UK and elsewhere doctors, nurses and others publish their own health information pages. Most focus on the particular interests of the author and may blur into the lay pages noted earlier when personal experience of illness is mixed in with professional advice. The Internet can therefore be a direct conduit for health and social care professionals to reach a global audience. However, there are ethical risks here as it is unclear how far a practitioner can (or should) provide information that may counter, for example, professional or institutional guidelines (Peacock 2001).

The voluntary sector covers a wide variety of organizations and includes international and national associations such as the Royal National Institute for the Blind (RNIB)[6] as well as small local groups. The use of the Internet largely reflects the size and campaigning power of the organization. Many charities make no or little active use of information and communications technologies although some groups share resources with local authorities and other organizations (Burt 2001). Two broad types of Internet presence can be identified. In the first type Internet resources may be devised to disseminate information about issues that concern the charity. The site for the mental health charity Mind[7], for example, provides descriptions of various mental health problems, available treatments, the obligations of health and social services to users and links to other Internet resources. Other sites are more interactive and provide chat rooms where users can interact with each other (e.g. National Schizophrenia Fellowship).[8] The second category of website is conceived of as primarily a campaigning tool. The Gulf War Syndrome web page, for example, publishes news, issues press notices and disseminates information to support the medical recognition in the UK of health problems experienced by ex-soldiers.[9]

Information and the dilemma of control

We have seen in the brief review of some of the main health and social care Internet resources that there is a diversity of forms of information, writers of information and readers of information. This contrasts with the closed knowledge base upon which professional expertise was founded. It also reflects a social change whereby the healthy body expresses and maintains a 'successful' lifestyle (Nettleton 1995; Shilling 1993; Turner 1995). What Baudrillard (1993) and other postmodern theorists have depicted as a social world engaged in an 'ecstasy of communication' includes new media with new ways of giving expression to individual fears and desires. The Internet has also given a new impetus to the long-established struggle over knowledge, information and expertise. This is manifest in the key medical debate about lay access to the Internet that is placed within a discourse about the 'quality' of information. Several organizations have developed mechanisms to evaluate and rate health-related Internet resources (e.g. HON Code, American Medical Association, Internet HealthCare Coalition, Hi-Ethics, MedCertain).[10] These follow more or less closely the hierarchy of evidence-based medical knowledge advocated by the Cochrane Centre and others. This confines positive ratings to medical sites and throws doubt on the veracity of, for example, complementary and alternative Internet resources. The site developed by a retired American psychiatrist aptly titled 'quackwatch'[11] follows the logic of this approach by condemning any Internet resources that are not based on evidence derived from randomly controlled trials (Vankevich 2002). Rating schemes remain largely dependent on voluntary self-assessments by web designers and clinicians, which has led to criticism about validity of their ratings (Kim *et al.* 1999).

Claims about altruism and the promotion of a culture that prioritizes the public interest and high quality, impartial service have been a central part of professional status (e.g. Parsons 1951). These are enshrined in the codes of practice of health and social care professions and form a key element of educational socialization into membership of the occupation (Crompton 1990; Harris 1989; Saks 1995). In effect, the public interest equates with a professional interest to define and maintain a sphere of expertise which others can access only through recourse to a recognized practitioner. The proliferation of information on the Internet represents a challenge to these professional monopolies. However, it would be simplistic to depict the concern about quality only in terms of professional self-interest. Research that has assessed medical information about specific conditions against established treatment protocols and guidelines suggests that many may not be wholly reliable even when distributed by medical institutions (Biermann, Golladay and Greenfield 1999; Griffiths and Christensen 2000). However, a dilemma here is the question of whose criteria it is appropriate to use to make such assessments. For example, a site originating in an Italian medical school will follow Italian rather than British or US protocols. Despite the debate about evidence-based practice in social work there has been no concerted attempt to establish an Internet content rating scheme like those found in medicine.

Bauman (2000) has noted that the appearance of 'ordinary' people on chat shows and reality television who, unlike experts or celebrities, share ordinary life with the viewers, may allow us to 'learn something *useful* from their victories and defeats alike' (p.68). Information within newsgroups and home pages is significant and useful to users because it presents embodied accounts of conditions, treatments and experiences that transcend an increasingly specialized and fractured expert knowledge system. It is this difference from professional expertise that is valued by both readers and writers of Internet information. The fact that the application of professionally developed scientific quality criteria would marginalize such resources is not relevant. This highlights the problem of the 'reality' of the experiences that are published on the Internet. The home page of a teenager in the US, who had leukaemia, took the form of a 'weblog' which she used to record her experiences over two years until she died. Her home page diary received many visitors and was discussed in newsgroups as people offered emotional and other support. However, the whole story was a complete fabrication. The fiction was created by a woman who was an active participant in newsgroups and chat rooms who initially adopted the virtual identity of the teenager as one of a number of Internet identities. A number of on-line support groups then sprang up where people could discuss their sense of betrayal in the wake of her unmasking.[12]

The space provided by the Internet is one within which people can remain anonymous and derive satisfaction from the disembodied interactions that take place. It is also a space that is strangely intimate, where experiences can be shared and feelings explored in ways not possible in other media. This highlights the way users may invest misplaced trust in the nature of the information they read. As the concern with quality criteria indicates, material on the Internet is not neatly or universally classified so that users can quickly identify a work of, for example, fiction from autobiography or journalism. Novels, films and the theatre have helped people to come to terms with difficult circumstances or enabled an audience to understand what it is like to cope with health or social problems. The 'reality' of, for example, a novel is not questioned because readers are clear about its status. However, it may draw on the author's experiences and, like narratives about health, seek to explain feelings and emotions to readers (see Bury 2001). This suggests that we need to focus attention on how people use the Internet and gain insights into how users select resources that shape their decisions and choices.

Conclusion

Within health and social care policy the Internet continues to be viewed as a means to promote the empowerment of users and support the seamless delivery of care. However, state resources are massively outnumbered by commercial, charitable and individual health and social care material that is available across the globe. As we have seen these include personal home pages, interactions in newsgroups and chat rooms, on-line consultations, the sale of pharmaceutical and alternative medicines, routes into international adoption and so forth. Samuel Smiles could never have imagined the contemporary mass consumer market for body maintenance, self-help and self-improvement. However, this market is orientated to those who have the cultural capital, financial resources and time to invest in their lifestyle to support their changing sense of self. This points to class-based differences that shape life chances and the extent to which opportunities and constraints are perceived and addressed. The Internet may not overturn or offer to lessen social and cultural differences and inequalities. Ownership of a computer and home access to the Internet is unusual in poorer communities although the relative income of new UK Internet users is decreasing (Foley 1999). Given the acknowledged association between poverty, sickness and use of social welfare services this information gap or 'digital divide' is a serious problem for those who advocate the Internet as an approach to creating greater social equality (Social Exclusion Policy Action Team 2001; see Please *et al.* in this volume). Moreover, as English is the predominate language used on the Internet, it can be forgotten that those who have no knowledge of the language are effectively excluded from most of the resources available (Berland 2001; Jorden 2001).

In his novel *The Constant Gardener* John le Carré (2000) coined the objurgation 'Big Pharma' to describe western pharmaceutical companies.

His novel revolves around the activities of companies which are engaged in testing new drugs in Africa that were too costly to be used on the continent. In April 2001 in the face of international criticism of 'Big Pharma' the Pharmaceutical Manufacturers Association dropped their case against the South African government's use of cheap AIDS drugs. Fiction had helped to shape the debate and outcome of a major international debate about health care.

As we have seen, a central debate about advice and information offered to users on the Internet concerns the 'quality' of material; this reflects a broader discourse about evidence-based practice. Framed in a concern to protect the public the mission of a number of organizations is to rate Internet information against an evidence-based gold standard. State-sponsored or authored sites are constrained by a concern not to stray from what is judged to be safe for users to read and not to deviate from current health or social care policy. In contrast, personal home pages may include elements of autobiography, fiction, pleas for understanding, exhortations, self-promotion and so forth. The extract from Ruth's home page and the text from the newsgroup can be deconstructed in any way the reader desires. In doing this the reader will reflect and use his or her experiences and the text in ways which may inform or shape his or her understanding of illness, young people or western society. In a similar way visitors to newsgroups or chat rooms are seeking information and advice to help them understand issues that involve their own or others' health and lifestyles. They may also contribute to the debates and construct their own web page to help others to share problems and support each other. Such information may closely reflect real lived experiences and expertise in a health or social problem or may be a more imaginative interpretation of events. However, fiction can inform and shape understandings about difficult health and social problems.

Lay narratives have always been central to health and social work research and practice. Following the Parsonian model (Parsons 1951), they constitute the raw material which experts use to uncover appropriate explanations or solutions. This is challenged by theoretical approaches that view accounts of individual problems and experiences as 'true' and as having meaning which does not need to be verified or interpreted through medical or other expert knowledge. This recognizes the expertise of users and recasts the lay–expert relationship as a dialectical one where shared explanations and courses of action are constructed. Such a user-centred approach has led some to argue that the general explanatory theories of modernity should be replaced in social work by local narratives (Parton 1998). However, a shift in the governance of professionals from a focus on practice within quality assurance frameworks to instrumental surveillance through audit strategies imposes a hierarchy of knowledge that leaves little space for negotiation or discretion.

There are tensions around the issues of increasing control and surveillance of health and social care professionals, and the expectation of many practitioners and patients of a dialectic relationship where their expertise is recognized remains (Beresford 2000; Smith 2001). Moreover, users who have gained information, advice and confidence from the Internet may challenge the authority of health and social care practitioners (Hardey 1999). As Giddens (1991) suggests, the Internet may provide the means for a partial or full-blown reskilling of lay users. As consumers of expertise we may not be willing to trust a system that fails to justify itself through reasoned dialogue. If we all at times make claims to expertise in some specialist area of knowledge we also take the lay role when we need to use other expertise. Identifying and using information and advice from the Internet and other sources may become a taken-for-granted part of self-reflexivity. The increasing fluidity of lay–expert relationships not only challenges many professional and institutional expectations but also creates opportunities to forge a genuine 'meeting of minds'.

The Internet can be used to promote user involvement in case management in social work and partnership in health care. Combined with the increased opportunities for self-help and support offered by the Internet this reinforces the reconfiguration of lay expertise. The context for this is the diversity and extent of information available on the Internet that draws attention to the way that scientifically informed expertise is essentially social, fluid and emergent. This is a characteristic of what Beck (1992) has described as the 'risk society' and has been given added poignancy by a series of well-publicized accounts of the failure of professionals to act in the public interest (e.g. the illegitimate removal and storage of organs, and even the mass murder of patients). If ambiguity and uncertainty, intimacy and estrangement are central to contemporary social life, these characteristics are reflected in the Internet. This poses major challenges and opportunities to all who consume or produce health and social care information, advice and services.

References

Baudrillard, J. (1993) *Symbolic Exchange and Death*. London: Sage.

Bauman, Z. (2000) *Liquid Modernity*. Cambridge: Polity Press.

Beck, U. (1992) *Risk Society. Towards a New Modernity*. London: Sage.

Beresford, P. (2000) '"Service users" knowledge and social work theory: conflict or collaboration.' *British Journal of Social Work 30*, 4, 489–504.

Berland, G. K. (2001) 'Health information on the Internet: accessibility, quality and readability in English and Spanish.' *Journal of the American Medical Association 285*, 2612–2621.

Biermann, S. G., Golladay, M. L. and Greenfield, L. B. (1999) 'Evaluation of cancer information on the internet.' *Cancer 86*, 3, 381–390.

Burrows, R., Nettleton, S., Pleace, N., Loader, B. and Muncer, S. (2000) 'Virtual community care? Social policy and the emergence of computer mediated social support.' *Information Communication and Society 3*, 1, 23–31.

Burt, E. (2001) 'When "virtual" meets values: insights from the voluntary sector.' *Information, Communication and Society 4*, 1, 231–309.

Bury, M. (2001) 'Illness narratives: fact or fiction.' *Sociology of Health and Illness 23*, 3, 263–285.

Crawford, R. (1987) 'Cultural influences on prevention and the emergence of a new health consciousness.' In N. Weinstein (ed) *Taking Care: Understanding and Encouraging Self-Protective Behaviour*. Cambridge: Cambridge University Press.

Crompton, R. (1990) 'Professions in the current context.' *Work, Employment and Society: Special Issue* 34–68.

Department of Health (1999) *Modernising Social Services*. London: The Stationary Office.

Department of Health (2000) *Information for Social Care*. London: HMSO.

Ehrenreich, B. (1990) *The Fear of Falling: The Inner Life of the Middle Class*. New York: Harper Perennial.

Featherstone, M. (1990) *Consumer Culture and Postmodernism*. London: Sage.

Featherstone, M. and Burrows, R. (1995) 'Cultures of technological embodiment: an introduction.' *Body and Society 1*, 3–4, 1–20.

Foley, P. (1999) *Whose Net? Characteristics of Internet Users in the UK*. London: Department of Trade and Industry.

Frank, A. (1991) *The Will of the Body*. Chicago: University of Chicago Press.

Giddens, A. (1991) *Modernity and Self-Identity*. Cambridge: Polity Press.

Giddens, A. (1994) *Beyond Left and Right*. Cambridge: Polity Press.

Glastonbury, B. and Gould, N. (1996) 'United Kingdom.' In D. Steyaert, D. Colombi and J. Rafferty (eds) *Human Services and Information Technology: An International Perspective*. Aldershot: Arena.

Goffman, E. (1967) *Interaction Ritual*. Harmondsworth: Penguin Books.

Griffiths, K. M. and Christensen, H. (2000) 'Quality of web based information of depression: cross sectional survey.' *British Medical Journal 321*, 1875–1879.

Hardey, M. (1998) *The Social Context of Health.* Buckingham: Open University Press.

Hardey, M. (1999) 'Doctor in the house.' *Sociology of Health and Illness 12*, 6, 820–835.

Hardey, M. (2001) 'E-health: the Internet and transformation patients into consumers and producers of health knowledge.' *Information, Communication and Society 4*, 1.

Hardey, M. (2002a) '"The story of my illness": personal accounts of illness on the Internet.' *Health: An Interdisciplinary Journal for the Social Study of Health, Illness and Medicine 6*, 1, 31–46.

Hardey, M. (2002b) 'Health for sale: quackery, consumerism and the Internet.' In W. Ernst (ed) *Plural Medicine, Tradition and Modernity 1800–2000.* London: Routledge.

Harris, N. (1989) *Professional Codes of Conduct in the United Kingdom: A Directory.* London: Mansell.

Jenkins, H. W. (1998) 'Is advertising the new wonder drug?' *Wall Street Journal,* 25 March, A23.

Jewson, N. (1976) 'The disappearance of the sick man from medical cosmology.' *Sociology 10*, 2, 255–274.

Jorden, T. (2001) 'Language and libertarianism: The politics of cyberculture and the culture of cyberpolitics.' *Sociological Review 49*, 1, 1–17.

Kim, P., Eng, T. R., Deering, M. J. and Maxfield, A. (1999) 'Published criteria for evaluating health related Web sites: review.' *British Medical Journal 318*, 647–649.

le Carré, J. (2000) *The Constant Gardener.* London: Hodder and Stoughton.

Loader, B.D. (1998a) 'Welfare direct: informatics and the emergence of self-service welfare?' In J. Cater (ed) *Postmodernity and the Fragmentation of Welfare.* London: Routledge.

Loader, B. D. (ed) (1998b) *The Cyberspace Divide.* London: Routledge.

Mapes, R. (1977) 'Patient manipulation of the system: an ethno-biographic account.' In A. Davis and G. Horobin (eds) *Medical Encounters: The Experience of Illness and Treatment.* New York: St Martin Press.

Mulrow, C. D. (1994) 'Systematic reviews: rational for systematic reviews.' *British Medical Journal 309*, 597–599.

Muncer, S., Burrows, R., Pleace, N., Loader, B. and Nettleton, S. (2000) 'Births, deaths, sex and marriage…but very few presents? A case study of social support in cyberspace.' *Critical Public Health 10*, 1, 1–16.

Nettleton, S. (1995) *The Sociology of Health and Illness.* Cambridge: Polity Press.

Parsons, T. (1951) *The Social System.* London: Routledge (1991 edition).

Parsons, T. (1978) 'Health and disease: a sociological and action perspective.' In T. Parsons (ed) *Action Theory and the Human Condition.* New York: Free Press.

Parton, N. (1998) 'Risk, advanced liberalism and child welfare: the need to rediscover uncertainty and ambiguity.' *British Journal of Social Work 28*, 2, 5–28.

Peacock, D. (2001) 'Legal aspects of developing a web site: a practitioner's viewpoint.' *He@lth Information on the Internet 21*, June, 7–8.

Reiner, D. A. (2000) 'The missing voice of the critically ill: a medical sociologist's first-person account.' *Sociology 22*, 1, 68–93.

Rheingold, H. (1994) *The Virtual Community: Finding Connection in a Computerised World.* London: Secker and Warburg.

Saks, M. (1995) *Professions and the Public Interest.* London: Routledge.

Schoech, D. (1996) 'America (USA).' In R. Steyaert, D. Colombi and J. Rafferty (eds) *Human Services and Information Technology: An International Perspective.* Aldershot: Arena.

Select Committee on Science and Technology (2000) *Complementary and Alternative Medicine. Sixth Report.* London: Stationary Office.

Shilling, C. (1993) *The Body and Social Theory.* London: Sage.

Smiles, M. (1857) *Self-help.* Oxford: Oxford University Press (2002 edition)

Smith, C. (2001) 'Trust and confidence: possibilities for social work in "high modernity".' *British Journal of Social Work 31*, 287–395.

Social Exclusion Policy Action Team (2001) *Closing the Digital Divide: Information and Communication Technologies in Deprived Areas.* London: Department of Trade and Industry. http://www.pat15.org.uk.

Turner, B. S. (1995) *Medical Power and Social Knowledge.* London: Sage (second edition).

Turner, J. W., Grube, J. A. and Meyres, J. (2001) 'Developing an optimal match within online communities.' *Journal of Communication 51*, 2, 231–251.

Vankevich, N. (2002) 'Limiting pluralism: medical scientism, quackery and the Internet.' In W. Ernst (ed) *Plural Medicine, Tradition and Modernity 1800–2000.* London: Routledge.

Webb, S. A. (2000) 'Avatar culture: narrative power and identity in virtual world environments.' *Information, Communication and Society 4*, 1, 56–74.

Webb, S. A. (2001) 'Some considerations on the validity of evidence-based practice in social work.' *British Journal of Social Work 31*, 1, 57–80.

Weber, M. (1976 [1904]) *The Protestant Ethic and the Spirit of Capitalism.* London: Allen Unwin.

Wright, K. (2000) 'Computer-mediated social support, older adults and coping.' *Journal of Communication 50*, 3, 100–118.

Endnotes

These sites were visited in September 2001. They may have considerably changed or moved to another URL since this time.

1.   http://www.nhsdirect.nhs.uk
2.   http://www.angelfire.com/on/teenfms/mystory.html
3.   http://netscan.research.microsoft.com/netscan/
4.   uk.people.support.mental-health
5.   http://www.pocketdoctor.co.uk
6.   http://www.rnib.org.uk/

7.   http://www.mind.org.uk/
8.   http://www.nsf.org.uk
9.   http://www.gulfveteransassociation.co.uk/
10. http:// www.hon.ch/HONcode; http://www.ama-assn.org;
     http://www.ihealthcoalition.org; http:// www.hiethics.com;
     http://www.dermis.net/aks/medcertain.html
11. http://www.quackwatch.com
12. http://groups.yahoo.com/group/kaycee-nicole

Technologies of Care

Stephen A. Webb

Much of what we know about the caring professions and welfare provision is open to question. The categories that seemed so natural are either rapidly converging or breaking up in one long stream of re-organization and new legislation. Policies on information technology often mirror *laissez-faire* approaches to the public sector. Inevitably, new information and communication technologies (ICTs) will come to have a decisive role in the complex field of transformations that are taking place in the caring professions. Niklas Luhmann (1998), one of the most sophisticated of contemporary social theorists, suggested that we live in an advanced modern age where factors that are not relevant to technological functioning have very little significance. Technology is always implicated in power relations and conceptions about our social identities. Speculation about the impact of ICTs, the 'Net' (the Internet and potentially associated networks), and its most rapidly developing dimension, the 'Web' (the World Wide Web), are symptoms and components of a broader reshaping of politics, economy, and culture. These changes challenge many of the categories within which we have previously thought about the shape and meaning of society and its future.

Governance and technologies of care

Of particular interest is the way in which new technologies interact with, and form part of, an assemblage of technologies of human governance – in short, the political dimension of technologies of ICTs and knowledge. This kind of exposition entails a conceptualization of governance as specific ways of intervening, shaping, regulating and directing the lives of people, through particular types of practical rationality (professional skills, expertise, knowledge, values), and by relying upon specific instruments, technologies and techniques of intervention, to shape behaviour. This shaping or standard-setting can take place either at a distance, as with health care telematics, or in close proximity, as in monitoring parenting skills through computer simulation exercises in family centres. In terms of health and social care these can be understood as 'technologies of care'. The work of Nikolas Rose (1999) and Dean Mitchell (1999) is crucial in the fashioning of this analysis. Rose's ground-breaking *Powers of Freedom* is highly suggestive for the analyses of changes in governance that are currently taking place in health and social care. It will be shown how strategies of governance produce reality through 'rituals of truth' and create a particular style of subjectivity to which one conforms or which one resists. Because individuals are assimilated within these forms of subjectivity they become part of its normalizing force. Social care, for instance, is not an unconditional right but is often dependent on the demonstration of moral improvement by service users. Governmentality (a neologism for governmental rationality) also includes a growing body of expert knowledge that presents itself as 'scientific' or 'technological' and which contributes to the power of human governance.

In the following, Rose (1999) makes the important link between governmentality and technologies of social regulation:

> Technologies of government are those technologies imbued with aspirations for the shaping of conduct in the hope of producing certain desired effects and averting certain undesired effects. A technology of government, then, is an assemblage of forms of practical knowledge, with modes of perception, practices of calculation, types of authority, forms of judgement, architectural forms, human capacities, non-human objects and devices, and so forth, traversed and transected by aspirations to achieve certain outcomes in terms of the conduct of the governed... Technologies are not realizations of any single will to govern. (pp.52–53).

Health policy in the form of medical preventive strategies can be understood from this technology of care perspective. Here the objectives are to reduce dangerousness or risks and the means are the shaping of people's motives, feelings of being clean and unclean, and their concepts of the healthy life. This is not just a question of implementing forms of knowledge; such means also appeal to feelings and models of identification. As a rationality of government this is a way of thinking, capable of making some form of that health-oriented activity thinkable and practicable both to the practitioners and to those upon whom it is practised. Technologies of care in health sow the seeds of judgement and invite normalizing prescriptions about what is acceptable and unacceptable in diagnosing health. In the US there are a number of privatized health care companies who go by names such as 'Total Care Technologies', 'Care Technologies Inc', 'Managed Care Technologies' and 'Patient Care Technologies'(see www.total-care.com/ and www.caretechnologies.com/).

Ethical issues at both a personal and professional level are not divorced from these technologies of care. Such ethical issues need to be located with what Dreyfus and Rabinow (1982) aptly call 'our regulative and welfare-oriented understanding of reality' (p.15). Care is implicated in what we can know about others and ourselves. It operates in a space that includes elements of both the official governmental and policy-making instruments, as well as in legitimizing norms of professional intervention. It is likely that the concept of care would not have emerged, either as an institutionalized professional practice or as a measure of the moral veracity of personal relations, without a corresponding change in definitions of subjectivity and liberal morality (see McBeath and Webb 1997). Liberal morality is inextricably linked to the activities of doctors, planners, teachers, social workers and managers. Its ethics of conduct are centred on the power to define appropriate and inappropriate behaviour and set the standards of what is considered normal. Thus, in our modern context, ethical conduct, our caring for and being cared for by others, becomes nearly impossible to disentangle from how power in its modern form operates.

Technical rationality as a technology of governance

'Social informatics' is the body of research that examines the design, uses, and consequences of information and communication technologies in ways that take into account their interaction with institutional and cultural contexts (see Kling 2000). In line with this, how is professional development in health and social care shaped by, and mediated through, new ICTs? There is, however, a more complex and challenging question that might be considered. The majority of studies of ICTs tend to focus narrowly on their impact, which seems one-dimensional. It is not very helpful to focus on the impact of ICTs in isolation because this kind of approach is blind to the real complexity of multi-causal change and influences. Influences do not occur naturally but are selectively produced within a matrix of multiple indices in order to realize some socially or politically defined goals. We know in the sciences, for example, that the practice of twentieth-century biology changed under the influence of physics rather than through its own internal dynamics (see Keller 1993). In consequence we have to ask, how do ICTs combine and configure with the wider complex of socio-cultural developments and formations?

Changes that are occurring in health and social care are best understood in terms of a newly fashioned configuration of forces set in motion by the dominance of a novel type of technical rationality. The configuration is formed through the cross-connections of interrelated and equivocal associations between ICTs, evidence-based practice, risk assessment and management, knowledge management, care management, decision regulation, performance frameworks and the hardening of protocols for standardized practice. These operations lead to a play of dependencies and correlations in order to fulfil the politics of technical rationality within a neo-liberal political agenda. Taken together, these might be usefully understood as 'new technologies of health and social care'. These new technologies of care – with ICTs as the central information hub – increasingly come to colonize policy making and front-line practice in welfare services. This new configuration is described as technological because it refers to aspects of practice which can be characterized in certain specific ways. Crucially they are end-oriented practices implying an underlying rationality or what Max Weber called purposive-rational (*zweckrational*). Practitioners and service users are expected to look at the world technologically, that is, to see it either as resources to be used or constraints to be overcome. Care planning, pathways and packages typically resemble this kind of end-oriented thinking about the social world. Simpson (1995) summarizes the step-by-step process of technological reasoning as follows:

> We can characterize the way that technology addresses its problems in the following way: a need is made explicit, or an opportunity, made available, by scientific or perhaps other technological developments, is articulated within the context of the need or opportunity, a clear and determinate goal is specified; the major steps to be taken and the major pieces of work to be done are identified; the plan is constantly made responsive to 'feedback' from the result of the work; and typically, the work is

organized so that each major segment is apportioned within a division of labour. This way of putting it highlights the important point that the end technology seeks to realize as efficiently and effectively as possible is one that is specified and determined beforehand. It further highlights the importance of planning, or of the rational orchestration of procedure, to the technological enterprise. (p.15)

This kind of rational planning and problem solving characterizes the very stuff of health and social care. Interventions in health and social care mimic this technological way of conceiving how an individual life should be codified, adjusted, modified and determined. On top of solution-focused, task and crisis-centred interventions, each of which specifies a desired outcome beforehand, an additional layer of new technologies of care have come into play, for example, evidence-based practice, knowledge management, decision pathways, and risk assessment (see Webb 2001). Taken together, this technical configuration of care comes to harden the remit of technical rationality and purposive rational action as a way of reframing expert interventions. Thus, the choice of means or methods of care is becoming more and more subject to the outcome of rational calculation: that is, it is increasingly becoming quantitatively determined in health and social care. This led Ellul (1967) to conclude that technological progress is now conditioned by nothing other than its own calculus of efficiency.

Health and social care are deeply implicated in the logic of this technical rationality. As part of this technology of care 'best practice' models of planning have grown enormously over the past decade. There is even an American nursing profession website, which is 'dedicated to address the entire care planning process including assessment, planning, implementation and evaluation as defined in the nursing process' (see http://www.careplans.com/pro/default.asp). Care planning adheres to this rationalist conception in that it involves separating knowledge from action. Conduct is conceived as 'grounded' in the systematic knowledge generated through rule-following procedures (e.g. identifying goals, setting standards of behaviour, proposing lines of action, estimating consequences and predicting outcomes), whereby practitioners or service users follow a predetermined and regulated model (e.g. an assessment model). Care planning generally involves an attempt to represent in systematic, rational terms the rules that should be followed to bring about certain effects in the lives of service users. Today the 'feedback' that Simpson talks of is written in the fashionable terms of stakeholder or service user involvement.

For some, ICTs are the ultimate planners' utopia in that they offer a projection of rational and effective planning, through the development of information systems and streamed data generation (see McBeath and Webb 2000). Some believe that ICTs will remove subjective bias and error in planning and assessment and that they will provide, for example, in decision analysis, for a full deliberative rationality, that is, a full account of the relevant facts after a careful consideration of the consequences. However, full deliberation cannot be more substantive than the premises from which it sets out. Therefore, planning decisions, which are subject to the endless flows and contingencies of time, are always likely to be contaminated by the limited information that is (narrowly) determined beforehand.

Health and social care planning is, however, not a flawless method for producing desired ends or even consent about the processes of intervention. Expert planners often fail to achieve their stated goals. Various plausible explanations for planning failures can be suggested. Planning is likely to be flawed because it relies on gathering 'adequate information' about the subjects of planning. Nevertheless, even with the most extensive efforts possible, there will always be an underestimated residue, which works imperceptibly to upset the implementation of plans. This is the 'beyond' of planning and may be called, in a general sense, 'political technology'. The rationality of planning can never achieve perfect information, and as such can never be entirely successful, because the individual and social work does not behave in a rational way. Social life itself is not properly the object of a plan. Care planning can be seen as one mechanism of the application of instrumental reason, which functions as a colonizing ideology. Habermas (1970) described the ability of instrumental reason to 'colonize' the 'lifeworld'. What this means is that the application of instrumental reason tends to negate, ignore and conquer alternative epistemologies. As can be seen in the drive towards evidence-based practice in health (through the National Institute of Clinical Excellence) and in social care (through the Social Care Institute for Excellence) only certain types of knowledge are permissible and only certain sorts of evidence will count in directing decision making.

The rise of actuarialism in welfare provision

There is a further complementary reading of these changes in health and social care that draws attention to the convergence of technical rationality with a politico-economic rationality that can be termed 'actuarialism'. This supporting analysis locates organizational changes in health and social care within the political programme of neo-liberalism. Crucially, the neo-liberal agenda problematized the welfare state and its key organizational components of bureaucracy, rigidity and centralization. It sought an extension of market rationality to all spheres of welfare society by focusing on individual choice, responsibility and efficiency. The political programme of neo-liberalism was initiated during the Thatcherite era of the early 1980s. It was particularly concerned with reducing 'welfare dependency' and curtailing professional power and autonomy in the public sector. More broadly, the major problem for social policy within the neo-liberal framework was not the anti-social effects of the economic market, but the anti-competitive effects of welfare society. As such, it advocated a kind of possessive and consumer individualism that systematically undermined traditional values of social solidarity and the common good. As Rose (1999) argues, neo-liberalism does not seek to govern through 'society', but through the deregulated choices of individual citizens, now construed as subjects of choices and aspirations to self-actualization and self-fulfilment. (See Ferguson 2001 for a version of this in social work, as encapsulated by the notion of 'life politics'.)

In the push towards neo-liberalism the welfare state comes to be seen as a liability as well as an economic luxury. In consequence, new measures such as the purchaser–provider split in health and social care were introduced. A key theme running through the neo-liberal agenda is that the welfare state is vulnerable to loss of authority and deference in advanced liberal societies (see Yudice 1995). Both government and service users have lost trust and faith in public sector professionals. Decisions made by social workers, nurses, teachers and medical doctors are increasingly challenged by sophisticated and sceptical service users. The gap between lay persons and experts has narrowed as consumer-oriented service users access their own expert technologies such as the Internet. New measures of accountability and performance become part of the governance of health and social care expertise. It is, perhaps, in response to the narrowing of the expert–lay gap and the burgeoning blame culture that ever more 'expert' technologies, preferably based on a more credible 'scientific rationality', are advanced to try to shore up fragile professional identities and public confidence.

As Colin Gordon (1991) has recognized, policy makers adopting a neo-liberal perspective propose that:

individual life be structured as the pursuit of a range of different enterprises, a person's relation to his or her self, his or her professional activity, personal property, environment, are all to be given the ethos and structure of the enterprise form. (p.42)

In plain terms, neo-liberalism marks the advent of the 'entrepreneurial self' interspersed in all walks of life. Direct payments made to adults in need of care are one very spectacular example of this mentality of the entrepreneurial self at work in social care. Here, service users design their own care packages, advertise, and interview and agree contract terms with potential service providers. They select and recruit 'personal assistants' who are issued with job specifications, their day-to-day management (e.g. time sheets, rotas and supervision) and make payments to them. The advanced liberal programme of governance constructs politics not through normative appeals to the greater good of society, but through the rational ordering of the calculating, private choices of entrepreneurial individuals (see Culpitt 1999, p.72). According to Leah Lievrouw (1998) communication using information technology mirrors this neo-liberal individualizing tendency. It encourages social separatism and parochialism, it inhibits the negotiation of disputes, and emphasizes competing interests. She describes the development of an 'heterotopic communication' in which we resort to our 'own devices', both in the sense of our personal agendas, strategies, interests, and interpretations, and in the sense of the ICT tools that help us realize them. In its path towards global dominance, the neo-liberal programme is increasingly circumventing new social movements based on disability, gender, ethnicity and environment. Taken together, this has led many theorists to argue that the 'death of the social' is no longer a proposition but an established fact in the world of possessive individualism (see Hindess 1997; Reddy 1996). Perhaps it is now accurate to say that we have entered the era of neo-liberal social care, rather than an era of liberal-humanist social work.

O'Malley (2000) extends these arguments to risk in his critique of neo-liberalism. He says that we have entered an era of neo-liberalism in which risk management is the dominant strategy for the governance of health and social care. This strategy is circular because the increasing accumulative effect of 'manufactured uncertainties' results in risk management being continuously undermined and then having to be renewed under new technologies of care. Expert systems crack under the weight of their own internal inconsistencies and the pressures of a deepening blame culture. The resultant effect leads to what O'Malley (1996) calls an 'enterprising prudentialism' in which stakeholders, service users and consumers become sovereign. O'Malley claims that risk management is increasingly tied to the desires and fears of consumer driven service users, who are constantly sampled by *ad hoc* surveys and focus groups to inform the way in which health and social care should be provided. Within the neo-liberal context an actuarial technology of risk practice develops out of this trend. O'Malley tells us:

> The prudent subjects of neo-liberalism should practice and sustain their autonomy by assembling information, materials and practices together into a personalized strategy that identifies and minimizes their exposure to harm. Such risk management is increasingly associated with access to statistical or actuarial technologies and expert advice that render measurable the probabilistic calculation of future harms… These precise forms of predictive calculation are only possible to the extent that the future is imagined to repeat the past. (O'Malley 2000, p.465)

Actuarial practice as a form of social insurance against risk is dependent on new technologies of care, as well as on new forms of subjectivity and methodologies of life planning. Francois Ewald (1991) defines the rationality of this emerging schema as follows:

> As a technology of risk, insurance is first and foremost a schema of rationality, a way of breaking down, rearranging, ordering certain elements of reality… One insures against accident through the probability of loss of some good. Insurance through the category of risk, objectifies every event as a potential accident. Insurance's general model is a game of chance. (p.199)

Within the neo-liberal context, direct service provision of social care increasingly comes to resemble a geometry of hazard, accident and risk. The new technologies are methodological variants of this changing geometry of heath and social care. What passes for face-to-face contact with service users increasingly takes the form of insurance against risk via the development of actuarialism. As Jock Young (1999) has argued:

> A major motif of social control in late modern society is actuarialism… This involves a transition to mores where there is no longer so much a concern with justice as with community defence and protection and where causes of crime and deviance are not seen as the vital clue to the

solution to the problem of crime. The actuarial stance is calculative of risk; it is wary and probabilistic; it is not concerned with causes but with probabilities, not with justice but with harm minimization. It does not seek a world free of crime but rather one where the best practices of damage limitation have been put in place; not a utopia but a series of gated havens in a hostile world. The actuarial stance reflects the fact that risk both to individuals and collectivities has increased, crime has become a normalized part of everyday life, the offender is seemingly everywhere in the street and in high office, within the poor parts of town but also in those institutions which were set up to rehabilitate and protect, within the public world of encounters with strangers but also within the family itself in relationships between husband and wife and parent and child. We are wary of scoutmasters, police officers, hitchhikers, babysitters, people who care for the elderly, husbands, dates, stepfathers and stepmothers; the 'other' is everywhere and not restricted to criminals and outsiders. Its causes are increasingly unsure and this uncertainty is compounded by its seeming ubiquitousness. (p.392)

New technologies of care, as they are moulded within the remit of actuarial culture, help to recast the nature of individual, family and community problems, as well as the purpose of welfare provision and intervention. These technologies are likely to entail an intensification of the government of conduct for the poorest members of society, the underclass and socially excluded. They aim to reshape moral and social responsibility, but do so within the respectable aura of expert objectivity. This is typical of neo-liberal Blairite rhetoric in the UK. In New Labour's New Deal policies, those who refuse to become responsible, to govern themselves ethically, or refuse to become active members of some imagined community, are penalized. For such morally irresponsible individuals harsh measures are considered entirely appropriate, and as Rose (1999) puts it, 'Three strikes and you're out: citizenship becomes conditional upon conduct' (p. 267).

Not only do new technologies of care account for changing face-to-face relations with service users, but also they account for the amount and type of work undertaken (Harlow 2002). Direct work, especially that involving in-depth intervention, is redefined along lines of resource or cost units in health and social care. It is likely that the amount of direct work with clients will decline in the caring professions as actuarial practice tightens its grip on the organizational remit. A visit to your local GP is enough to give a sense of this actuarial rationality at work. On entering the consulting room, one usually discovers the GP glued to the flat-face screen computer interface. An occasional sideways glance may be offered whilst you narrate your symptoms. The relevant data, bringing the computerized medical records up to date, is keyed in. In his essay 'From dangerousness to risk', Robert Castel (1991) makes the following very telling observation:

> I would like to put forward a line of reflection on the preventive strategies of social administration which are currently being developed, most notably in the United States and France, and which seem to me to depart in a profoundly innovatory way from the traditions of mental medicine and social work. The innovation is this. The new strategies dissolve the notion of the *subject* or a concrete individual, and put in its place a combinatory of factors, *the factors of risk*. Such a transformation carries important practical implications. The essential component of intervention no longer takes the form of the direct face-to-face relationship between the carer and the cared, the helper and the helped, the professional and the client. It comes instead to reside in the establishing of *flows of populations* based on the collation of a range of abstract factors deemed liable to produce risk. (p.281)

Medical and health care professionals have endured this actuarial culture for some time now, largely because it sits very comfortably with models of forensic science and clinical governance. GiRAffe (Generic Integrated Risk Assessment for Forensic Environments), for example, is a self-funded project developed by Julian Fuller, a consultant clinical psychologist at the Forensic Psychiatric Service at Langdon Hospital, London, which is the original pilot site. It is an all-singing, all-dancing facility described as a 'computer aided risk assessment, risk communication and research tool for use with forensic client populations, combining clinical and actuarial approaches' (www.giraffeonline.co.uk). The aim of GiRAffe is to 'co-ordinate the work of multidisciplinary staff teams in the complex process of appraising clinical risk'. The software has been developed for use in residential forensic environments such as medium and low-security NHS psychiatric units, high-security hospitals, prisons and young offender institutions.

Actuarial practice has developed out of the dominance of the empirical movement in the caring professions, and from a preoccupation with new forms of 'scientific expertise' that aims to offset the blame culture surrounding much of the public sector. As a type of social insurance it groups together specific types of service user. Sometimes the grouping process is crudely conceived as 'high' or 'low' risk groups, as with recent models of child care assessment and work with sex offenders. Thus actuarial practice, as a form of social insurance against risk, adopts a technical rationality that is formulated through the calculus of probability. The empirically driven 'what works' movement provides the legitimation for the deepening of actuarial practice in health and social care. Preoccupied as it is with calculating probability, constructing controlled environments which try to remove chance and measuring potential through evidenced-based outcomes, it is transposed within the neo-liberal programme into a technology of risk and methodology for life planning. Tele-healthcare is an example of actuarial practice in gatekeeping and regulating processes of health care provision at a distance. It encompasses a broad spectrum of telecommunications and information technologies, which regulate access to health care expertise at a distance, by a wide variety of means ranging from real-time video-conferencing to transmission of real-time or prerecorded images and/or data. For clinicians and policy makers in the NHS, these information systems have the advantage of rationalizing 'throughput' in specialist clinics, reducing waiting times and producing streamed data, allowing for the calculation of flows of risk populations that can be targeted as presenting typical medical problems.

Knowledge management (KM) combines technical and economic rationality with this deepening of actuarial culture. KM is not new in that it has grown and developed from existing practices, and it is already well established in many organizations – notably, the 'know-how' services, which sell off-the-shelf legal knowledges in big city law firms. KM is a convergence of ideas promulgated over the past decade including: core competencies and resource-based theories of the firm; 'info-mapping' and information resource management; the 'balanced scorecard' and intangible/intellectual assets; the learning organization and 'communities of practice'; total quality management and business process re-engineering; the networked organization and the 'boundary-less' firm. Irrespective of the terms used, the practical management objectives are actuarial: to convert human capital (tacit learning/team-shared capabilities) into structural capital (organizational knowledge or 'what is left when people go home', such as documented processes and knowledge bases) and thereby move from tacit to explicit knowledge, and reduce the risk of losing valuable knowledge if people leave the organization. It also has the effect of reducing professional autonomy and discretion once tacit knowledge is formalized within information systems.

The knowledge-creating organization depends on the interaction between explicit knowledge and tacit knowledge as a source of innovation. On-line communication and computerized storage capacity are important tools in developing the complexity of organizational links between tacit and explicit knowledge (see Castells 1996, p.160). Loss of 'corporate memory' – in other words, loss of control to competitors – as a result of downsizing is one of the prime reasons given for adopting formal knowledge management practices. From the KM perspective, organizations have a valuable asset in the informal knowledge that is the daily currency of their knowledge workers, but this asset usually lives only in the collective human memory, and thus is poorly preserved and managed. Other factors often mentioned include global competition and the pace of change. Organizations see KM as a means of avoiding the repetition of mistakes, reducing the duplication of effort, saving time on problem solving and getting closer to customers.

All of these perceived benefits comply with the logic of actuarial practice. KM encourages the competitive use of knowledge as a commodity to be bought or sold. Under the regime of KM it is likely that practitioners in health and social care will be increasingly recast as 'knowledge workers' in the application of evidence-based information systems. This will affect individual work practices and resources required to do the job. It will also require local re-negotiation of resource allocation, staff development and other forms of policy setting. Finally, it will affect health and social care as a whole, reconfiguring traditional boundaries and challenging assumptions about interprofessional knowledge. We can observe from this vantage point how KM fits neatly with Castell's (1996) perspective, that functions and processes in the information age are increasingly organized around networks. In the US, for example, the health insurance industry has been transformed in recent years with the rise of managed care networks and health maintenance organizations. Here knowledge is a part of the causal power of network flows which, as flows of power, become more important than the specific interests they represent (e.g. patients' needs). In trading knowledge as a commodity participation in the network becomes essential.

Conclusion

It is easy to see how new technologies of care comfortably fit with the defining features of the culture of actuarial practice. Under actuarial conditions of professional practice, meaningful social relationships give way to functional relationships at the level of front-line practice. We have seen this to be the case in social care particularly in adult services. The life-world of service users is transformed into an objective component of administrative, technical and organizational systems organized along functionalist lines. This results in what many front-line practitioners refer to as the 'tick-box culture' of assessment. New ICTs become a crucial part of the machinery for achieving these ends. As Suzanne Iacono (1996) noted:

> From information acquisition and anxiety to information warfare and weapons, there are few areas of social life that are left untouched by the mechanistic and instrumental rhetoric of computational information processing and the associated ways we humans traffic and trade in it. (p.449)

ICTs promise, unlike the immediacy of face-to-face work, a built in reflexivity that purports to give us control over the interface and, by extension, over information itself. The suggestion is that controlling the interface gives us control over the information it mediates. Information society relies heavily on ICTs as examples of science, technology and systems analysis. These tools of control are used to rationalize and simplify social activities, to make them more readable for decision makers, and to direct them toward achieving a narrow set of predetermined goals.

With the hardening of actuarialism in health and social care, a concomitant decline in the value of professional values will be witnessed. Codes of conduct will increasingly replace the more ubiquitous codes of ethics. The value base of social work, as the single defining feature of professional identity, particularly in relation to anti-oppressive and anti-discriminatory practice, will be disregarded. The changes predicted here will result in a marked reframing of professional identities in health and social care. In an important sense actuarialism is morally neutral; it is part of an advanced liberal sensibility which Zygmunt Bauman (1995) terms 'adiaphorization' – the stripping of human relationships of their moral significance, exempting them from moral evaluation, rendering them 'morally irrelevant' (p.133).

References

Bauman, Z. (1995) *Life in Fragments*. Blackwells: Oxford.

Castel, R. (1991) 'From dangerousness to risk.' In G. Burrell, C. Gordon and P. Millar (eds) *The Foucault Effect: Studies in Governmentality*. London: Harvester Wheatsheaf.

Castells, M. (1996) *The Information Age: Economy, Society and Culture. Volume I. The Rise of Network Society*. Oxford: Blackwell Publications.

Culpitt, I. (1999) *Social Policy and Risk*. London: Sage Publications.

Dreyfus, H. and Rabinow, P. (1982) *Michel Foucault: Beyond Structuralism and Hermeneutics*. London: Harvester Wheatsheaf.

Ellul, J. (1967) *The Technological Society*. (trans John Wilkinson) New York: Vintage Books.

Ewald, F. (1991) 'Insurance and risk.' In G. Burrell, C. Gordon and P. Millar (eds) *The Foucault Effect: Studies in Governmentality*. London: Harvester Wheatsheaf.

Ferguson, H. (2001) 'Social work, individualization and life politics.' *British Journal of Social Work 31*, 1, 41–56.

Gordon, C. (1991) 'Governmental rationality: an introduction.' In G. Burrell, C. Gordon and P. Millar (eds) *The Foucault Effect: Studies in Governmentality*. London: Harvester Wheatsheaf.

Habermas, J. (1970) *Toward a Rational Society*. (trans J. Shapiro) Boston: Beacon Press.

Harlow, E. (2002) 'The future of social work?' Paper given to the International Symposium on Social Work and Late Modernism, April, Ambleside, Cumbria, UK.

Hindess, B. (1997) 'A society governed by contract.' In G. Davis, B. Sullivan and A. Yeatman (eds) *The New Contractualism*? Melbourne: Macmillan.

Iacono, S. C. (1996) 'The demise of meaning-making and social agency as critical concepts in the rhetoric of an information age.' *The Information Society 12*, 4, 449–450.

Keller, E. F. (1993) 'Fractured images of science, language and power: a postmodern optic or just bad eyesight?' In E. Messer-Davidow, D. R. Shumway, and D. J. Sylvan (eds) *Knowledges: Historical and Critical Studies in Disciplinarity*. Charlottesville: University Press of Virginia.

Kling, R. (2000) 'Learning about information technologies and social change: the contribution of social informatics.' *The Information Society 16*, 3, 25–27.

Lievrouw, L. A. (1998) 'Our own devices: heterotopic communication, discourse and culture in the information society.' *The Information Society 14*, 2, 68–75.

Luhmann, N. (1998) *Observations on Modernity*. (trans W. Whobrey) California: Stanford University Press.

McBeath, G. B. and Webb, S. A. (1997) 'Community care: a unity of state and care? Some political and philosophical considerations.' In R. Hugman, M. Peelo, M. and K. Soothil (eds) *Concepts of Care*. London: Arnold.

McBeath, G. B. and Webb, S. A. (2000) 'On the nature of future worlds? Considerations of virtuality and utopia.' *Information, Communication and Society 3*, 1, 1–16.

Mitchell, D. (1999) *Governmentality: Power and Rule in Modern Society*. London: Sage Publications.

O'Malley, P. (1996) 'Risk and responsibility.' In A. Barry, T. Osborne and N. Rose (eds) *Foucault and Political Rationality.* London: UCL Press.

O'Malley, P. (2000) 'Uncertain subjects: risks, liberalism and contract.' *Economy and Society* 29, 4, 460–484.

Reddy, S. (1996) 'Claims to expert knowledge and the subversion of democracy: the triumph of risk over uncertainty.' *Economy and Society 25*, 2, 222–254.

Rose, N. (1999) *Powers of Freedom.* Cambridge: Cambridge University Press.

Simpson, L. C. (1995) *Technology, Time and the Conversations of Modernity.* London: Routledge.

Webb, S. A. (2001) 'Some considerations on the validity of evidence-based practice in social work.' *British Journal of Social Work 31*, 1, 41–56.

Young, J. (1999) 'Cannibalism and bulimia: patterns of social control in late modernity.' *Theoretical Criminology 3*, 4, 387–407.

Yudice, G. (1995) 'Civil society, consumption, and governmentality in an age of global restructuring: an introduction.' *Social Text 45*, 2–15.

The Contributors

Roger Burrows is Co-Director of the Centre for Housing Policy and a Reader in Social Policy at the University of York in the UK. He has published widely on health, housing and social aspects of ICTs.

Joe Cullen is Director of the Collaborative Learning Unit (CO-LEARN) at the Tavistock Institute, London, in the UK, and is the Institute Scientific Dean. He is co-ordinator of a number of research and research and development projects in the field of health technologies. These include: SEAHORSE (an EU project in HIV/AIDS); HERO (an EU project providing health and educational support for offenders in a range of European prisons) and an ESRC project on motivation and empowerment, within the ESRC Innovative Health Technologies (IHT) Programme.

Nick Gould is Reader in Applied Social Studies and Head of the Department of Social and Policy Sciences at the University of Bath in the UK. He has published widely in the fields of professional learning and information management, and is currently part of an EC funded project developing new approaches to measuring the 'digital divide'.

Michael Hardey is a Lecturer in Sociology at the University of Southampton in the UK. He has published widely in the areas of: identity; health and ICTs; user and patient narratives of health and social care; professional territories of care; new media; and ethnography. He is currently writing a book on e-health, knowledge and expertise that will be published by Routledge.

Elizabeth Harlow is a Senior Lecturer in Social Work at the University of Bradford in the UK. In addition to information and communications technologies in the welfare services, her research interests include: gender, organizations and careers; new public sector managerialism; and the changing nature of social work.

Annie Huntington is a Lecturer in the Directorate of Health and Social Care at the University of Salford in the UK. Before this she worked as a social worker, psycho-therapist and nurse, and has over twenty years experience of work in the statutory, voluntary and private health and social care sectors. She completed her PhD in 1999.

Brian Loader is Director of the Community Informatics Research and Application Unit (CIRA) at the University of Teesside in the UK. He is the editor of the journal *Information, Communication and Society.*

Steven Muncer is a Lecturer in the Department of Psychology at the University of Durham, Stockton on Tees, in the UK.

Sarah Nettleton is a medical sociologist and is currently a Senior Lecturer in Social Policy in the Department of Social Policy and Social Work at the University of York in the UK.

Nicholas Pleace is Research Fellow in the Centre for Housing Policy at the University of York in the UK. He has published widely on homelessness, welfare aspects of housing and social aspects of ICTs.

Suzanne Regan is a principal lecturer in Health and Social Services Management at St Martin's College Lancaster. Her research interests are in the analysis of the organization and management of health and welfare services undertaken in local practice settings.

Brian Relph is Children Service Manager with Luton Borough Council in the UK. He is responsible for the Child Protection and Looked After Children's Conference and Reviewing Service. A qualified social worker with several years experience in child care and child protection work at field and managerial levels, Mr Relph holds postgraduate degrees from Oxford and St Andrews, and is currently researching integrated family support services.

Bob Sapey is a Lecturer in Applied Social Science at Lancaster University in the UK. He is interested in the impact of technology on social work practice, in particular on work with disabled people. He is co-author, with Michael Oliver, of *Social Work with Disabled People* (second edition).

Walter Sermeus is Professor in Nursing Management and Research at the Centre for Health Services and Nursing Research at the Catholic University of Leuven in Belgium.

Mark Watson has been providing electronic and traditional information services to social workers for twenty years, initially at Essex Social Services Department, then at the National Institute for Social Work. Having helped to establish the Social Care Institute for Excellence, he has recently moved to OLM Systems in the UK to take forward new developments in this area.

Stephen A. Webb teaches social work and social policy at the University of Sussex in the UK. He is completing a book called *Social Work in a Risk Society: Social and Cultural Perspectives* for Palgrave. His research interests include: risk society; social work ethics; evidence-based practice; new communication technologies and subjectivity; the history of social work ideas.

Subject Index

Abidjan 161
access to knowledge
  prior to Internet 50–3
  through Internet 54–61
access points 83
actuarialism in welfare provision, rise of 228–35
ADSL cable satellite 173
advice, lay knowledge and 203–6
Africa 17
AgeInfo database (Centre for Policy on Ageing) 53, 54, 55
Agency for Health Quality and Research 148
AIDS *see* HIV/AIDS
AIM (Telematics Systems for Health Care Programme) 160
Alcohol Concern 55
American Hospitals Association 149, 154
American Medical Association 214
Archie 53
Arden Syntax 149
Area Child Protection Committees (ACPCs) 127, 130
Arnold, Stephen 124
Asia 213
assessment in social work
  informationalisation 74–6
  models and arguments 70–4
Association of Chief Police Officers (ACPO) 127
Association of Directors of Social Services 49
Audit Commission 40, 47

'Balanced Scorecards' 152
BBC OnLine site 211–12
Benefits Agency 184
Best Practice guidelines 150
Best Value 29, 57
  as sign 89
'Big Pharma' 216–17
BITnet 58
Blair (New Labour) governments 9, 83
BOS (Bill of Service) 153
branding 88
Bristol Royal Infirmary Inquiry 148, 154
British Library 51
British Medical Journal see eBMJ
bullying 89

CABG, New York 144
Cabinet Office 183, 196

Canada 123, 124, 143
Canadian Charter of Rights and Freedoms 124
Cancerfacts.com 149
care
  concepts of 145–6
  information systems and evaluation of 152–4
  information systems in delivery of 152
  provision of, and organizational processes 146–8
  technologies of 223–38
    and governance 223–5
Care and Health 13
Caredata database (NISW) 53, 54, 55, 61, 62
Care Technologies Inc. 225
caring professions and IT 29–48
case management 146
CCETSW (Central Council for Education and Training in Social Work) 70, 71, 79
CDC 150
CEBSS (Centre for Evidence Based Social Services) 49, 52, 60, 62
Census (UK) 54
Central Council for Education and Training in Social Work *see* CCETSW
central duty teams 83
Centre for Evidence-Based Practice, University of Exeter 201
Centre for Evidence Based Social Services *see* CEBSS
Centre for Human Services Technology (University of Southampton) 60
Centre for Policy on Ageing 53
  AgeInfo database 53, 54, 55
Chatdanger.com 112
chat rooms and newsgroups 206–10
'Chat Wise, Street Wise' 130
child abuse 102, 107
  Internet 111–34
ChildData database (National Children's Bureau) 53, 54, 55
Child Net International 130
child pornography
  national and international law 122–6
  proliferation of 114–15
Child Pornography Prevention Act (1996) 123
child protection *see* CP
child protection agencies, challenges of Internet to 114–17
  increased opportunities for contact provided by Internet 115–17
    opportunities for contact between offenders 115–16
    opportunities for offenders to contact children 116–17

proliferation of child pornography 114–15
Children Act 1989 102
Children's Society 38
Child Trafficking and Pornography Act (Republic of Ireland, 1998) 122
Christianity 177
Clearing House for Local Authority Social Services Research 57
clinical decision making and information systems 148–9
clinical outcome 153
clinical pathways 146–7
Clinical Pathway ConstructorTM 151
Clinician Information Exchange 173
CMMS (computer mediated social support) 15
Cochrane Centre 214
Cochrane Database, University of York 148, 150, 201
code
   definitions 87
   technology and strengthening control of 85–91
collaborative learning
   health and collapse of professionalism? 157–82
   policy background to health informatics 160–2
   telediagnosis and 165–9
Community Care 12–13, 90
   'Research Matters' 56
   website 56
Community Development Foundation 53
   Volnet database 53, 54
confidentiality 33, 41–2
Conservative governments 9
Constant Gardener, The 216
consumer culture and expertise 200–2
contact
   increased opportunities for provided by Internet 115–17
   opportunities for between offenders 115–16
   opportunities for offenders to contact children 116–17
control, information and dilemma of 214–16
COPINE Project (Combating Paedophile Information Networks in Europe) 114, 119, 121
CP (child protection) 89, 90, 100
CPMC medical entities dictionary 149
CPS (Carte Professional Sante) card 169
Criminal Code (Canada) 124
Criminal Justice Act 1988 123, 124
Criminal Justice and Public Order Act 1994 123
Critical Appraisal Skills Programme 60
Crossing the Quality Chasm: A New Health System for the 21st Century (IOM) 137
Crumpton, Martin 124

Curapath 151
Cussnet (Computer Users in Social Services Network) 58
customer-facing settings 95
customer services 83
   transferring referrals to local team 99–106
cyborg 186

Dartington Social Research Unit 52, 58, 64
Data Protection Act 1984 42
Data-Star 54
db@socialworkalliance.net 85, 108
Deja News 206
delivery of services 14–16
demeanour work 95
Denmark 178
Department for Education and Employment 71, 80, 133
Department for Education and Science 130
Department of the Environment, Transport and the Regions 77, 79
Department of Health 12, 29, 30, 31, 39, 42, 46, 49, 52, 60, 61, 62, 64, 70, 71, 73, 79, 85, 89, 90, 91, 100, 106, 109, 110, 111, 116, 127, 130, 133, 159, 181, 201, 211, 219
Department of Health and Social Security (DHSS) 51, 55
   Library 54
Department of Trade and Industry 159, 181
detection, assessment and investigation of Internet child abuse 126–8
DHSS-DATA database 54
Dialog 54
DIOGENE (Digital Imaging Unit, University Hospital of Geneva) 168–9
Diploma in Social Work (DipSW) 70, 71
DiTV (Digital Interactive Television) 159, 165, 172
domestic violence 89
Drugscope 55
DW (data warehouse) 153

Eastern Europe 121, 213
eBMJ (British Medical Journal) 55, 211
EC (European Community) 43, 160
ECDL ('European Computer Driving Licence') 59
Economic and Social Research Council see ESRC
EDI (electronic data interchange) 164
effectiveness paradigm 35
efficiency paradigm 35
e-government Interoperability Framework 85
eLSC (Library for Social Care) 56, 60, 61
England 127

ENITH (European Network for Information Technology in the Human Services) 8, 34, 35
EPRs (Electronic Patient Records) 159, 163
ESRC (Economic and Social Research Council) 56, 59, 185
  REGARD database 56
Essex SSD 52
EU (European Union) 159, 175, 176
Euro-ISDN 163, 180
Europe 143, 160, 164
European Computer Driving Licence see ECDL
European Network for Information Technology in the Human Services see ENITH
Evidence Bank 58
Excelcare 151
expertise
  and consumer culture 200–2
  reconfiguration of 199–222

Fabian Society 45, 46
FBI 116
Fellows, Allan 124
Fidonet 58
financial outcome 153
'Findings' (Joseph Rowntree Foundation) 56
Fordist networks 31
Forensic Psychiatric Service, Langdon Hospital, London 233
France 126
FriendsReunited website 54

gender and sexuality 16–19
General Social Care Council 62
Geneva Canton University Hospital 168
Germany 126, 176, 177
GIF (e-Government Interoperability Framework) 159
GiRAffe (Generic Integrated Risk Assessment for Forensic Environments) 233
GLIF 149
Gopher 53
governance
  technical rationality as technology of 225–8
  and technologies of care 223–5
Greater Manchester Police Obscene Publication Squad 114
Greece 175
Green, Patrick (paedophile) 112, 116
Guardian 157, 181
  Society supplement 56
Gulf War Syndrome web page 213

Hampshire SSD 52

HBOC 151
health
  collaborative learning and collapse of professionalism? 157–82
  and welfare 135–222
health care model 143–8
  concepts of care 145–6
  focus of hospital 144
  organizational support systems 148
  provision of care and organizational processes 146–8
Healthfinder 149
health informatics
  policy background to 160–2
  typology of systems 162–5
Health Professional Information Exchange 174
Healthwise 149
Hertfordshire Constabulary 118
Hi-Ethics 214
'Highlights' series (National ChildrenÆs Bureau) 53
Hines, David (paedophile) 115
HISs (hospital information systems) 163, 164
HIV/AIDS 161
  and SEAHORSE 173–6
HL-7 152
HMSO 109, 211
Home Office 71, 80, 118, 133
HON Code 214
hospital, focus of 144
House of Lords 67
human capital 11
Human Services Information Technology Application see HUSITA
HUSITA (Human Services Information Technology Application) 8, 34
hypomnemata 178

ICTs
  and delivery of services 14–16
  gender and sexuality 16–19
  welfare organizations and their management 8–14
IDS 86, 92, 109
ILRT (University of Bristol) 56
information and dilemma of control 214–16
Informational Age Government 89
informational age 68–70
informationalisation 74–6
Information Exchange: Swamp or Desert? 51
Information for Health (DoH) 61, 159
Information for Health Strategy 60
Information for Social Care (DoH) 31, 62, 85
Information Needs of Social Workers 50

information systems
  and clinical decision making 148–9
  in delivery of care 152
  in design of patient care programmes 149–52
  and evaluation of care 152–4
    clinical outcome 153
    financial outcome 153
    process 152–3
    service outcome 153–4
  and patient care 148–54
Ingenta initiative 55
INISS *see* Project INISS
Institute for Clinical Improvement 148
Institute of Medicine *see* IOM
International Classification of Diseases 72
International Telecommunications Union 160
Internet 15, 18, 22, 49, 50, 54, 56, 57, 63, 117,
      119, 121, 124, 127, 129, 130, 131, 132,
      157, 172, 173, 177, 185, 193, 195, 200,
      205, 206, 211, 213, 216, 218, 223, 229
  access to knowledge prior to 50–3
  case studies on sex crimes 117–22
    case A 117–18
    case B 118–19
    case C 119–20
    case D 120–2
  challenges of, to child protection agencies
      114–17
  child abuse 111–34
    detection, assessment and investigation of
        126–8
    development of technological responses
        130–1
    practice issues arising from challenges and
        case studies 122–6
    raising of public awareness 130
    treatment and monitoring arrangements for
        sex offenders 129
    treatment of victims 129
  consumers and reconfiguration of expertise
      199–222
  increased opportunities for contact provided by
      115–17
  lay expertise: newsgroups and chat rooms
      206–10
  personal home page 203–6
  professional expertise: state, commercial and
      voluntary sectors 210–13
  using for evidence-based practice 49–65
'Internet Detective' learning module 59
Internet HealthCare Coalition 214
Internet Relay Chat 185
'Internet Tutorial for Social Workers' 59
Internet Watch Foundation 112, 121, 130

INTERPOL 122
intrahospital communication 163
IOM (US Institute of Medicine) 137, 148, 154,
      155
Irish Republic 123
IRM (information repository management system)
      173
ISDN 171
Italy 175
IUMT (Interactive User Monitoring Tool) 173–4

JANET 58
Japan 18, 111, 122
Johns Hopkins Hospital 141
Joint Commission for the Accreditation of
      Healthcare Organisations 149
Joint University Council – Social Work Education
      Committee 59
Joseph Rowntree Foundation 56
  'Findings' 56
Joseph Rowntree Memorial Trust 52
Journal of Social Forces 50

Kantian principle-based approach 41
'Keisha' child protection module 57
KM (knowledge management) 11, 38–41, 234,
      235
knowledge
  access to prior to Internet 50–3
  lay knowledge and advice 203–6
  management *see* KM
  power and professional ethics 41–5

Langdon Hospital, London 233
LANs (local area networks) 163
lay expertise: newsgroups and chat rooms 206–10
lay knowledge and advice 203–6
learning organizations 36–8
LGR (local government review) 96
Library for Social Care *see* eLSC
literature of the self 178
London Lighthouse 174
Looked After Children Assessment and Action
      Records 20

McDonald's 88, 107
McLeish, Father Adrian 125–6
Managed Care Technologies 225
management of welfare organizations 8–14
MANs (metropolitan area networks) 163
MAPI 121
Mayo Foundation 139
MBA 73
MedCertain 214

MEDCOM 178
Medline database 55
Medlineplus 149
MEDLINK initiative 170
MELIC Consortium 176, 181
Microsoft 90

'name and shame' 89
Napoleonic Code 169
National Assistance Act 1948 89
National Association of Social Workers,
    Washington DC 54
National Children's Bureau 53
    ChildData database 53, 54, 55
National electronic Library for Health *see* NeLH
National Electronic Library for Learning Disability
    61
National Electronic Library for Mental Health 61
National Health Service *see* NHS
National Health Service and Community Care Act
    31, 88
National Institute of Clinical Effectiveness 148
National Institute of Clinical Excellence 228
National Institute for Social Work *see* NISW
*National Plan for Safeguarding Children from
    Commercial Sexual Exploitation* (DoH) 111,
    127, 130
National Research Register 56
National Schizophrenia Fellowship 213
National Society for the Prevention of Cruelty to
    Children *see* NSPCC
NeLH (National electronic Library for Health) 12,
    60, 61, 62
network agency 36
network organizations 31
New Labour (Blair) governments 9, 83, 183, 232
'New Literature on Old Age' (Centre for Policy on
    Ageing)53
new managerialism 19
newsgroups and chat rooms 206–10
New York Presbyterian Hospital 149
NHS (National Health Service) 9, 13, 39, 61–4,
    159, 233, 234
    Executive London 61, 64
    Information Authority 63
    Information Strategy 61
    Workforce Development Confederation 62
NHS Direct Online 13, 149, 159, 200, 210–11
NHSnet 30
NISW (National Institute for Social Work) 51–2,
    53, 57
    Caredata database 53, 54, 55, 61, 62
    Information Service *see* NISWIS
    Library 52, 62

Library Advisor 61
    Practice and Development Exchange 51, 52
NISWIS (National Institute for Social Work
    Information Service) 52, 53, 62
No Logo (Klein) 90
North America 164
Northern Ireland 127
NSPCC (National Society for the Prevention of
    Cruelty to Children) 55, 90
    Virtual Children Centre 131

Obscene Publications Act (1959) 123, 124
offenders
    opportunities for contact between 115–16
    opportunities to contact children 116–17
Office of Scientific and Technical Information 50
Omnibus Bill (Canada) 123
one stop shops 83
Operation Cathedra 115
Operation Starburst 124, 125
Orchid Club 116
organizational support systems 148
organization of patient care and IT 137–56

PACS (picture archiving and communication
    systems) 165
'Paedophiles: Assessing the Risk' (C4) 111
PathCare 151
Pathlinks 151
patient care
    from functional departments to 138–43
    organization of and IT 137–56
        from functional departments to
            patient-focused care 138–43
        health care model 143–8
        information systems 148–54
Patient Care Technologies 225
PDCA (Plan–Do–Check–Act) cycle 150
Pennsylvania Health Care Cost Containment
    Council 149
personal home page 203–6
Pharmaceutical Manufacturers Association 217
pharmacists 169–72
'Pocket Doctor' 212
Pocket Oxford Dictionary 89, 109
policy background to health informatics 160–2
Poor Laws 89
Portugal 176
post-Fordist networks 31, 36
power, knowledge and professional ethics 41–5
Powers of Freedom (Rose) 224
PPPs (private/public sector partnerships) 172
Price Waterhouse 90, 109
professional ethics, knowledge and power 41–5

professional expertise: state, commercial and
voluntary sectors of Internet 210–13
Project INISS (Information Needs and Information
Services in Social Services) 51
Protection of Children Act 1978 114, 123, 124
public awareness of Internet child abuse, raising of
130
Public Health Laboratory Service 211
PubMed 148

Quality Checks 149
Quality Protects 29, 89
Quality Strategy for Social Care (DoH) 62
Q.works 151

R. v. Gloucestershire County Council 67
R. v. Sharpe in Supreme Court of Canada 124
'Race and Social Work' multimedia package 58
RCTSs (randomised controlled trials) 201
redesigning care delivery paradigm 35–6
referral systems
    technology and social services 83–110
    transferring from customer services to local
        team 99–106
REGARD database 56
Register of Social Care Research 57
Regulation of Investigatory Powers Act 2000 127
Research Findings Electronic Register 56
'Research Mindedness' web module (DoH) 58, 60
Research Policy and Planning 56, 61
Resource Discovery Network 59
RNIB (Royal National Institute for the Blind) 213
Romania 175
RTD (research and technology development) 159,
160

Scandinavia 178
SCIE (Social Care Institute for Excellence) 12, 53,
61, 62, 228
Scotland 127
Scottish Intercollegiate Guidelines Network 148
Scottish Office 70, 80
SEAHORSE (Support, Empower and Awareness for
HIV/AIDS: the Online Research and
Self-help Exchange) 173–6, 177, 178, 179
search engines 206
Select Committee on Science and Technology 210,
221
Self-Help (Smiles) 205
self-service welfare to virtual self-help 183–97
service(s)
    delivery of 14–16
    outcome 153–4
SESAME/VITALE system 169–72

sex crimes, case studies on Internet-based 117–22
sex offenders, treatment and monitoring
arrangements for 129
sexuality and gender 16–19
Sharp, Christopher 124
Shouldice Hospital, Toronto, Canada 143
signs, codes and brands 88–91, 107
SLAs (service level agreements) 152
smartcards 169–72
SOAPs (electronic seals of approval) 173
social care and social work 27–134
Social Care Institute for Excellence *see* SCIE
'Social Care Update' (NISW) 53
Social Exclusion Policy Action Team 216, 221
social informatics 33–36, 225
social services, technology and referral systems
83–110
Social Services Abstracts (DHSS) 51
Social Services Inspectorate 39, 40, 70
Social Services Research Group 56, 57, 61
Social Services Research 57
social support, VHS and provision of 187–91
social work
    assessment in 70–6
    and social care 27–134
Social Work Abstracts database 54
Society supplement to *Guardian* 56, 111, 133
Sociology Online 211
South Africa 217
Spain 175, 176
SSDSs (social service departments) 9–10, 11, 34,
51–2
structural capital 11
'Superhighway Safety Guidance' (DFES) 130
support systems 148
Supreme Court of Canada 124
Sure Start 9
surface of production 94
Sweden 122, 126
Switzerland 54

Taylorism 31, 37
TEAM (Tele-Education and Medicine) 168
technical rationality as technology of governance
225–8
technological responses to Internet child abuse,
development of 130–1
technology, referral systems and social services
83–110
    background to research 91–9
    strengthening control of code 85–91
    transferring referrals from customer services to
        local team 99–106
telematics 167

Telemedicine 154
Telnet 53
Thames Valley Police 112
'Theorizing Social Work Education' seminar series
    59
Third Generation (G3) phones 183
To Err Is Human: Building a Safer Health System (IOM)
    137
Total Care Technologies 225
Training Organization for Personal Social Services
    63
treatment
    and monitoring arrangements for sex offenders
        129
    of victims of sex offenders 129

UNESCO
    Conference in Paris 122
United Kingdom 9, 12, 39, 42, 49, 54, 58, 69,
        111, 114, 123, 124, 127, 130, 141, 159,
        175, 176, 186, 193, 200, 211, 212, 213,
        215, 216, 232
United Nations 122
    Conventions on the Rights of the Child 122
United States 58, 69, 74, 126, 137, 143, 178,
        185, 212, 213, 215, 225, 235
University of Birmingham 124
University of Bristol 56
University College Cork 114
University of Exeter 201
University Hospital of Geneva 168
University of Southampton 60
University of Texas in Arlington 57
University of York 201
US House Commerce Committee Report 172
USA Today 172, 181
'Use of the Internet' (ECDL module) 59
Usenet 185, 186, 206
Utrecht Academic Centre 139

Value Compass 152, 153
Venezuela 18, 122
victims of sex offenders, treatment of 129
Volnet database (Community Development
        Foundation) 53, 54
VSH (virtual self-help) 184–6
    alternative perspective 191–3
    meanings of 186–7
    and provision of social support 187–91

Wales 127
WANs (wide area networks) 163
WAP mobile phones 212
welfare

and health 135–222
    organizations and their management 8–14
    provision, rise of actuarialism in 228–35
West Midlands Police 124
Wider Strategy for Research and Development Relating to
        Personal Social Services (DoH) 49, 52
Wonderland Club 114, 115
Worker Safety Advisor resource 57
Working Together to Safeguard Children (DoH) 127,
        130
World Congress Against Commercial Sexual
        Exploitation of Children
    Stockholm, Sweden, 1996 (1st) 122
    Yokohama, Japan, 2001 (2nd) 111, 127, 130
World Health Organization 31, 33, 48
World Wide Web 54, 58, 185, 186, 223

X-ray examination 139

Author Index

Abbott, V.P. 192, 195
Abell, A. 11, 12, 14, 23, 26
Abercrombie, N. 84, 108
Abersnagel, E. 139, 154
Adam, A. 87, 108
Akdeniz, Y. 124
Amin, A. 7, 23
Anderson, R. 77, 78
Argyris, C. 31, 45
Arriagada, R. 155
Atherton, C. 58, 60, 64

Bagley, C. 114, 132
Bainbridge, W.S. 13, 23
Baker, W.E. 128, 132
Banks, S. 41, 45
Bannister, A. 70, 78
Barnes, M. 71, 78
Bates, J. 77, 79
Baudrillard, J. 20, 23, 87, 88, 91, 108, 214, 219
Bauman, Z. 104, 108, 215, 219, 236, 237
Beck, U. 87, 108, 134, 191, 195, 218, 219, 200
Beijers, R.P. 141, 154
Bell, 7, 23
Bellamy, C. 22, 23
Beresford, P. 218, 219
Berland, G.K. 149, 154, 216, 219
Berliner, L. 117, 132
Berman, Y. 21, 23, 59, 64
Bernstein, B. 219
Beveridge, W.H. 9
Beynon, H. 37, 45
Biehal, N. 81
Biermann, S.G. 215, 219
Biestek, F.P. 41
Bikson, T. 78
Bilson, A. 134
Bindel, J. 18, 23
Blackler, F. 45, 46
Blaug, R. 70, 79
Blaxter, M. 219
Blichert-Toft, M. 155
Boberg, E. 181
Bosworth, K. 181
Bower, K. 152, 156
BPRC 23
Brantingham, M. 125, 132
Braverman, H. 46
Brennan, T. 144, 154

Briceland, L. 139, 155
Bricker, E. 181
Bridget, M. 78
Brittain, J. 50, 64
Brosnan, M.J. 17, 23
Brown, M.J. 50, 64
Bryant, C. 113, 133
Burchell, D. 81
Burnes, B. 78, 79
Burrows, R. 183–95, 196, 197, 202, 210, 219, 221, 239
Burt, E. 213, 219
Bury, M. 216, 219

Callaghan, P. 188, 196
Cant, S. 219
Carew, R. 13, 23
Carr, J. 114, 115, 116, 127, 132
Carter, D. 22, 23
Carter, P. 87, 109
Castel, R. 233, 237
Castells, M. 7, 8, 10, 15, 16, 18, 23, 24, 67, 69, 74, 76, 79, 86, 108, 111, 196, 235, 237
Catchpole, P. 14, 24
Chassin, M. 144, 155
Children's Society 38, 46
Chilvers, R. 65
Christensen, H. 215, 220
Cooner, T.S. 58
Cullen, J. 157–80. 181
Culpitt, I. 230, 237, 239

Danziger, J.N. 24
Davidson, M.J. 17, 23
Davies, N. 115, 133
Deering, M.J. 196, 220
Denzin, N. 88, 109, 185, 196
De Paepe, L. 153, 154
de Vries, P. 141, 154
Dominelli, L. 38, 47
Donaldson, M. 137, 155
Dosi, G. 160, 181
Douglas, M. 88, 109
Dovey, K. 45, 46
Dreyfus, H. 225, 237
Duncle, D.E. 17, 24
Durkin, K. 113, 133
Dyson, G.E. 13, 24

Easterby-Smith, M. 37, 46
Ehrenreich, B. 202, 219
Ellis, K. 71, 80
Ellul, J. 227, 237
Eng, T.R. 196, 220

Erooga, M. 118, 133
Evers, G. 146, 155
Ewald, F. 231, 237

Faulkner, R.R. 128, 132
Featherstone, M. 186, 196, 202, 219
Felson, D. 121, 133
Ferguson, H. 229, 237
Fetter, R. 138, 155
Finkelhor, D. 116, 125, 133
Finkelstein, V. 77, 80
Finn, J. 185, 188, 194, 196
Fisher, M. 49, 64
Flynn, N. 85, 109
Foley, P. 216, 219
Forrest, J. 52, 58, 64
Foucault, M. 23, 157, 158, 165, 177, 178, 181
Francis, J. 52, 64
Frank, A. 205, 219
Freddolino, P.P. 14, 24
Freeman, J. 138, 155
Frissen, P. 10, 24
Froggett, L. 71, 73, 80
Fuller, J. 233

Gaintner, J. 155
Galinsky, M.J. 14, 26
Gammon, D. 182
Garrett, P.M. 20, 24
Geertz, C. 96, 104, 109
Gelman, S.R. 21, 24
Gherardi, S. 37, 45, 46
Ghoshal, S. 40
Giddens, A. 15, 23, 24, 158, 181, 191, 196, 199, 200, 202, 205, 218, 220
Giffords, E.D. 13, 24
Glastonbury, B. 7, 25, 30, 35, 43, 46, 47, 63, 64, 211, 220
Glennerster, H. 34, 47
Goffman, E. 209, 220
Goldstein, H. 13, 25
Golladay, M.L. 215, 219
Gomm, R. 74, 80
Goodinge, S. 70, 80
Goossens, L. 156
Gordon, C. 229, 237
Goschenberg, E. 181
Gott, M. 162, 181
Gould, N. 8, 12, 29–45, 46, 47, 211, 220, 239
Graaf, H. de 35, 47
Greenfield, L.B. 215, 219
Griffiths, R. 31, 46, 215, 220
Grint, K. 85, 86, 107, 110
Grose, D. 51, 64

Grube, J.A. 209, 221
Grumet, G.W. 14, 25
Gulia, M. 187, 191, 197
Gustafson, D. 161, 181

Habermas, J. 158, 160, 181, 228, 237
Halm, E. 144, 155
Hampton, K. 191, 196
Han, A.S. 14, 24
Hansard 114, 133
Hapgood, M. 14, 25
Hardey, M. 14, 15, 192, 196, 199–218, 220, 239
Harlow, E. 7–23, 25, 232, 237, 239
Harris, J. 19, 25
Harris, K. 53
Harris, N. 214, 220
Harrison, M. 176, 181
Harvey, D. 10, 25
Haughton, E. 16, 25
Hawkins, R. 181
Hearn, J. 18, 25
Henderson, V. 145, 155
Herring, S. 121, 133
Herzlinger, R. 138, 155
Heskett, J. 143, 155
Heyssel, R. 141, 155
Hill, M. 152, 155
Hill, S. 84, 108
Hindess, B. 230, 237
Holland, G. 114, 134
Holman, B. 67, 80
Howell, J. 15
Hudson, J. 183, 196
Hughes, D.M. 18, 25
Hughes, J. 91, 94, 95, 109
Hughes, L. 9, 25
Hughes, R. 21, 25
Huntington, A. 11, 20, 67–78, 80, 239
Hyden, L.C. 220

Iacono, S.C. 236, 237
Isherwood, B. 88, 109
Itzin, C. 115, 133

Jackson, N. 87, 109
James, A. 31, 46
Jarvis, P. 36, 46
Jellineck, D. 13, 15, 16, 25
Jenkins, H.W. 213, 220
Jenkins, P. 134
Jewson, N. 199, 220
Jones, A. 155
Jones, C. 21, 25
Jones, Insp. T. 114

Jonscher, C. 80
Jorden, T. 216, 220

Kaplan, R. 152, 155
Karlen, H. 18, 25
Kearney, N. 156
Keller, E.F. 225, 237
Kelly, A. 9, 25
Kempf, K. 129, 133
Kerslake, A. 31, 34, 47
Keyworth, G. 13, 24
Khan, P. 38, 47
Kiesler, S. 196
Kim, P. 192, 196, 214, 220
King, J.L. 24
King, S. 185, 188, 196
Kinnunen, J. 156
Kirby, S. 171, 181
Klein, N. 90, 109
Kling, R. 86, 109, 225, 237
Knights, D. 78, 79
Kohn, L. 137, 155
Kosarajhu, S. 176, 181
Kraemer, K.L. 24
Kraut, R. 195, 196
Krebs, V.E. 128, 133
Kues, I. 155
Kumar, K. 7, 25

Laird, N. 154
Lambden, P. 13, 25
Lathrop, J. 138, 139, 140, 155
Lave, J. 175, 181
Law, J. 104, 108
Law, S. 78
Lawler, J. 9, 25
Lawton, A. 10, 25
Le, M. 155
Leape, L. 154
Le Carré, J. 216, 220
Lee, C. 144, 155
Leonard, P. 8, 25
Lesar, T. 139, 155
Lewis, J. 34, 47
Lievrouw, L.A. 230, 237
Lilley, R. 13, 25
Line, M.B. 50, 64
Lineham, C. 134
Lingus, A. 94, 109
Lipstein, S. 155
Loader, B. 183–95, 196, 197, 211, 219, 220, 221,
    240
Lockard, J. 186, 197
Luhmann, N. 223, 237

Lundmark, V. 196
Lyotard, J-F. 13, 25

McBeath, G.B. 225, 228, 237
McCartney, I. 85
McCulloch, J.W. 50, 64
McCurry, P. 77, 80
Macdonald, K. 31, 47
McDonald, S. 45, 46
McHugh, D. 10, 26
Mackay, H. 44, 47
Manning, B. 72, 80
Mapes, R. 205, 220
Marsh, P. 81
Marshall, L.E. 134
Marshall, W.L. 115, 116, 133, 134
Maslow, H. 37, 47
Mason, H. 118, 133
Maxfield, A. 196, 220
Meyres, J. 209, 221
Michelet, E. 181
Miller, A. 16, 26
Miller, M. 156
Milne, J. 73, 80
Mintzberg, H. 138, 155
Mitchell, D. 224, 237
Morris, A.D. 145, 155
Morris, R. 155
Morrison, D. 76, 77, 80
Morrissey, J. 196
Moultrie, K. 33, 47
Moursund, J. 185, 188, 197
Mukopadhyay, T. 196
Mulrow, C.D. 201, 220
Muncer, S. 183–95, 196, 197, 209, 219, 221, 240

Nellis, M. 70, 80
Nelson, E.C. 152, 155
Nettleton, S. 183–95, 196, 197, 210, 214, 219,
    221, 240
Newman, J. 9, 24
Nite, G. 145, 155
Norton, D. 152, 155
Nurius, P.S. 17, 26

Oakland, J.S. 11, 26
O'Brien, J. 109
O'Byrne, P. 73, 80
O'Connor, R. 116, 117, 129, 133
O'Higgins, M. 14, 24
Okunieff, P. 155
Oliver, M. 67, 80
O'Malley, P. 230, 231, 238
Oxbrow, N. 11, 12, 23

Paccagnella, L. 195, 197
Parker, R. 52
Parkin, W. 18, 25
Parry, L.E. 17, 26
Parsons, T. 201, 214, 217, 221
Parton, N. 102, 109, 218, 221
Pashley, G. 81
Paterson, E. 219
Patterson, M. 196
Peacock, D. 213, 221
Peeters, G. 156
Peters, T.J. 11, 26
Pleace, N. 15, 183–95, 196, 197, 216, 219, 221,
    240
Pollack, D. 21, 24
Prahalad, C.K. 145, 155
Preston-Shoot, M. 21, 26
Pringle, K. 118, 133
Pugh, R. 31, 36, 47

Quaethoven, P. 154
Quayle, E. 114, 134
Quilgars, D. 194, 197
Qvortrup, L. 35, 47

Rabinow, P. 225, 237
Rafferty, J. 8, 24, 26, 31, 35, 46, 47
Ramaswamy, V. 145, 155
Ravetz, J. 19, 26, 72, 80
Raynsford, N. 85
Reddy, S. 230, 238
Regan, S. 10, 11, 83–108, 109, 110, 240
Regan-Shade, L. 77, 80
Reid, E.M. 195, 197
Reiner, D.A. 205, 221
Relph, B. 18, 111–32, 240
Remotti, L. 181
Revans, R. 37, 47
Rheingold, H. 186, 197, 209, 221
Riley, L. 17, 26, 30, 47
Rose, A. 10, 25
Rose, N. 224, 229, 232, 238
Rosengarten, P. 38, 47
Ross, L. 71, 80
Rouncefield, M. 109
Rushdie, S. 157

Saks, M. 214, 221
Salter, A.C. 117, 119, 133
Sapey, B. 11, 19, 20, 26, 67–78, 74, 75, 77, 78,
    81, 240
Sarup, M. 91, 109
Sasser, W. 143, 155
Scarborough, H. 47

Scherlis, W. 196
Schesinger, L. 143, 155
Schoech, D. 57, 212, 221
Schoenfeld, A. 176, 181
Schon, D. 31, 37, 45, 47
Schopler, J.H. 14, 26
Semke, J.I. 17, 26
Senge, P. 31, 36, 37, 47
Sermeus, W. 10, 137–54, 240
Sharif, B.F. 195, 197
Sharkey, P. 65
Sharma, U. 219
Sheldon, B. 49, 65
Sherman, C. 81
Shilling, C. 202, 214, 221
Siddall, A. 9, 26
Simpson, L.C. 87, 110, 226, 238
Smale, G. 51, 60, 65, 71, 81
Smiles, M. 205, 216, 221
Smith, C. 218, 221
Smith, G. 17, 26, 30, 47, 86, 110
Snell, R. 37, 46
Somer, T. 171, 181
Sparrow, M.K. 127, 133
Spath, P. 153, 156
Spender, D. 191, 197
Stein, D. 139, 155
Steinberg, S. 155
Steiner, J.F. 50, 63, 65
Steyaert, J. 8, 24, 26, 31, 33, 35, 36, 46, 47
Straw, J. 111
Streatfield, D.R. 65
Strydom, P. 160, 181
Sundin, E. 17, 26
Svennevig, M. 76, 77, 80

Tapscott, D. 38, 39, 47
Taylor, C. 73, 81
Taylor, M. 114, 115, 116, 118, 119, 121, 129,
    134
Taylor, T. 145, 156
Thompson, P. 10, 26
Thornton, P. 70, 77, 81
Thorpe, D. 91, 101, 102, 106, 109, 110
Tijdens, K.G. 17, 26
Times, The 40, 48
Toffler, A. 10, 13, 24, 26
Tolmie, P. 109
Troyen, A. 154
Turner, B. 84, 108, 214, 221
Turner, J.W. 209, 221
Tuson, G. 81

Upton, A. 63, 65

Van Dongen, J. 155
Vanhaecht, K. 150, 156
Vankevich, N. 214, 221
Van Loon, J. 87, 108
van Vliet, J. 139, 154
Vasagar, J. 39, 48, 115, 133
Vleugels, A. 154, 156
Vorderman, C. 112

Waine, B. 9, 24
Wajcman, J. 17, 26
Walsh, D. 122, 134
Warren, L. 71, 78
Waterman, R.H. 11, 26
Watson, M. 10, 12, 49–64, 65, 240
Wattam, C. 102, 109
Webb, S.A. 7, 12, 18, 19, 26, 49, 65, 111–32,
       201, 206, 221, 223–36, 237, 238, 240
Weber, M. 37, 48, 201, 221, 226
Webley, M. 65
Weick, K. 175, 181
Weiner, A. 21, 24
Wellman, B. 187, 191, 196, 197
Wenger, E. 175, 181
Wharton, R.R. 17, 26
White, J. 155
White, S. 73, 81
Whitfield, D. 70, 81
Wiener, L.S. 14, 26
Williams, N. 116, 130, 134
Williams, S. 52, 58, 64
Willis, M. 75, 81
Willis, T. 187, 188, 196
Wilmot, H. 78, 79
Wilson, G. 75, 81
Wilson, J. 155
Wilson, T.D. 65
Woolgar, S. 85, 86, 107, 110
Woolham, J. 76, 81
Wright, K. 210, 222
Wulff, R. 141, 156
Wyre, R. 115, 134

Yalom, I. 74, 81
Young, J. 231, 238
Ypren, T.A. van 72, 81
Yudice, G. 229, 238

Zander, K. 152, 155, 156